"DALLAS AND WATERGATE ARE CONCRETE LINKS IN A CHAIN OF OMINOUS EVENTS...A HIDDEN DRAMA OF COUP AND COUNTERCOUP WHICH REPRESENTS THE LIFE OF AN INNER POWER SPHERE, AN 'INVISIBLE GOVERNMENT,' CAPABLE OF ANY ACT, SETTING ITSELF ABOVE THE LAW AND BEYOND MORAL RULE: A CLANDESTINE AMERICAN STATE."
—from *The Yankee and Cowboy War*

No writer of fiction could have conjured the nightmare events of our recent past. Only an entirely new way of looking at them could make sense out of what on the surface seems an insane pattern of violence, villainy and horror.

The Yankee and Cowboy War provides the approach and the evidence we need to understand what is happening in America. We urge you to read it—if you have the nerve to take the naked truth.

"The most readable book on conspiracies and assassinations I have read and also the most stimulating. I think Oglesby is one of our first-rate political writers, skilled, always interesting, and with a rare gift for making political theory as lucid and exciting as a good narrative."
—Norman Mailer

THE YANKEE AND COWBOY WAR

★★★★★★★★★★

Conspiracies from Dallas to Watergate and Beyond

★★★★★★★★★★

CARL OGLESBY

A BERKLEY MEDALLION BOOK
published by
BERKLEY PUBLISHING CORPORATION

To my mother

Library of Congress Catalog Card Number: 76-23321
SBN 425-03493-3

BERKLEY MEDALLION BOOKS are published by
Berkley Publishing Corporation
200 Madison Avenue
New York, N.Y. 10016

BERKLEY MEDALLION BOOK ® TM 757,375

Printed in the United States of America

Berkley Medallion Edition, SEPTEMBER, 1977

ACKNOWLEDGMENTS

Grateful acknowledgement is made to the following sources for permission to quote from published material:

Carroll Quigley for excerpts of his book *Tragedy and Hope,* copyright © 1966 by Carroll Quigley.

Carl Bernstein and Bob Woodward for excerpts of their book *All the President's Men,* copyright © 1974 by Carl Bernstein and Bob Woodward.

Walter Cronkite for permission to quote from his March 1974 interview with Robert Vesco, copyright © 1974 by CBS Evening News with Walter Cronkite.

Doubleday & Company, Inc. for use of excerpts from *Just About Everybody versus Howard Hughes* by David B. Tinnin. Copyright © 1973 by David B. Tinnin. Reprinted by permission of Doubleday & Company, Inc.

Andrew St. George for permission to quote from his article "The Cold War Comes Home," copyright © 1973 by *Harper's* magazine. Reprinted from the November 1973 issue by special permission.

Bernard Barker and Eugenio Martinez for permission to use excerpts of their article "Mission Impossible," copyright © 1974 by *Harper's* magazine.

Acknowledgments

Many people helped. Special thanks for the special help from Bob Katz, Ann Koutso, Toby Kranitz, and Jim Kostman.

Contents

IV
NEITHER YANKEE NOR COWBOY

Preface to the Berkley Edition

The apperance of this new edition of *The Yankee and Cowboy War* confronts me with the temptation to update the book across the board. Since publication, Carter has become president, the JFK and King assassination cases have been reopened by the Congress, there has been more heavy commotion within the Hughes empire, and accounts published by such Watergate heroes as John Dean (*Blind Ambition*, 1976) and Fred Thompson (*At That Point in Time*, 1976) have further strengthened the view that there is some important, still-concealed connection between Watergate and the CIA. These matters tie directly to the themes explored in this book. But since a general update would still be premature, I decided to restrict my textual changes to a few corrections of fact and adjustments of style, except for the insertion of one new passage, a Yankee-Cowboy analysis of the coming of President Carter, at the end of chapter 8. This addition allows me to bring to a fuller close my argument that Watergate, like Dallas, was a coup d'etat, culminating in the installation of a new president and a new executive elite.

C.O.
March 1977

I

Clandestine America

Yankees and Cowboys:
A Perspective on the
Dallas-Watergate Decade

The assassination of John Kennedy and the downfall of Richard Nixon have both been viewed as isolated moral disasters for American democracy: Kennedy's murder as a demonstration of our continuing national inability or unwillingness to cope with violence; Nixon's downfall as a demonstration of the failure of our democratic institutions to overcome the abuses of secret intelligence and electronic surveillance at the seat of national power.

But these two events represent neither isolated disasters nor a generalized failure of American institutions but something almost beyond the ability of ordinary people even to see, much less control. The two events—Dallas and Watergate—are actually concrete links in a chain of related and ominous events passing through the entire decade in which they occurred and beyond. And this chain of events itself represents only the violent eruptions of a deeper struggle of rival power elites identified here as Yankees and Cowboys.

This book proposes to show that Dallas and Watergate are intrinsically linked conspiracies in a hidden drama of coup and countercoup which represents the life of an inner oligarchic power sphere, and "invisible government," capable of any act in the pursuit of its objectives, that sets itself above the law and beyond the moral rule: a clandestine American state, perhaps an embryonic police state.

We see the expressions and symptoms of clandestine America in a dozen places now—the FBI's COINTELPRO scheme, the CIA's Operation Chaos, the Pentagon's Operation Garden Plot, the large-scale and generally successful attempts to destroy legitimate and essential dissent in which all the intelligence agencies participated, a campaign whose full scope and fury are still not revealed. We see it in the ruthlessness and indifference to world, as well as national, opinion with which the CIA contracted its skills out to ITT to destroy democracy's last little chance in Chile. We see it as well, as this book argues, in the crime and cover-up of Dealey Plaza, the crime and cover-up of Watergate.

How could the clandestine state have stricken us so profoundly? How could we—as we might have fancied, "of all people"—have given way with so little resistance, in fact with so little evident understanding of what was happening? What accounts for the way the various organs of state force—defense and security alike—became so divided against each other? CIA-Intelligence against CIA-Operations, the CIA, the Pentagon, the FBI, and the presidency at one time or another against each other—what is this internal conflict all about? Why should the country's premier political coalition, formed after Reconstruction and reformed by Franklin Roosevelt, have begun to destabilize so badly in the 1960s and 1970s?

The intensification of clandestine, illicit methods against racial and antiwar dissent as a "threat" to the (secret) state precisely coincided with the intensified use of such methods in conflicts for power and hegemony taking place *within* the secret state, against a background of declining consensus.

The Dallas-to-Watergate outburst is fundamentally attributable to the breakdown taking place within the incumbent national coalition, the coalition of the Greater Northeastern powers with the Greater Southwestern powers, the post-Civil War, post-Reconstruction coalition, the coalition of the New Deal, of Yankees and Cowboys.

This is the theme, at bottom, of the entire narration to follow. The agony of the Yankees and the Cowboys, the "cause" of their divergence in the later Cold War period, is that there was finally too much tension between the detentist strategy of the Yankees in the Atlantic and the militarist strategy of the Cowboys in the Pacific. To maintain the two lines was, in effect, to maintain two separate and opposed realities at once, two separate and contradictory domains of world-historical truth. In Europe and the industrial world, the evident truth was that we could live with communism. In Asia and the Third World, the evident truth was that we could not, that we had to fight and win wars against it or else face terrible consequences at home.

As long as the spheres of detente and violence could be kept apart in American policy and consciousness, as long as the Atlantic and Pacific could remain two separate planes of reality wheeling within each other on opposite assumptions and never colliding, then American foreign policy could wear a look of reasonable integration. But when it became clear that the United States could not win its way militarily in the Third World without risking a nuclear challenge in the North Atlantic, the makings of a dissolving consensus were at hand.

I argue in Part Two of this book that the power-elite collision one sensed at Dallas on November 22, 1963, was real. It was no chance collision of a lone political maniac with a lone political star. It was a collision anchored in the larger social dialectic that propels the life of the national ruling elites. The conspiracy to kill JFK and the much larger conspiracy to keep official silence embodied this collision and had their being in this, the opposition of Yankee and Cowboy.

The lines of division became clear early in 1968 with the rapid crystallizing of a whole new front of opposition to the war, that of the "corporate liberals." Formerly, the established liberalism of the sort we associate with Xerox and Harvard had been inclined to defend the U.S. position in Vietnam as a part of its long-standing general commitment to anticommunism. The Yankee lights had made the usual arrangements to provide world banking services to a Free South Vietnam and take the oil from its waters, and it was always clear that there would be no serious objection from the Yankees as a whole if the Vietnam War turned out to be winnable.[1] But now in 1967-68 a new line of criticism of Johnson and his war policy opened up.

The war's costs had exploded out of all proportion to the original objective, one now heard. No vital American interests were being attacked or defended in Vietnam, after all. Europe was appalled at us. Our European alliances were suffering. Our young people were strenuously alienated. Our economy was hurting. Other problems were lying neglected. We needed to wrap up the bleeding stump and move to a better position. General James Gavin, for example, one of President Kennedy's chief military advisers, developed these and related ideas about the war in various public forums during that period.

But the strategy that was continued by Nixon in 1969 in the aftermath of the Martin Luther King and Robert Kennedy assassinations and Nixon's resultant reelection, was, of course, escalation—the secret air war, the invasion of the "sanctuaries" in Cambodia and Laos, the Christmas bombings, etc. But for a moment in 1968, Johnson had suddenly and strangely abdicated, stopped the bombing, and opened the Paris peace talks, and Robert Kennedy had assembled an electoral coalition reaching from Mayor Daley to the liberal peaceniks, if not Tom Hayden, a New-Politics-style coalition that appeared easily capable of beating

Nixon, taking office, and stopping the war with a thump.

So whereas there had formerly appeared to be essential agreement at the top of the American power structure on the Vietnam question, now we had two "ruling-class" voices to account for, one demanding more military effort and insisting upon the necessity of the original objective, the other tiring of the frustrations and costs of the attempt, unwilling to sacrifice resources at a yet higher magnitude, and wanting to be free to worry about other things—oil, gold, the Mideast, Europe, the economy, and so on.

It was directly clear that there was a regional component to this difference. Of course there are major points that do not fit the Yankee/Cowboy curve. The West Coast Bank of America, for example, spoke throughout the period of maximum unrest over the war with an essentially liberal voice. And Fulbright is from Arkansas. But on balance, the souls most fervently desirous of decisive military measures to prevent a Communist takeover tended to argue from a Frontierist, China-Lobby kind of position, and the souls most calmly able to accept losses and pull back tended to argue from an Atlanticist, Council on Foreign Relations, NATO-haunted kind of position.

The Yankee/Cowboy split thus suggested itself as a not-too-simplistic way to indicate in swift, available terms the existence of a rich and complex rivalry, the general cultural disposition of its chief contending principals, and the jointly historical and mythic character of their struggle, commingling John Wayne fantasies with real bloodshed, real genocide.

The profile of these types is best suggested in the persons and relationship of corporate-banker/monopolist David Rockefeller and tycoon entrepreneur Howard Hughes. An inquiry into their long rivalry is the first step in our exposition of Watergate in Part Three. But the spirit of Yankeeness is given off by many things besides the Chase Manhattan and of Cowboyness by many things besides the Hughes empire. Yankeeness is the Ivy League and

Cowboyness is the NFL. Yankee is the exclusive clubs of Manhattan, Boston, and Georgetown. Cowboy is the exclusive clubs of Dallas and New Orleans, Orange County East and West. Yankee is the Council on Foreign Relations, the secret Round Table, Eleanor Roosevelt, Bundles for Britain, and at a certain point, the Dulles brothers and the doctrine of massive retaliation. Cowboy is Johnson, Connally, Howard Hunt and the Bay of Pigs team. Yankee is Kennedy, Cowboy is Nixon.

But I stress my purpose is not to name a concrete group of conspirators and assassins, though I do not doubt that the conspiracies I speak of are actual. My aim rather is to call attention to the persistence of Civil War splits in the current situation and to the historical ideological substance of the positions at play.

It must be often the case, as it was with me and the Yankee/Cowboy idea, that one's fresh insight turns out to be already well mapped and settled. I first proposed the Yankee/Cowboy references in early 1968[2] but wrote nothing of any account on the theme until a series of articles about Watergate for the Boston *Phoenix* in 1973 and 1974. A reader of one of those pieces informed me of the similarity of my views with those of Professor Carroll Quigley, a historian at Georgetown.

Quigley is the author of a huge book about the contemporary world, *Tragedy and Hope*, to which I will return in chapter two. I begin my debt to Quigley here by borrowing the following observation from his summary. Noting that since 1950 a "revolutionary change" has been occurring in American politics, Quigley says this transformation involves "a disintegration of the middle class and a corresponding increase in significance by the petty bourgeoisie at the same time that the economic influence of the older Wall Street financial groups has been weakening and been challenged by new wealth springing up outside the eastern cities, notably in the Southwest and Far West." He continues:

* * *

These new sources of wealth have been based very largely on government action and government spending but have, none the less, adopted a petty-bourgeois outlook rather than the semiaristocratic outlook that pervades the Eastern Establishment. This new wealth, based on petroleum, natural gas, ruthless exploitation of national resources, the aviation industry, military bases in the South and West, and finally on space with all its attendant activities, has centered in Texas and southern California. Its existence, for the first time, made it possible for the petty-bourgeois outlook to make itself felt in the political nomination process instead of in the unrewarding effort to influence politics by voting for a Republican candidate nominated under Eastern Establishment influence.... By the 1964 election, the major political issue in the country was the financial struggle behind the scenes between the old wealth, civilized and cultured in its foundations, and the new wealth, virile and uninformed, arising from the flowing profits of government-dependent corporations in the Southwest and West.[3]

The whole point of introducing the Cowboy/Yankee language, of course, is to bring precisely that old-money/new money, Atlanticist-Frontierist tension into focus in the plane of current events.

The main idea of looking at things this way is to see that a sectional rivalry, derived from the patterns of the Civil War, still operates in American politics, indeed that at the altitude of national power elites, it may be the most sensitive and inflamed division of all, more concentrated than race and class and more basic than two-party system attachments and ideologies. The argument of this book is that the emerging clash of Yankee and Cowboy wills beneath the visible stream of events is the dominant fact of real U.S. political life since 1960. The dissolution of the Yankee/Cowboy consensus of

World War II and the Cold War until 1960 is behind the
Dallas of Kennedy and the Watergate of Nixon.

Let us go a step further with these types, Cowboy and
Yankee, and sketch a first outline of the differing worlds they
see.

The Yankee mind, of global scope, is at home in the great
world, used to regarding it as a whole thing integrated in the
far-flung activities of Western exploration, conquest, and
commerce. The Yankee believes that the basis of a good
world order is the health of America's alliances across the
North Atlantic, the relations with the Western Democracies
from which our tradition mainly flows. He believes the
United States continues the culture of Europe and relates to
the Atlantic as to a lake whose other shore must be secured as
a matter of domestic priority. Europe is the key world
theater, and it is self-evident to the Yankee mind that the fate
of the United States is inevitably linked up with Europe's in a
career of white cultural destiny transcending national
boundaries: that a community of a unified world civilization
exists, that there is such a thing as "the West," "One World."

The Cowboy mind has no room for the assumption that
American and European culture are continuous. The
Cowboy is moved instead by the discontinuity of the New
World from the Old and substitutes for the Yankee's
Atlantic-oriented culture a new system of culture (*Big Sky*,
Giant) oriented to an expanding wilderness Frontier and
based on an advanced Pacific strategy.

The Yankee monopolists who first broke faith with the
goal of military victory in Vietnam did so in view of what
they saw as the high probability of failure and the certain
ambiguity of success. The Cowboy entrepreneurs who
fought hardest to keep that faith alive did so out of
conviction of the *necessity* of success. Said the
multicorporate-liberal Yankee (about 1968): "The United
States cannot wage a winning nonnuclear land campaign in
Asia. It will destroy its much more essential relations in
Europe if in spite of all wisdom its leadership continues to

siphon off precious national blood and treasure to win this war. It is necessary to stand down." Said the Cowboy: "Only the strong are free."

The distinction between the East Coast monopolist and the Western tycoon entrepreneur is the main class-economic distinction set out by the Yankee/Cowboy perspective. It arises because one naturally looks for a class-economic basis for this apparent conflict at the summit of American power. That is because one must assume that parties without a class-economic base could not endure struggle at that height. It is then only necessary to recall that antiwar feeling struck the Eastern Establishment next after it struck the students, the teachers, and the clergy—struck the large bank-connected firms tied into the trans-Atlantic business grid. During the same period, industrial segments around the construction industry, the military-industrial complex, agribusiness, the Southern Boom of the sixties and seventies, and independent Texas/Southwest oil interests—i.e., the forces Quigley calls "new wealth"—never suffered a moment of war-weariness. They supported the Texan Johnson and the Southern Californian Nixon as far as they would go toward a final military solution.[4]

Why should this difference have arisen? After a century of Northeastern leadership, and one-quarter century of Cold War unity, why should the national ruling coalition of the old and new owning classes, Yankee and Cowboy, have begun pulling apart? But then we have to go back: What was the basis of their unity to begin with?

William Appleman Williams deals with a variation of this question when he argues that the basis for the long-term general (or "pluralist") coalition of the forces of capitalism (or "plutocracy") with the forces of democracy in American politics is the constant companionship of the expanding wilderness frontier. Williams thus stands the Turner Frontier on its head, correcting it.[5] I add that another and cognate effect of the frontier in American economic development was to preserve the entrepreneurial option long after the arrival of the vast monopoly structures which tend to consume entrepreneurs. In the states whose political-economic histories Marx studied, for example, the frontier was never the factor that it was in America, except as America itself was Europe's Wild West. The rugged-individualist self-made rich man, the autonomous man of power, the wildcatter, began to drop out of sight, to lose presence as individual, type, and class, with the rise of the current-day computer-centered monopoly-corporate formations. The tycoon-entrepreneur is of course disappearing as a type in America too, at least as a political force in national life. The Hughes empire, at last, has been corporatized. Old man Hunt is dead. His sons are bringing Harvard Business School rational bureaucracy to the operation. But that only makes it all the more curious that political power continued to emanate from the type and the person, the image and the reality, the ghost perhaps, of a creature like Hughes as late as the second victorious presidential campaign of Nixon. Why should the Cowboy tycoon have persisted so long as a political force, competent to struggle against the biggest banking cartels for control of the levers of national power?

As others have argued, the Frontier was a reprieve for democracy. We may note here that it was also a reprieve for capitalism as well, whose internal conflicts were constantly being financed off an endless-seeming input of vast stretches of natural riches, having no origin in capitalist production. All that was needed was for the settlers to accept the genocidal elimination of the native population and a great deal became possible—the purple mountains, the fruited plains. And generation after generation of American whites were able to accept that program. The Indian wars won the West. The railroads and highways were laid. The country was resettled by a new race, a new nation.

Energies of expansion consumed the continent in about two centuries, pushing on to Hawaii and Alaska. There is no way to calculate the impact of that constant territorial expansion on the development of American institutions.

There is no way to imagine those institutions apart from the environment created by that expansion. It is a matter our standard national hagiography paints out of the picture, though we make much of the populist-saga aspect of the pioneering (never "conquering") of the West. How can we congratulate our national performance for its general democracy and constitutionalism without taking into account the background of that constant expansion? We do not teach our children that we are democrats in order to expand forever and republicans on condition of an unfrozen western boundary with unclaimed wilderness. To the extent that the American miracle of pluralism exists at all, we still do not know how miraculous it would be in the absence of an expanding frontier, its constant companion till the time of the Chinese revolution.

The overwar in Asia has its internal American origin in the native reflex to maintain the Western Frontier on the old terms and to do so at all cost, since our whole way of life hinges on the Frontier. What the late-blooming Yankee liberal critics of the Vietnam war refused to hear and recognize between the lines of the prowar arguments of the more philosophical Cowboy hawks was this essential point about the importance of Frontier expansion in American life from the beginning.

In the nature of things, the American Frontier continued to expand with the prosperity it financed. Now, in our generation, it has brought us to this particular moment of world confrontation across the Pacific, fully global in scale for both sides, fully modern in its technological expression for both sides—the old Westward-surging battle for space projected onto the stage of superpowers.

The success and then the successful defense from 1950 to 1975 of the Asian revolutionary nationalist campaigns against further Western dominance in Asia—China, Korea, Vietnam—means that all that is changed. What was once true about the space to the west of America is no longer true and will never be true again. There will never be a time again when the white adventurer may peer over his western horizon at an Asia helplessly plunged in social disorganization. In terms of their social power to operate as a unified people and in the assimilation of technology, the Chinese people are, since 1950, a self-modernizing people, not colonials any more. And instead of a Wild West, Americans now have a mature common boundary with other *moderns* like ourselves, not savages, not Redskins, not Reds, only *modern people like ourselves in a single modern world*. This is new for us, a new experience for Americans *altogether*.

Our national transformation from an unbounded to a bounded state will of course continue to stir the internal furies. No one interpretation of the event will be able to establish itself. No one will agree what the end of the Frontier means, what it will lead to, what one ought to do about it. But all will agree that it is upon us and past, whether it is called one thing or another. And now *after* Vietnam, as though it were not clear enough before, it is apparent beyond any possibility of doubt that whatever this force of Asian self-modernization is, whether it is evil or good or beyond good and evil, it is assuredly *not* a force that United States policy-makers can manhandle and manipulate and hold back through diplomatic chicanery and military force. Even if it were still *advisable* for the United States to stop "the march of Asian communism," if that is what we are really talking about, it is not *possible* for the United States to do that. Look and see: China, Korea, Vietnam.

I have not written this book to say at the end, choose sides between Cowboy and Yankee for Civil War II. My less bloody belief is that ordinary people all over the map, Northeast by Southwest, have a deep, simple, and common need to oppose all these intrigues and intriguers, whatever terms one calls them by and however one understands their development. But this need of course must be recognized, and that is why I write: to offer an analysis of the situation of domestic politics from the standpoint of power-elite collisions taking place at the top, and then, at the end, to suggest that democracy's first response must be to demand a realistic reconstruction of the assassination of President Kennedy. To comprehend his murder (as with the murder of Lincoln) is to comprehend a very basic event in the history of American government, as well as the crimes that came after it. The comprehension of these covert political actions is the absolute precondition of self-government, the first step toward the restoration of the legitimate state.

More broadly I write to say that we are the American generations for whom *the frontier is the fact that there is no more frontier* and who must somehow begin to decide how to deal with this.

What shall America do about the loss of its wilderness frontier? Can we form our nation anew, on new, nonexpansionist terms without first having to see everything old swept violently away? The unarticulated tension around that question undermined the long-standing Yankee/Cowboy coalition and introduced, with President Kennedy's assassination, the current period of violent and irregular movement at the top of the power hierarchy. It is the precipitous and at the same time unfocused character of this question of the closed, lost frontier that has created such a challenge, such a threat, to traditional American values and institutions, the threat of a cancerously spreading clandestine state within.

2

Clandestine America: Three Sources

What is actually *possible* on the stage of American politics? Can presidents be assassinated by conspirators who go free and win out in the end? Are events which the media soberly report on often little more than playshows contrived by Machiavellian power elites for the manipulation of mass consciousness?

Even after Watergate, the idea that there may be a clandestine American state vastly predating Nixon's arrival in the White House, transcending Nixon and lingering beyond him, will seem too wild, will seem "to go too far," unless we come upon it as the wind and the rain fashioned the thing itself, bit by bit. The following three stories about how that happened could be followed by thirty more rather like them; I am not trying to be definitive or exhaustive, only to exemplify the steps taken, now well behind us, that pointed us down the path toward Dallas and Watergate, toward COINTELPRO, Chaos, Garden Plot, and the secret state:

1.   The long-term penetration of the American foreign-policy bureaucracy by a secret group of Anglophiles operating worldwide as the "Round Table."

2.   The so-called "Operation: Underworld" of the World War II years, a secret but evidently formal and binding compact linking the federal police apparatus and the crime syndicate of Meyer Lansky.

3.   The secret submission of the U.S. World War II command to the astonishing demands of Nazi Germany's top spymaster, General Reinhard Gehlen, who leapt from Hitler's sinking general staff to become unrivalled chief of American, West German and NATO intelligence systems in the Cold War years.

But as these narratives will be appreciated better in view of their distance from standard ideas, we will first take up two other responses to this question, one by a conservative CIA sophisticate, Miles Copeland, a retired CIA official, and the other by his liberal counterpart, Andrew St. George, a journalist specializing in CIA themes. The Copeland piece appeared in the October 1973 issue of William Buckley's *National Review*. St. George's piece came out a month later in *Harper's*. Both articles were cited in the report of Senator Howard Baker's special Watergate subcommittee looking into the CIA's role at Watergate.[1] Both writers were questioned in secret by Congressional investigators. And as we shall see, despite their conservative-liberal opposition, the men are ideological bookends. Both assure us—I almost said *reassure*—that in terms of Big Brotherism and the police state, things will be getting worse.

Copeland opens his explanation of clandestinism in U.S. politics by setting out a picture of concatenating world-scale disasters mounting over the coming years and battering with cumulative force against the foundations of human society everywhere. He sees this process of breakdown as leading inevitably to the world-wide escalation of left-wing terror-ism. In response to this forthcoming contagion, the governments of the world one after the other will be forced to the use of totalitarian methods of social control. Watergate gives us, he says, a slice-of-life look at the way these forces were developing (i.e., shows us that Nixon was provoked to the police state by those who opposed him). The inevitability of terror in a collapsing situation culminates in the inevitability of a gestapo response. "The only answer to the problem [of terror]," Copeland writes, "seems to be to keep whole communities under surveillance. 'This means we are subscribing to police-state methods,' says Mother, 'but what else can we do?'"

Copeland does not stop to consider that for some of us this might not be a self-answering question, or whether, person for person, it might not be braver and better for a people and a society to endure terror, if that is indeed the only alternative, than to countenance tyranny. The point he is in a rush to make is that, for the ruling classes with whom he identifies, it is better to impose a police state than to suffer a revolution. He is also saying that even in the United States, the people will tolerate or welcome this police state as the only alternative to revolution. "With intelligence on the 'people's war' pouring in as it presently is," he writes, "even the most liberal-minded CIA officers feel that they have no choice but to do *whatever* is necessary to deal with it." [Copeland's emphasis.]

They believe that, sooner rather than later, the public will swing over to sharing the alarm, and will become suddenly unsqueamish about police-state methods or whatever it takes to give them a good night's sleep. The CIA, the FBI, and other security agencies had better be prepared. They had better have in readiness methods of "community surveillance" which have in them only such invasions of privacy as are absolutely necessary, and which ensure that the invasions are handled with such discretion and delicacy that even the most ardent liberal can't object to them.

These still-to-be-demonstrated "methods," as Copeland airily calls them, are at the same time, so he assures, essentially benign, in some respects benevolent, and efficient in implementation. "The FBI has a comparatively simple problem," he writes. "Provided it can be assured of freedom from political influences, it can easily administer a system of community surveillance which will be pervasive enough to check terrorist influences in the United States yet not constitute more than a minor departure from our traditional ways of doing things."

Thanks to the Seymour Hersh/ *New York Times* disclosures of Christmas 1974, showing a vast CIA-run domestic-intelligence activity, we now understand of course that the presumptively futuristic scenes promoted by Copeland, wherein the CIA enters massively into domestic intelligence operations to stop some future crescendo of terrorism, were already old hat when he was writing. "Intelligence leans toward keeping discreet track of terrorist groups and neutralizing them quietly while policemen think in terms of evidence that will stand up in court," he writes. "In the future, these distinctions will become less and less important—and extra-legal (i.e., intelligence) actions against terrorism will be closely coordinated with legal (police) actions against them."

Nothing futuristic about all this at all, as it turned out. All ancient history. Witness the Hoover memos of May 1968 inaugurating a massive program of FBI aggression against the antiwar and civil-rights movement—*not* against "terrorism," by the way, but against "dissent," against *a rival political standpoint*. Witness the Huston Plan and Operation Gemstone and Octopus and all the rest that came with the succession of Nixon to the Johnson throne. We have a concrete sequence of repression, of the use of police-state methods, exactly along Copeland's lines, undertaken exactly with his kind of self-flattering and historically ignorant posturings about keeping order and giving people "a good night's sleep," as though that were a fit image of a self-governing people, a nation asleep.

A current failure of Buckleyite conservatism as a serious political philosophy is that it refuses to dissociate itself from

this anticonstitutional mania for the state-financed subversion of political dissent and radical-popular movements of
reform. It has no values to propose other than the one single
flattened-out value of the total security of the state. The
more traditional and substantial conservative values of
republicanism, limits, and constitutionality are all reduced
in the *National Review* to the one imperious demand for
order, silence, sleep.

Tyranny was never a remedy for terror. Tyranny *is* terror.
Tyranny and terror promote and multiply each other so well
because each is the other's only possible "legitimation." But
if they are actually the same, as any Socrates could show,
then they cannot "legitimate" each other. The choice
between terror and totalitarianism is a choice that can only
be made—can·only be identified *as a choice*—by terrorists
and tyrants. The democrat, the republican, and the
independent among us will not be so quick to see terror and
tyranny as opposite alternatives, but only as two sides of one
coin, a single composite choice against liberty and humanity.
The authentic rejection of terror mandates the rejection of
tyranny. The authentic rejection of tyranny mandates the
rejection of terror. There is no way to defend the democracy
by the use of antidemocratic means. There is no antirepubli-
can method corresponding to a republican purpose. There is
no furtherance of national and personal, political and social
independence through submission to national police
controls. The state cannot at the same time uphold the law
and trample it underfoot.

The liberal survey of the same forces, however, is
disquietingly similar. As Copeland finds totalitarianism
necessary, Andrew St. George finds it irresistible. Too
enlightened to fall back on Copeland's all-vindicating
menace of Red terror as the legitimating raison d'être of the
clandestine American police state, St. George rather sees a
monster he calls *technofascism* as emerging from the
material conditions of ultramodern production, from the

computerization of everyday life. His position is sociologi-
cally sophisticated. He borrows knowledgeably from the
Weberian literature and incorporates the pessimism of
current observers like Jacques Ellul and Hannah Arendt
without a trace of unconfidence.

St. George calls Watergate "the poisonous afterbirth of
Vietnam.... An end to external conflict, the inward-turning
of the nation's aggressions, the unmistakable first step
toward genuine convergence with our erstwhile totalitarian
opponents." He quotes Patrick McGarvey's 1972 work, *The
C.I.A.: The Myth and the Madness*, "United States
intelligence is now turning inward on the citizens of this
country.... The next logical step would be for an administration to do exactly what its people suspect it of doing—
start mounting intelligence operations against citizen groups
and assemblies."

"Richard Nixon and John Mitchell," continues St.
George, "may have been instinctively, if not consciously,
motivated toward Watergate by an intuitive sense that the
era of foreign intervention was drawing to a close. [He is
writing before the CIA-Chile exposures.] From now on
America would have to generate the climate of defactualization and policeness [St. George finds the Hannah Arendt
coinage useful] right at home if it wanted continued progress
toward fully achieved, seamlessly engineered, cybernetically
controlled techno-totalitarianism."

Taking as his given the rapid growth in funds and prestige
technology available to the national security complex, St.
George asks how this complex arose, where it came from,
and "what history is trying to tell us" about it. He writes,
"Technological society is a matter of internal controls. The
very concept of national security has changed; its focus is no
longer on spies and seditionists, but on the bureaucracy's
internal power arrangements and hierarchical structures."
How has this transformation come about?

"Within a year of the Bay of Pigs," he writes, "the CIA
curiously and inexplicably began to grow, to branch out, to

gather more and more responsibility for 'the Cuban problem' etc. . . . By the time of the 1965 U.S. military intervention in the Dominican Republic both the good guys and the bad guys—i.e., the 'radical' civilian politicos and the 'conservative' generals—turned out to have been financed by La Compania. . . . Owing largely to the Bay of Pigs, the CIA ceased being an invisible government: it became an empire."

Now he approaches a mysterious question. "The Agency had become a tireless data digger and interviewer and fact collector about the smallest details of life in Cuba under Castro—until the landing preparations began in earnest in early 1961. Then intelligence collection began to drop off: the 'operators' took over. It seemed that when the operational side of the Agency cut in, the intelligence side cut out. It was baffling. . . . The real question was: Why?"

Why did CIA-*Intelligence* "cut out" of the Bay of Pigs invasion at roughly the moment Kennedy was inaugurated, and why did CIA-*Operations* then "cut in"? To go to the heart of it, what seems strange on the assumption that the CIA is an integrated bureaucratic entity ceases to seem strange on the assumption—*our* assumption—that it is a house divided against itself. St. George might have been about to lay this important distinction bare. But he goes wrong. He chooses the path of "psychohistorical analysis" over the path of political criticism.

Arming himself pretentiously with Arendt's "magisterial" concept of "defactualization" (information deteriorates upwards through bureaucracies), he sets out to treat the problem of clandestinism as a *syndrome* belonging to the domain of psychological aberration. St. George knows or surmises that a conflict shoots through the CIA, through the presidency, through the entire executive system, and that effective presidential command and control are the more deeply in doubt the deeper one goes into the heart of the national defense and security establishments. Then why try to explain breakdowns, when they occur, as though they were the result of "turning away from reality, from empirical data, provable facts, rational truth, toward image-making and self-deception.'"? Why ignore the overwhelming differentials of policy and faction at play in these breakdowns?

It is not Nixon himself, the Joint Chiefs, or the CIA whom Nixon, the Chiefs, and the CIA are deceiving, it is only ordinary people. Nixon knew he was secretly bombing Cambodia. The Joint Chiefs knew they were secretly bombing exempted targets in North Vietnam. The defense and security establishment knew that "peace with honor" was a slogan with a hatch in the bottom, and that the "peace" mandate Nixon would secure with it was prestructured for easy transmutation into a war mandate. Watergate cannot be reduced to a question of Nixon's personal psychology. He was not deceiving himself, only others. He was not deceiving his class.

St. George lets the fashion for *psychohistory* guide him to the belief that the hero of the story will turn out to have been J. Edgar Hoover. St. George says Hoover distrusted and hated the CIA.

> He thought of it as a viperine lair of liars and high-domed intellectuals, of insolent Yalies who sneered at Fordham's finest, of rich young ne'er-do-wells who dabbled in spy work because they could not be trusted to run the family business, of wily "Princeton Ought-Ought" himself, "Dickie" Helms, who spun his tweedy web from an ultramodern, electronically secured enclave up the river in Virginia. . . . Hoover realized that inevitably, disastrously, the CIA's tainted ways were seeping back home to America; there is a vengeful law of historic osmosis about these things.

"Hoover was proven fatally right," St. George continues, blithely putting his own ideas into the dead director's mind and altogether overlooking the fact that it was the director himself who already launched in May 1968 a concerted, all-out FBI "counterintelligence" campaign "to expose, disrupt and otherwise neutralize the activities of the various New Left organizations, their leadership and adherents."[2] Certainly Hoover struggled with the CIA about domestic intelligence, just as he opposed the Huston Plan, but that was because he saw the CIA and the White House as rivals to the FBI, as rival *power bases*, not because he had suddenly grown sentimental about the Constitution and democracy.

Yet St. George's larger point about the growth of the national-security complex stands up. Estimating the CIA staff at 150,000 and the total national security budget at $10 billion a year, he confronts the meanings of this with honest emotions: "One should pause to absorb this in its full...innovative enormity," he writes, "a United States Senator tapped and trailed on his legislative rounds by *American* Army agents?—but there are facts and figures to back up the claim: Senator Ervin's *other* investigating committee, the Subcommittee on Constitutional Rights, revealed last year, in a report that went largely unnoticed, that by 1969 the Army—not the Defense Department [and not the CIA], just the Army—had built up a 'massive system' for keeping watch on U.S. politics.... The simple fact is that as the Sixties turned into the Seventies, America became a nation under surveillance." Say it with trumpets. Blow the alarm. This did not stop with Watergate.

No doubt, as Copeland's example teaches, the persistence of left-wing terror in the world scene will make an easy excuse for totalitarian-minded persons. No doubt, as St. George's example teaches, the computerization of everyday life will seem to embody an irresistibly transcendent force. But let us remember that we are actually looking back on *the certain knowledge* of a clandestine America which these writers can still pretend to see as a *future* threat. We are trying to understand the onset of an *achieved*, not merely a prognosticated, predicament. So we may not be so abstract. We must find the concrete mechanisms. The way into the blind snarls of clandestinism was not led by pious elders seeking to quiet the public sleep or by robots programmed with a contempt for democracy. The way was taken step by step by ordinary human beings acting under the burden of ordinary human motives. The following three examples will bear out the importance of this innocuous reminder.

The Round Table

The John Birch Society maintains that linked up with, if not actually behind, the International Communist Conspiracy is a higher-level supercabal of internationalists of the United States and Western Europe, led here by the Rockefeller-Morgan group and there by the Rothschilds, whose purpose is to create a unified world political order. "This myth," writes its most temperate and only first-hand historian, Carroll Quigley (*Tragedy and Hope*, Macmillan, 1966), "like all fables, does in fact have a modicum of truth. There does exist, and has existed for a generation, an international Anglophile network which operates, to some extent, the way the radical right believes the Communists act. In fact, this network, which we may identify as the Round Table Groups, has no aversion to cooperating with the Communists, or any other groups [e.g., as we see below, the Nazis] and frequently does so."

Quigley studied the operations of the Round Table first hand for twenty years and for two years during the early 1960s was permitted access to its papers and secret records. He objects to a few of its policies (e.g., its conception of England as an Atlantic rather than a European power), but says his chief complaint about the Round Table is its secrecy, a secrecy which he comes forward to break. "The American branch of this organization, sometimes called 'The Eastern Establishment,' has played a very significant role in the history of the United States in the last generation," he writes, "and I believe its role in history is significant enough to be known."

The Round Table Groups, by Quigley's detailed report,[3] are semicovert policy and action groups formed at the turn of the first decade of this century on the initiatives of the Rhodes Trust and its dominant Trustee of the 1905-1925 period, Lord Milner. Their original political aim was federation of the English-speaking world along lines laid down by Cecil Rhodes.

By 1915, Round Table Groups were functioning in England and in six outposts of the Empire— South Africa, Canada, Australia, New Zealand, India, and the United States. The U.S. group included George Louis Beer, Walter Lippmann, Frank Aydelotte, Whitney Shepardson, Thomas W. Lamont, Jerome D. Greene, and Erwin D. Canham of the *Christian Science Monitor*, a Yankee bouquet.

The organization was originally financed by the associates and followers of Cecil Rhodes, chiefly from the Rhodes Trust itself, but since 1925, according to Quigley, substantial contributions have come from wealthy individuals, foundations, and firms associated with the international banking fraternity, especially the Carnegie United Kingdom Trust, and other organizations associated with J. P. Morgan, the Rockefeller and Whitney families, and the associates of Lazard Brothers and of Morgan, Grenfell, and Company. The chief link-up in this organization was once that of the Morgan Bank in New York to a group of international financiers in London led by Lazard Brothers, but at the end of the war of 1914, the organization was greatly extended. In England and in each dominion a group was set up to function as a cover for the existing local Round Table Group.

In London, this front was the Royal Institute of International Affairs, which had as its secret nucleus the existing Round Table Group. The New York group was the Council on Foreign Relations. The Morgan men who dominated the CFR went to the Paris Peace Conference and there became close to a similar group of English experts recruited by Milner. There thus grew up "a power structure" linking London and New York banks and deeply penetrating "university life, the press, and the practice of foreign policy."

The founding aims of this elaborate, semisecret organization were "to coordinate the international activities and outlooks of all the English-speaking world into one... to work to maintain peace; to help backward, colonial, and underdeveloped areas to advance toward stability, law, and order and prosperity, along lines somehow similar to those taught at Oxford and the University of London...." These aims were pursued by "gracious and cultured gentlemen of somewhat limited social experience.... If their failures now loom larger than their successes, this should not be allowed to conceal the high motives in which they attempted both."

Quigley calls this relationship between London and New York financial circles "one of the most powerful influences in twentieth-century American and world history. The two ends of this English-speaking axis have sometimes been called, perhaps facetiously, the English and American Establishments. There is, however, a considerable degree of truth behind the joke, a truth which reflects a very real power structure. It is this power structure which the Radical Right in the United States has been attacking for years in the belief that they are attacking the Communists."

Am I borrowing on Quigley then to say with the far right that this one conspiracy rules the world? The arguments for a conspiracy theory are indeed often dismissed on the grounds that no one conspiracy could possibly control everything. But that is not what this theory sets out to show. Quigley is not saying that modern history is the invention of an esoteric cabal designing events omnipotently to suit its ends. The implicit claim, on the contrary, is that a multitude of conspiracies contend in the night. Clandestinism is not the usage of a handful of rogues, it is a formalized practice of an entire class in which a thousand hands spontaneously join. Conspiracy is the normal continuation of normal politics by normal means.

What we behold in the Round Table, functioning in the United States through its cover organization, the Council on Foreign Relations, is one focal point among many of one among many conspiracies. The whole thrust of the Yankee/Cowboy interpretation in fact is set dead against the omnipotent-cabal interpretation favored by Gary Allen and others of the John Birch Society, basically in the respect that it posits and divided social-historical American order, conflict-wracked and dialectical rather than serene and hierarchical, in which results constantly elude every faction's intentions because all conspire against each and each against all.

This point arose in a seminar I was once in with a handful of businessmen and a former ambassador or two in 1970 at the Aspen Institute for Humanistic Studies. The question of conspiracy in government came up. I advanced the theory that government is intrinsically conspiratorial. Blank incredulous stares around the table. "Surely you don't propose there is conspiracy at the top levels?" But only turn the tables and ask how much conspiring these men of the world do in the conduct of their own affairs, and the atmosphere changes altogether. Now they are all unbuttoned and full of stories, this one telling how he got his competitor's price list, that one how he found out whom to bribe, the other one how he gathered secret intelligence on his own top staff. Routinely, these businessmen all operated in some respects covertly, they all made sure to acquire and hold the power to do so, they saw nothing irregular in it, they saw it as part of the duty, a submerged part of the job description. Only with respect to the higher levels of power, around the national presidency, even though they saw their own corporate brothers skulking about there, were they unwilling to concede the prevalence of clandestine practice. Conspiratorial play is a universal of power politics, and where there is no limit to power, there is no limit to conspiracy.

The Round Table is not the only source of American

clandestinism. As we are to see, there are other main roads to the self-same city. I call attention to it because it is precisely the kind of semihidden organization that standard consciousness does not recognize as a force in the flow of events, and yet whose influence is vast. When I read in Quigley's account of the Round Table that it was "concerned only to bring the English-speaking world into a single power unit, chiefly by getting the United States and Great Britain to support common policies," I suffer a painful shock of recognition: How much of what we most take for granted about the political world, how much of standard thought, is the artifact of Yankee bankers?

The Derivation of Kennedy

John Kennedy was not by personal heritage a Round Tabler any more than his family was by type or beginnings an Establishment Yankee family. On the contrary. He was the great-grandson of an emigrant Irish cooper and the grandson of a ward-heeling East Boston saloonkeeper. His father Joseph, the founder of the dynasty (if indeed the family is to prove dynastic), was an operator, speculator, wheeler-dealer and Prohibition-era smuggler whose drive for wealth, power and social status was easily worthy of any new-rich Cowboy, and who was in fact often snubbed by the Boston brahminate.

According to Quigley, JFK's "introduction to the Establishment arose from his support of Britain in opposition to his father [FDR's ambassador to the Court of St. James and an ardent anti-interventionist] in the critical days at the American Embassy in London in 1938-40. His acceptance into the English Establishment opened its American branch as well" (p. 1245). But maybe this rounds off the corners too much. At that time, JFK was a mere Harvard stripling, and according to his father's biographer, Richard J. Whalen (*The Founding Father*, New American

Library-World, 1964), he was wholly influenced by his father's political views. According to Whalen (p. 294), JFK's senior thesis, published in 1940 as *Why England Slept*, "was almost a carbon copy of his father's position." JFK followed his father in excusing Munich, defending Chamberlain, and blaming Britain's military unpreparedness for World War II on "the slowness of the British democracy to change from a disarmament policy."

How could the Founder have so misread the situation of European spirit? Whalen says (p. 348) that Joseph "might have muddled through—except for one failing. He identified himself with the 'top people' in England and moved to embrace their views. But these men and women of lofty rank and distinguished lineage belonged to a dying England. Dazzled, charmed, delighting in his acceptance, Kennedy spent little time at other levels of society, in the company of men holding radically different (though not necessarily 'radical') opinion, who would lead England's struggle and revive her spirit in the days of supreme trial. The intimate of those who first lost their function, then their faith in themselves and in their country, Kennedy rode high and handsome at their side, and shared their fall."

Thus, a rather more likely explanation of the British Establishment's initial interest in seeing the Kennedys elevated socially and thus politically in the United States is that the aristocrats in whom the *arriviste* ambassador took such delight were themselves mesmerized by Hitler's military power and spiritually incapable of challenging it.

"Operation Underworld"

German U-boats had already been sinking defenseless U.S. merchants within sight of East Coast beaches when a string of sabotage incidents on the East Coast docks climaxed in 1942 in the burning of the French liner *Normandie*, just on the eve of its rechristening as an Alli freighter. The event showed Roosevelt how easily Mussolini's saboteurs could strike at the base of U.S. shipping.

Meyer Lansky, meanwhile, chief minister of organized crime, was troubled because certain Mafia families were proving reluctant to join the larger Syndicate which he had been building since Prohibition under the yellow and black colors of Lucky Luciano. Luciano had been jailed in 1937 by New York D.A. Thomas Dewey, and Lansky had been operating since as his top man in the world of the other capos, where his main problem was how to persuade the Sicilian holdouts to accept the executive leadership of a Jew.

Lansky's leadership. Different students of organized crime in America interpret Lansky's role in different ways. The perceptive and original Alfred McCoy, for example, in *The Politics of Heroin in Southeast Asia* (1972), treats Luciano himself, not Lansky, as the first wholly modern executive of crime and attributes to him, not Lansky, the insights that led to the current federation of previously autonomous criminal groups around particular rackets and particular cities.

But Hank Messick, who develops the point in a string of unique books of crime reportage, notably *Lansky* (1971) and *John Edgar Hoover* (1972), thinks Luciano's greatest genius lay in his grasp of Lansky's greater genius, and that Lansky was always the main strategist in bringing big crime to accept the standpoint of the Harvard Business School and the necessity of monopoly-style business rationalization. McCoy would agree that Lansky at least became the top boss after Luciano's sudden death by heart attack in a Naples airport in 1962. I follow Messick on the point if only because Lansky was Luciano's front man in the real world during the nearly ten years Luciano was imprisoned and carried out the concrete tasks that actually brought the new supercorporate organization, "the Syndicate," into existence.

But this difference matters little for the current point. Whether it was Lansky's or Luciano's doing or the doing of "social forces" pushing towards "multicorporatism" in every sphere of exchange, in business and politics as well as in crime, in Hughes's and Rockefeller's and Nixon's worlds as well as Lansky's, the fact of expansion and integration, of the centralizing of business authority in an unimpeachable bureaucracy, is the main fact of organized crime's inner life from Prohibition on, and it seems appropriate to associate this general movement with the long period of Lansky's preeminence.

Roosevelt's problem then was how to guarantee the security of the docks against Fascist sabotage. Lansky's problem was how to complete the organization of the Syndicate. What artist of the possible saw the convergence of these two problems in a common solution?

The precise origins of *"Operation: Underworld"* are not public knowledge. Both McCoy and Messick fasten upon a Brooklyn shipyards office of U.S. Naval Intelligence. That would not mean the initiative was necessarily federal or the Navy's. The idea could have been dropped there by any messenger. In any case, it came down to a straightforward proposition. Lansky first turns to the reluctant capo and says: What if I can free thy leader, Luciano? Then he turns to the anxious Roosevelt and says: What if I can secure thy docks against sabotage?

The offer Lansky made in particular was simply for Roosevelt to intervene in the Luciano matter, although from the prosperity enjoyed by organized crime during World War II, it may appear to imply that the deal went much further and actually entailed federal protection for certain areas of Syndicate wartime activity, e.g., smuggling.

Luciano was moved right away from the remote Dannemora Prison to the more comfortable and spacious Great Meadow Prison north of Albany. His accessibilities thus improved, he lived out the war years in a style befitting the prisoner who is also the jailer's benefactor and a party to a larger arrangement with the throne. Promptly on V-E Day, his lawyer filed the papers that opened the doors for his release and deportation to Sicily. He would shortly return to his Godfatherly duties in the exile capital Lansky had been preparing all the while in Havana. Lansky delivered Luciano and won federal protection. The Syndicate was made.

But that only began it. Syndicate collaboration with the American war effort went much further.

The Sicilian Mafia, for example, had been all but wiped out by Mussolini in fascism's long violent rise to power. The Mafia was a power rival and Mussolini crushed it bloodily. But when General George Patton landed on Sicily with the Seventh Army's Third Division in 1943, he came with instructions to fly Luciano's black and yellow scarf along with the Stars and Stripes and to seek out the tactical support of local Mafiosi, who would offer themselves as guides and informants. This support may or may not have been of measurable military value. The Kefauver Committee theorized later that it was too slight to have justified the release of Luciano on patriotic grounds. But what Patton's tanks meant to the Mafia was purely and simply its restoration to power in Sicily.

Then in 1944 Roosevelt wanted Batista to step aside in Cuba. The most persuasive confidential ambassador he could think of, the best man for delivering such a message to Batista, Messick reports, was Lansky himself. Whom else would Batista listen to?

Lansky and Batista had first met ten years before in the year of Repeal, 1934. Lansky had seen that the coming legalization of liquor might give an enormous business opportunity to those who had run it when it was illegal. So as Repeal drew nearer, he started shopping for raw material sources, for all the world like a run-of-the-mill corporate-imperial businessman.

He got to Havana in 1934 shortly after Batista first won power. The two men found themselves in deep harmony. Lansky stayed three weeks and worked out with Batista the arrangements that would bring molasses from Cuban cane to Syndicate-controlled distilleries and set up Havana as a major gaming capital of the Western hemisphere.

From these beginnings, the Lansky-Batista association prospered greatly over the next decade. No one better than Lansky could have carried Roosevelt's message, nor could Batista have wiled away his exile period in a more appropriate or comfortable setting than the Palm Springs mansion which Lansky made available. When the wind changed yet another time in the early 1950s and it was time for Batista to go back to Cuba and resume command, it was again Lansky who gave Batista the word to move.

In France, too, the forces of crime were integrated into U.S. efforts to establish anti-Communist postwar governments, notably at Marseilles, where the World War II CIA (OSS) employed Corsican Syndicate goonsquads to break the French Communist Party's control of the docks. It was another twisted situation. The main serious wartime resistance to European fascism was that of European Communists. Their resistance was militarily and therefore politically significant. Beyond Communist Party activity, resistance to Nazi Germany had been fragmentary or weak-willed and ineffectual. The non-Communist left (e.g., the groups around Jean-Paul Sartre and Albert Camus) had prestige but little combat or political-organizational capability. The rest of the country collaborated.

With no interference from outside, the natural result of this disposition of factors in postwar Europe might easily have been the immediate rise of the Communist Party to great power if not dominance in French affairs.

The same thing was threatening to happen all across Europe. Given that American policy was committed to the achievement of a non-Communist postwar Western Europe, there was possibly no way for the pacification effort to have avoided collusion with crime. *Besides the Corsican Syndicate, there was no other group sufficiently organized and disciplined to challenge the French CP for control of the Marseilles docks*. A result is that Marseilles became within a few years the heroin-manufacturing capital of the Western world and the production base of the Lansky-Luciano-Trafficanto heroin traffic into the American ghetto.

The integration of the forces of law with the forces of organized crime extends from the municipal to the federal level. It takes in vast reaches of the law-enforcement and security establishment: police, military, paramilitary, and private alike. It constitutes a burden of corruption possibly already too heavy to be thrown off.

When we look back from Watergate to find the causes of it all, the Yankee wartime leadership's amazing opportunism looms large. With Operation Underworld, Roosevelt made the Mafiosi all but official masters of the U.S. East Coast docks and gave implicit protection to their activities everywhere. With his instructions to Patton in 1943, he restored the Mafia to power in Sicily. When he sent Lansky to Batista in 1944, he paved the way for the spread of Syndicate influence throughout the Caribbean and Central America. When he directed the CIA to use Syndicate thugs at Marseilles in 1945, he licensed the heroin factories that would be feeding the American habit into a contagion virtually unchecked over the years of the Cold War.

One can easily enough sympathize with Roosevelt's desire to strike at the Axis powers with whatever weapons came to hand, and especially to do something to protect the docks. But we must also judge his acts by their longer-term consequences. Certainly we cannot say it is all Nixon's fault if during his novice and formative years in political administration, when he and Rebozo may have found themselves in a relationship around black market tires in wartime Miami (see below), he should have come upon the idea, FDR-sponsored, that some crooks were patriotic, and the patriotic ones were okay to do business with, just as though a few purchased gestures of patriotism could make crime itself legitimate. Fine word, legitimate. Operation Underworld is one of the roots of Operation Gemstone. Roosevelt is one of the authors of Watergate.

The Derivation of Nixon

> Tricky is perhaps the most despicable President this
> nation has ever had. He was a cheat, a liar and a crook,
> and he brought my country, which I love, into
> disrepute. Even worse than abusing his office, he abused
> the American people.
>
> —Earl Warren[4]

Nixon is commonly supposed to have been introduced to
Bebe Rebozo by Richard Danner, the courier and connecter
who left the FBI to become city manager of Miami Beach at
a time when it was under the all-but-open control of the
Mob.[5]

Danner first met Nixon at a party thrown in Washington
in 1947 by another newly elected congressman, George
Smathers. Smathers was by that time already an intimate
friend and business partner of Rebozo and a friend of
Batista. When Nixon vacationed in Havana after his 1952
election to the vice-presidency, Syndicate-wise Danner used
his clout with Lansky's man Norman "Roughhouse"
Rothman to get gambling credit at the Sans Souci for
Nixon's traveling companion, Dana Smith.[6] We recall Dana
Smith as the manager of the secret slush fund set up to
finance Pat Nixon's cloth coats, the exposure of which led to
the famous Checkers TV speech during the 1952 campaign.
Smith dropped a bundle at the Sans Souci and left Cuba
without paying it back. Safe in the States, he repudiated the
debt. That infuriated Rothman. Nixon was forced to ask the
State Department to intervene in Smith's behalf.[7]

It is poetically satisfying to imagine Nixon and Rebozo
meeting through Danner. When Danner reenters in the next
to last act of Watergate with the $100,000 from Hughes
which only he seems to have been able to deliver, we may
sense a wheel coming full circle. But there is the possibility
also that Rebozo and Nixon actually connected in Miami in

1942, and it is almost certain that they knew of each other then, as will emerge.

Here are the fragments with which we reconstruct Rebozo: (a) he is associated with the anti-Castro Cuban exile community in Florida; (b) an all-Cuban shopping center in Miami is constructed for him by Polizzi Construction Co., headed by Cleveland Mafioso Al "The Owl" Polizzi, listed by the McClellan crime committee as one of "the most influential members of the underworld in the United States"; (c) his Key Biscayne Bank was involved in the E. F. Hutton stock theft, in which the Mafia fenced stolen securities through his bank.[8]

Rebozo's will to power appears to have developed during the war, when he made it big in the "used-tire" and "retread" business. Used-tire distributors all over the country, of course, were willingly and unwillingly turned into fences of Mafia black market tires during the war. Rebozo could have been used and still not know it.

He was born in 1912 in Florida to a family of poor Cuban immigrants, was ambitious, and by 1935 had his first gas station. By the time the war was over, his lucrative retread business had turned him into a capitalist and he was buying up Florida land. Before long he was buying vast amounts of it in partnership with Smathers and spreading thence into the small-loans business, sometimes called loan-sharking.[9] From lending he went to insuring. He and Smathers insured each other's business operations. His successes soon carried him to the sphere of principalities and powers the likes of W. Clement Stone of Chicago and the aerosol king Robert Abplanalp, both of whom met Nixon through him. Also during the war, Rebozo was navigator in a part-time Military Air Transport Command crew that flew military transports to Europe full and back empty, which some find a Minderbinderesque detail.

During the first year of the war, before going into the Navy, Nixon worked in the interpretations unit of the legal section of the tire-rationing branch of the Office of Price

Administration. Investigator Jeff Gerth has discovered that three weeks after Nixon began this job, his close friend-to-be, George Smathers, came to federal court for the defendant in this case, *United States* vs. *Standard Oil of Kansas*.[10] U.S. Customs had confiscated a load of American-made tires reentering the country through Cuba in an "attempt to circumvent national tire rationing," i.e., bootleg tires. Smathers wanted to speed up the case for his client, and so wrote to the OPA for a ruling. His letter must have come to Nixon, who, OPA records show, was responsible for all correspondence on tire rationing questions. It was therefore Nixon's business to answer Smathers. Especially since this was the first knock on the door, it would be nice to know what Nixon said and how the matter was disposed of. "Unfortunately," reports Gerth, "most OPA records were destroyed after the war. The court file for this case is supposed to be in the Atlanta Records Center, but a written request submitted to the clerk of the civil court on July 6, 1972, has not been honored, despite the usual one week response time. Written questions submitted to President Nixon and Bebe Robozo have also gone unanswered. Among the relevant questions is whether Miami was one of the regional offices Nixon set up."[11]

Was this the bending of the twig? And if Rebozo and Nixon actually did meet then, even if only through bureaucratic transactions around the flow of tires, then they met within the sphere of intense Syndicate activity at a time when Roosevelt's Operation Underworld had conferred immense prestige and freedom of movement on Syndicate activities. Could the Nixon-Rebozo relationship escape being affected by FDR's truce between law and crime?

Let us spell out this theory of Nixon's beginnings in A-B-C simplicity.

Prohibition: Organized crime takes over the distilleries industry.

Repeal: Bootlegging goes legit, the Syndicate thereby expanding into the sphere of "legal" operations. This is the first big foothold of organized crime in the operations of the state.

Cuba/Batista: Lansky goes to Cuba in 1934 in search of a molasses source, meets and courts the newly ascendant strongman Batista, stays three weeks and lays plans for developing Havana into the major off-shore freezone of State-side organized crime, Cuba playing the role in the Caribbean of Sicily and Corsica in the Mediterranean.

World War II: In despair of otherwise securing the physical security of the docks against sabotage which may or may not have been Fascist-inspired, Roosevelt accepts a secret arrangement with organized crime. He comforts Luciano in prison and agrees to release him to exile at the end of the war. He generates an atmosphere of coalition with crime for the duration. In that atmosphere, Syndicate projects prosper. But one of the smugglers, Kansas Standard, gets too brazen and is caught, perhaps, by naive customs officials. Smathers takes the case for the defendant and thus comes into contact with Nixon.

Noting Gerth's discovery that the records of this case have inexplicably disappeared from the files, noting Rebozo's involvement in the tire business and his rapid enrichment during World War II, and noting Smathers's well-known affection for Cuban associations, we generalize to the straight-forward hypothesis that Nixon may have been fused to the Syndicate already in 1942. Was his 1944 stint in the Navy a sheep-dipping? Look at this rise: 1946: Nixon for Congress; 1948: Nixon for Congress (II); 1950: Nixon for Senate; 1952: a heartbeat away.

So it is another Dr. Frankenstein story. The Yankees beget in sheer expediency and offhandedness the forces that will later grow strong enough to challenge them for leadership. Operation Underworld was the supreme pioneering joint effort of crime and the state, the first major direct step taken toward their ultimate covert integration in the Dallas-Watergate decade.

The Gehlen Organization

Recall two generals of World War II. First, General Andrei Vlassov, a Red Army officer secretly working with an extensive anti-Bolshevist spy ring.[12] He joined up his forces with the advancing Germans during the invasion of the Ukraine, where Russian forces antagonistic to Stalin and anxious to overthrow the Bolsheviks had collected. Vlassov commanded the so-called Army of Liberation, a full division of more or less well equipped troops fighting under the flag of Great White Russian reaction for the restoration of the Czar.

And second, General Reinhard Gehlen, the famous "superspy" of the same war, master of Hitler's powerful Soviet intelligence apparatus. The practical basis of the great success of Gehlen's Soviet intelligence system was his relationship to Vlassov. Through Vlassov, Gehlen had access to the Russian anti-Bolshevist underground network that had long since penetrated if not captured key departments of the Soviet regime. At a moment in their invasion when the Nazis still thought themselves on the brink of triumph, Gehlen proposed to Hitler that Vlassov be made the head of the forthcoming provisional government. Hitler declined, presumably out of respect for Vlassov's power, but the relationship between Gehlen and Vlassov and their spy systems remained intact, even after the defeat of the Wehrmacht in the Battle of Stalingrad, winter of 1942-43.

By Christmas 1944 Gehlen had reached the belief that Germany's cause was hopeless. Against the certainty of national defeat, he decided that his only personal choice lay between surrender to the Russians and surrender to the Americans.

In April 1945, with the Russian army closing on Berlin, Gehlen gathered together with his top aides in a hotel room in Bad Elster, Saxony, to carry out the decisive and most dangerous step of their decision. They stripped their archives of the intelligence information that would be most useful to them in subsequent negotiations. Burning tons of other documents, they stored their basic intelligence cache in fifty-two crates and with elaborate security measures moved these crates south into the Bavarian Redoubt and buried them in a high mountain field called Misery Meadow, overlooked by a chalet which Gehlen's foresight had long before provisioned. Safe there with his forty top aides and his buried spy treasures, Gehlen settled down to await the Americans.

By May Day 1945 the Red Army was in Berlin and Hitler was dead. Three weeks later, columns of the 101st Airborne moved up the valley below Gehlen's mountain fortress. Gehlen's aides descended from the upper slopes to present themselves for capture and arrange an appointment for the capture of their commander, the highest-ranking German officer and Hitler's only staff general yet to make his way to safety in American hands.

No ceremonies were slighted. One interview followed another. Captured in May, Gehlen arrived in Washington three months later, August 22, 1945, in the uniform of a general of the United States Army, flown there in the command transport of Gen. Walter Bedell Smith. In a series of secret meetings with the American staff, beginning with Allen Dulles and Wild Bill Donovan of the OSS, he laid out in detail the proposal—the surrender conditions, essentially—which he was offering the Americans.[13]

Postwar Europe, he pointed out, as everyone knew, was certain to become the arena of a confrontation between the United States and the Soviet Union ultimately even greater than the confrontation just ending between the victorious Allies and the vanquished Axis powers. The Soviets, he said, were well prepared for this new confrontation from an intelligence standpoint, as who better than he could say, and the Americans were not. The Russians had a crack spy network in West Europe and America, but the Americans did not have a spy network of any kind or quality in East

Europe and Russia. Did that not put the Americans at an important disadvantage in the forthcoming struggles?

Then where and how could the Americans procure the needed capability? Recruiting and training a corps of Russian and Central European intelligence agents and building a network of reliable sources and experts nearly from scratch would take years, generations. The Americans agreed with Gehlen that they did not have that much time.

Very well, Gehlen had a practical solution to this very problem. His own intelligence apparatus was still intact within the collapsing Hitler government. It was as capable as ever of delivering large masses of high-quality intelligence data on all aspects of Soviet life. Hitler had never taken advantage of this capability, Gehlen explained. Hitler had ignored Gehlen's organization and had gone on to ruin. Still it was there. It might have been put to better use. It still could be, should the Americans accept his offer.

Gehlen's offer was for the Americans to pick up his organization bodily and bolt it into the empty space in their own intelligence system, as though it were one of the spoils of the war. Gehlen could plausibly guarantee his network's unmatched and unbending loyalty to the cause of anti-Bolshevism, and the fifty-two crates he had buried in Misery Meadow were tangible proofs of his power and a foretaste of secret knowledge to come.

All the Americans had to do was to meet Gehlen's four conditions. First, Gehlen was to have complete autonomy within his organization and total control over its activities. The Americans would tell him what they wanted and they would get it, satisfaction guaranteed, but they would have to know nothing about the process by which Gehlen got it to give them; that knowledge was Gehlen's own. He even reserved the right to approve U.S. liaison officers assigned to him. Second, the Americans would agree to use Gehlen only against the USSR and the East European satellites. Third, when a new German government was set up, the Americans would constitutionally install the Gehlen organization in it as its official central intelligence agency and cancel automatically all outstanding Gehlen commitments to the United States. Fourth, the Americans would never require Gehlen to do anything he considered against German national interests.

In the long and the short, our guys fell for it. Even as the United States was publicly proclaiming a policy of unconditional German surrender, Gehlen's incredible conditions were met and his organization was being established at the very core and seat of the American system of foreign intelligence under the responsibility of Allen Dulles's Secret Intelligence Branch of the OSS.[14] By the time of the transformation of the OSS into the CIA in 1948, Gehlen had grown tight with Dulles and his organization had become in effect the CIA's department of Russian and East European affairs. Soon after the formation of NATO, it became the official NATO intelligence organization. And as per Gehlen's third condition, his organization was installed as the core and he as the director of the West German CIA, the *Bundesnachtendienst* (BND).

We need go no further into the exploits of this last long improbable phase of Gehlen's career, save to note that it spans the Cold War, that it was current as of Watergate, and that Gehlen had to be pried out of a spy's "retirement" in 1974 to testify in the sensational West German spy scandal that brought down Willy Brandt. Look what power the victors conceded the vanquished. Exclusive purveyor of intelligence on the Soviet Union and East Europe to the United States, West Germany, and NATO, Gehlen and the spirit kept alive in him and his staff had more power over official American perceptions in the postwar world than even a German victory could have given them. The Gehlen-Vlassov intelligence system had become a main source and fountain of official American consciousness.

Behold the span of this concatenation. First in the time of Trotsky there is General Vlassov and his anti-Bolshevist army and spy ring. The Vlassov apparatus is then at a certain later point assimilated to the Gehlen apparatus. Then just as the White Russian spies jumped to the Nazis when their own army went down, so now the German Nazi and Russian Czarist spies together jumped to the American army as the Wehrmacht was falling. Vlassov first became a department of Gehlen, then Gehlen became a department of Allen Dulles.

This is how it came to pass that a Czarist spy ring inside a Nazi spy ring took up the inner seats in the American foreign intelligence apparatus at the precise moment that this apparatus was starting to come forward as a major player in the great policy wars of Washington and the world. This is how it came to pass that everything official Washington would know about the Soviet Union and East Europe on most believable report, everything about the enemy our policymakers would most confidently believe, would come by way of Czarists and Nazis installed at the center of our national intelligence system. That was a buzzard that would come home to roost again and again.

Clandestinism is a disease of republican twilight. Its coming bespeaks the degeneration of the constitutional republic into the military empire. It worsens when the empire shakes, as in the Vietnam war America was shaken. In the American case, it does not arise from the mere accident of the Round Table's domination of the foreign service or FDR's ready capitulation to Syndicate extortion or the ideological gullibility of America's wartime espionage elite before the rational blandishments of a Nazi superspy. Rather, such accidents themselves were given significance by the larger transformation taking place around them: the dissolution of the wartime alliance between the United States and the Soviet Union and the crystallizing in its place of the Cold War conflict between them. But one must always return to the specific events in which these larger forces unveiled themselves. Otherwise we repeat the conservative's error of assuming that state clandestinism results from the struggle against subversive terror instead of the struggle to maintain illegitimate state power, and the liberal's error of thinking that fascism is a result of the high-technology era instead of the domination of this era by the activities of self-serving power elites.

II

Dallas

During this long period of delay and potential litigation, ugly passions would again be aroused. And our people would again be polarized in their opinions. And the credibility of our free institutions of government would again be challenged at home and abroad. . . . My conscience tells me clearly and certainly that I cannot prolong the bad dreams that continue to reopen a chapter that is closed. My conscience tells me that only I, as President, have the Constitutional power to firmly shut and seal this book. My conscience tells me that it is my duty, not merely to proclaim domestic tranquility, but to use every means I have to ensure it.

—President Ford pardons Nixon,
September 8, 1974

3

"The Whole Bay of Pigs Thing"

At the 10:00 A.M. Oval Office meeting of June 23, 1972, the fifth day of Watergate, alone with Haldeman, Nixon said, "Of course, this Hunt, that will uncover a lot of things. You open that scab, there's a hell of a lot of things, and we just feel that it would be very detrimental to have this thing go any further. This involves these Cubans, Hunt, and a lot of hanky-panky that we have nothing to do with ourselves. . . ."

Moments later Nixon returned to this problem: "When you get in—when you get in (unintelligible) people, say, 'Look, the problem is that this will open the whole, the whole Bay of Pigs thing, and the President just feels that ah, without going into the details—don't, don't lie to them to the extent to say there is no involvement, but just say this is a comedy of errors, without getting into it, the President believes that it is going to open the whole Bay of Pigs thing up again. And ah, because these people are plugging for (unintelligible) and that they should call the FBI in and (unintelligible) don't go any further into this case period! . . ."

Then at the 1:00 P.M. meeting that same day, again alone with Haldeman, Nixon said, "O.K., just postpone (scratching noises) (unintelligible) Just say (unintelligible) very bad to have this fellow Hunt, ah, he knows too damned much, if he was involved—you happen to know that? If it gets out that this is all involved, the Cuba thing would be a fiasco. It would make the CIA look bad, it's going to make Hunt look bad, and it is likely to blow the whole Bay of Pigs thing, which we think would be very unfortunate—both for the CIA, and for the country, at this time, and for American foreign policy. Just tell him to lay off. . . ."

At the meeting of 2:20 P.M., the same day, Haldeman said to Nixon: "Gray called Helms and said I think we've run right into the middle of a covert CIA operation."

Nixon: "Gray said that?"

Haldeman: "Yeah. And (unintelligible) said nothing we've done at this point and ah (unintelligible) says well it sure looks to me like it is (unintelligible) and ah, that was the end of that conversation (unintelligible) the problem is it tracks back to the Bay of Pigs and it tracks back to some other, the leads run out to people who had no involvement in this, except by contracts and connection, but it gets into areas that are liable to be realized. The whole problem (unintelligible) Hunt. . ."

What could all this be about? What does Hunt know about some still-secret "thing" associating Nixon in some new, dreadful way with the invasion of Cuba of April 1961? Was the Bay of Pigs Fiasco not Kennedy's fiasco? By the time of the invasion, Nixon had already been out of office for three months. What did Nixon have to do with it? And whom exactly does Haldeman protect with this haunting phrase, "except by contracts and connection"?

True, as vice president, Nixon had been chief political officer on the National Security Council's Special Group (5412/2) in which the Cuban invasion was conceived, decided upon, planned, and directed. He has written of flying from California to Washington on the day of the invasion and that evening receiving CIA Director Allen

Dulles, who brought the news that all was lost.[1]

But there was nothing secret about any of this. What could Hunt now add to the story of the Bay of Pigs that would put Nixon in such steep new peril?

So far in the national analysis of Watergate, this question has been largely overlooked. What was fastened upon in the June 23 tapes was rather the brief passage in which, unmistakably, Nixon tells Haldeman to cover up White House complicity in the Watergate cover up. That bit of evidence convicted Nixon in the public mind of an impeachable offense and remaining salvos were left unfired.

So what could "the whole Bay of Pigs thing" be? The book of standard American impressions badly overstates the respect in which the Bay of Pigs Fiasco was a Cold War confrontation between the Free World and communism and understates the respect in which it was also a confrontation between rival American power elites, each with its strengths and weaknesses, Kennedy on one side and Nixon on the other, and as I would say, Yankee and Cowboy in makeup. That is why the operation turned out the "Fiasco" which all parties promptly agreed to call it.

To unravel this, start with the conventional picture of the Bay of Pigs as a Cold War confrontation. In the 1960 campaign, Kennedy promised to get tough with Castro, trying to get to the right of Nixon on the Cuban issue at the very moment that Nixon was secretly operating as the chief political officer in the invasion planning group. Within scant months of taking office, Kennedy seemed to keep his promise; within hours more, he had failed to make it good. As a result of the Fiasco ending, the Russians got more deeply involved in Cuban affairs and brought Kennedy to the test of wills of the October Missile Crisis a year and a half later, in which Kennedy is supposed to have stood his ground and regained his manhood.

To this general picture, the activists of the anti-Castro invasion, such as Nixon and Hunt, add a critical detail, namely, that the fault for the failure of the Cuban invasion lies with Kennedy. Kennedy, they say, cut back on critical U.S. support to the invasion forces at the last moment and thereby doomed to failure a project they believe could otherwise have succeeded easily.

This theory suffers from the crude partisanship which keeps it from looking beyond such notions as cowardice and treachery to explain Kennedy's apparent about-face at the beach. But it does recognize that the Kennedy administration was in sharp internal conflict over what to do about Cuba, and that the formulation and implementation of Frontier Camelot Cuban policy were affected by this conflict or, as might be said, disfigured by it.

That is the key point which the Cold War conception of the Bay of Pigs Fiasco cannot bring into focus: that the Cuban question and the question of hemispheric revolution so divided the Kennedy administration that the United States could neither accept Castro nor act with a will to destroy what Castro stood for. The cause of Nixon's panic a decade thereafter about what his comrade Hunt knew of "the whole Bay of Pigs thing" may thus lie within the terms of this conflict, which we now explore.

Nixon testified offhandedly to this division in his November 1964 *Reader's Digest* piece, "Cuba, Castro, and John F. Kennedy." He wrote:

But, as had happened in the Eisenhower administration, a sharp difference of opinion about Castro developed among President Kennedy's advisors. One group of activists urged him to go forward with the invasion plan. His liberal advisors . . . advised that the United States should either try to get along with Castro or find some other method of dealing with him. . . . Kennedy finally over-ruled his soft-line advisors and decided to go forward with the plan. . . . But in the end the soft-liners won their point and, by last-minute compromises, doomed the operation to failure.

* * *

Thus, in the eyes of the invasion's self-styled "strongest advocate," Kennedy did *not* go forward with the agreed-to plans, he went forward with a new and different set of plans, plans that no one had actually proposed or defended or thought would work, plans (a) minus the use of the B-26s ready and waiting in Central America and (b) minus a CIA subplot to assassinate Castro.

What was the actual significance of these two last-minute changes? For an insight into this, we first have to sketch out the CIA's most probable invasion scenario. From the sophistication, if not the overwhelming competence, it has shown in other such operations, the CIA should not be thought vain enough to think its Free Cuba exile army could actually endure against the arms of the Cuban revolution, much less march to the capital. The CIA strategy was more roundabout: "to maintain an invasion force on Cuban territory for at least 72 hours and then to proclaim the Free Government of Cuba there on that bit of territory."[2] From there it would unveil a worldwide network of Free Cuba exile government offices, already assembled, in an effort to pull the U.S. military into demonstration-state alert and exert U.S. diplomatic influence with the OAS, and UN, the Soviet Union, and other countries to move "the Cuban situation" to an international-negotiations setting. It would thus throw open again the whole political question of Cuba's internal direction, with many opportunities for counterrevolutionary maneuver.

The fate of such a strategy would hinge on the missions of the B26s and the assassination squad.

The B-26s were important because in order for the invading forces to hold a position on the beach without direct U.S. aerial support, it was necessary for Castro's air force to be suppressed. This amounted only to two trainer jets left behind by Batista on which Cuban mechanics had mounted rudimentary armament systems. But if the invaders were to have a chance at their basic positional objectives, those two little jets would have to be kept out of the air. Crude as they were, unopposed against ground forces on a beach, they could be decisive in the battle. Had the B-26s flown in from the Atlantic out of the sunrise, as first planned, and caught the Cuban jets on the ground, the landing forces would have encountered no Cuban air resistance. That might have made it possible to hold the beachhead a little longer.[3]

From a technical standpoint, the assassination of Castro was equally important to the success of the invasion. The revolutionary government was at that time a little more than two years old. It still consisted in some part of antagonistic groupings held together mainly by Castro's great prestige. Wouldn't the elimination of the Castro brothers encourage fragmentation? Look at the CIA's broad-daylight murder of Allende in 1973 for the component of the Bay of Pigs invasion plan that Kennedy vetoed in 1961: the assassination of the leader.

The particular importance of the Castro hit to the overall success of the invasion may be inferred from the intensity of the struggle about it. Journalist Cuba-watcher Tad Szulc reported thirteen years later that in a private Oval Office interview with Kennedy in November 1961, with Richard Goodwin present, seven months after the invasion had been repulsed and/or betrayed, Kennedy said to him, "What would you think if I ordered Castro to be assassinated?" Szulc says he objected to this idea and that Kennedy "leaned back in the chair, smiled, and said that he had been testing me because he was under great pressure from advisors in the intelligence community (whom he did not name) to have Castro killed, but that he himself violently opposed it on the grounds that for moral reasons, the United States should never be party to political assassinations."[4]

Another anecdote has Florida's Senator Smathers pressing Kennedy for Castro's head at a formal White House dinner. Kennedy is finally infuriated and breaks plates and scatters flowers to convince Smathers he must stop asking.[5]

The intensity of feeling no doubt flowed both ways. Early in 1975 an item long familiar to conspiracy researchers became big-time news: It was that around the time of the Bay of Pigs the CIA used Howard Hughes's special agent Robert Maheu to contract the services of Syndicate Capo John Roselli to get rid of Castro. The immediate question posed by this now-authenticated story is whether it was Kennedy who actually authorized the CIA to use a Syndicate hitman to liquidate Castro, or somebody else. Why should the CIA have to rent assassination capabilities from the Syndicate?

The timing of these events is uncertain. We do not know at what moment Kennedy vetoed the Castro assassination plot or at what moment the CIA used its Hughes-Maheu connection to retain a Syndicate assassination squad. It appears that Kennedy first told the CIA not to carry out the assassination, and that the "activist" elements of "the intelligence community" then took it upon themselves to mobilize Syndicate resources to the task.

"By the advent of the Kennedy administration," writes R. Harris Smith, "the CIA had indeed become a schizophrenic organization, torn between political left and right. Yet few outside the government understood these divisions. The CIA conservatives and swashbucklers found warm support for their position in Congress; the Agency liberals were forced to fend for themselves."[6] The basis of the CIA's need for the Syndicate may lie ultimately in the politics of that split.

In any case, there was no internal Frontier Camelot consensus on Cuba or on the Bay of Pigs invasion project. Kennedy's veto of the B-26 raids and the assassination plot embodied a basic change from the original invasion plan. The judgment of Nixon and Hunt is surely borne out in this respect if in no other, that is, Kennedy's veto of these two moves did indeed "doom the invasion to failure." The quarrel between Nixon and Kennedy was thus a quarrel of basic political and operational substance, not merely a technical falling-out among comrade militarists. And if an epitaph makes it clearer, there is Nixon's memorable remark to Dean and Haldeman in the Oval Office on February 28, 1973: "...I was reading a book last night. A fascinating book, although fun book, by Malcolm Smith Jr. on Kennedy's Thirteen Mistakes, the great mistakes. And one of them was the Bay of Pigs. And what happened there was Chester Bowles had learned about it, and he deliberately leaked it. Deliberately, because he wanted the operation to fail. And he admitted it! Admitted it!"

That is the whole point. From the standpoint of the Nixon side, the Kennedy side *wanted* the Cuban invasion to fail. There is no other explanation for the quickness and venom with which the proinvasion side fastened on Kennedy's "betrayal" of their project.[7]

Nixon tells us the conflict about Castro began in the State Department before Kennedy came on. Obviously it sharpened with his arrival. We know Kennedy was furious in the Bay of Pigs aftermath and felt betrayed—betrayed by the CIA and the larger clandestine state in fact—and that he tried to reorganize the overall clandestine apparatus, and especially the CIA, precisely to make it responsive and accountable to the White House.

Yet the left denounces Kennedy for invading Cuba as casually as the right denounces him for invading it too timidly. One side sees Kennedy's "betrayal" and the other sees his "failure to understand the situation." The idea that the actual policy as carried out was the free synthesis of a totally absorbing internal conflict over which neither side had complete control does not seem to be widely entertained.

David Halberstam, to take an important liberal example, writes that "the crux of [the Bay of Pigs] was how the U.S. government could have so misread the Cuban people." Was Kennedy not the founder of the Peace Corps and the Alianza? "How a President so contemporary could agree to a plan so obviously doomed to failure, a plan based on so little understanding of the situation, was astounding."[8]

Rather more astounding looking back post-Watergate is the insensitivity of liberal commentary to the importance of the internal conflict that wracked Frontier Camelot from the first. It is general knowledge that Kennedy was at odds with powerful hawks from the outset of his administration on the question not only of Cuba but of Laos, Vietnam, and the Congo, on the questions of the Third World as a whole, disarmament, Berlin, nuclear weapons, etc., that he came to mistrust the whole security-intelligence apparatus, and that he finally sought to reduce the influence of Johnson and his circles. Halberstam's book is actually a treasure chest of examples of that mistrust and shows clearly the general Yankee/Cowboy outlines of the Kennedy Administration. Why then do Halberstam and other liberals not weigh this division in with the other forces acting on policy?

We see Kennedy's Cuban policy better if we simply recognize that it was formed under conditions of internal conflict, conflict within the executive policy apparatus itself. Frontier Camelot was the Kennedys' attempt to transform an exaggeratedly wide *electoral* coalition—the Kennedy/ Johnson, Yankee/Cowboy coalition—into an effective *governing* coalition, an attempt which failed at the Bay of Pigs, its first test, as it ultimately failed in Vietnam, its most tragic test. Thus, we simply put what we know about the "irrationality" of Kennedy's policy together with what we know about the conflict within which the "irrational" policy was formed, and we answer Halberstam's question about how Kennedy "could have so misread the Cuban people" with another question: How could the liberals have so misread Kennedy's situation? And still misread it a decade and more later? How could they have read the Bay of Pigs invasion as a Camelot project while at the same time claiming to be baffled at the inconsistency of that invasion with Camelot values and consciousness? Yes, Kennedy would have been foolish some other way. The Bay of Pigs seemed Nixon's way of being foolish.

The trick to how the invasion could come about nevertheless, how there could be a Bay of Pigs against the will of the president, is that the president is not an absolute

monarch ruling a submissive bureaucracy. Rather, a
"corporate" presidency is nested within the federal power
grid along with a variety of institutional strongholds, such as
the Pentagon, the CIA, the Department of Transportation,
the Texas Railroad Commission, etc. The president in
person proper is only one among many others on the larger
board of national directors—a special stronghold clearly but
by no means the only power source on the scene. The
presidency of the corporate state is the presidency of
factional and bureaucratic coalitions that can weaken, grow
old and brittle, fail in crises. The tragedy of Frontier
Camelot, whose prince is said to have sought the presidency
"because it's where the action's at," unfolds in the prince's
gradual discovery of the *corporate* and *limited* nature of his
office, then more particularly of its relative *weakness* against
the will of the clandestine establishments of defense and
security.

The Bay of Pigs invasion project began on April 19, 1960,
in the vice-president's office at the Capitol at some point in
Nixon's celebrated interview with Castro. At Nixon's
insistence, only interpreters were present, so there is no
record of the meeting other than his recollection of it. "After
3½ hours of discussion," write Nixon four years later, "I
summed up my impressions in this way—he looked like a
revolutionary, talked like an idealistic college professor and
reacted like a communist.... At the conclusion of our
conference I wrote a four-page secret memorandum, and
sent copies to President Eisenhower, Secretary [of State]
Herter and Allen Dulles.... My conclusion was, 'Castro is
either incredibly naive about communism or is under
communist discipline.'"[9]

Nixon proceeds to describe the "spirited policy discussions on Cuba" that then took place within the Eisenhower
foreign-policy establishment and tells how his position
hardened around the conviction that Castro was not naive,
while (as he says) "the majority view in the State Department
was in sharp disagreement with my appraisal of Castro." He

says the foreign-policy elite harbored the view that Castro was "liberal" (Nixon uses the word with quotes).

Nixon says Eisenhower realized the majority view was wrong: "By early 1960 President Eisenhower reached the conclusion that Castro was an agent of international communism and a menace to peace in this hemisphere. In a top-secret meeting in his office, at which I was present, he authorized the CIA to organize and train Cuban exiles for the eventual purpose of freeing their homeland from Castro's communist rule."

Then came the agony of the TV debate in which Kennedy (says Nixon) "emerged as the man who was advocating a 'get-tough policy' toward Castro. I was the man who was 'soft' on Castro—the exact opposite of the truth." Nixon says he had to pretend to be "soft" in order to protect the security of the invasion project then going forward. "The irony was," writes Nixon, "that I had been the strongest and most persistent advocate for setting up and supporting such a program."

Nixon does not record the evidence for this self-estimate, but we have no reason to challenge it, and we know that someone in a position to do something about it was doubtful enough of JFK's commitment to a winning invasion to take steps toward implementing the plans for it before the election, thus obviating the question of Kennedy's will. That was the discovery of *Washington Post* reporter Haynes Johnson, who wrote in his book, *The Bay of Pigs*, that "on November 4, 1960, four days before the Presidential election, the CIA sent a long cable to Guatemala informing its men there of the decision to carry out the Cuban invasion plans." Johnson quotes Cuban exile commanders as saying their "CIA advisers ordered them to continue with the invasion even if Kennedy called it off altogether, that if this happened the Cubans were to rebel against their CIA instructors and present Kennedy with a situation in which he would have no political alternative to supporting them."[10]

We do not know that Nixon was the author of this

decision, but we do know that Nixon was the chief political officer of the decision-making body, the Special Group of the National Security Council. Further, Johnson writes that "in reconstruct[ing] the process by which the 'Special Group' made its decision, one impression comes through very strongly: Dwight D. Eisenhower was not a major participant. Eisenhower himself has said publicly that there was no plan for an invasion while he was in office; that the only plan was to train guerrillas. His contention varies so sharply with the facts that an explanation for the discrepancy must be sought, for Eisenhower's integrity cannot be questioned."

Such an explanation is offered by Air Force Colonel L. Fletcher Prouty (ret.), now an executive at Amtrak. Prouty is one of several intelligence-community insiders who have come forward over the past several years with exposé-memoirs variously supporting the theme that there is, in Prouty's phrase, "a Secret Team" operating clandestinely within governmental structures toward ends it unilaterally defines as "vital to the national interest." Prouty worked as the DIA's "Focal Point Officer" for all interaction between the CIA and the Pentagon. If the CIA needed something from the Navy for project x, or something from the Army for project y, Prouty knew. He did this kind of work for some eight years, operating as a staff-briefing officer to the Joint Chiefs and the secretary of defense on vital policy memoranda. His claims therefore have a certain interest. (At one point in his book, *The Secret Team*, he uses the phrase, "my membership in the Secret Team." He never goes into this or tells us why, when, how or indeed *if* he left it, why he is telling on it now, etc.)

Prouty's main purpose in this book is to counter Daniel Ellsberg's thesis that the CIA was largely right about Vietnam and the Department of Defense largely wrong. Prouty says it was the other way around. It was in reality such "hardnosed liberals" as the CIA's Tracy Barnes and Edward Lansdale (for whom Ellsberg worked in Vietnam) and Kennedy's chief military adviser Maxwell Taylor who advocated clandestine war, or Special Forces warfare, as an alternative to conventional military and diplomatic options and thus got the U.S. involved untenably in Cuba and Vietnam. This is an intriguing and subtle dispute: the spies proving we should trust them and not the soldiers, the soldiers proving the spies lie and it is they who saw the truth.

Prouty supports Haynes Johnson's view that Eisenhower did not support the decision to invade Cuba. He writes, "In fact, all of the Eisenhower-era schemes were extremely modest when it came to action against Cuban soil and property."[11] In an interview I had with Prouty in Washington in May 1973, he added an interesting detail. What Eisenhower had approved in the way of an anti-Castro action program, said Prouty, was a thirty-three man project looking toward the feasibility of forming a guerrilla base in the countryside. But within days of the election of Kennedy, says Prouty, "orders came down" (he does not say from where) to change the 33s on the program's personnel records into 3300s.

One might find it an incredible spectacle were it not before us as a *model*, so to speak, that Howard Hunt himself, black-propagandist par excellence, sat down with gluepot, a typewriter, a Xerox copier, a light-table, an X-acto knife, and sample and related communiques from the inner-sanctum files of the State Department to prove in 1972 that the Kennedys in 1963 had ordered the assassination of Diem and his brother-in-law Nhu *as well as* the coup that toppled them from power. This makes it easier to picture someone like Prouty—big, distinguished, honorable—sneaking around the office at night with a flashlight carefully typing in two zeros after every 33 in all the records of the anti-Castro guerrilla project, records which may for that matter at that moment have been few.

Thus it was, in any case, according to Prouty, that the myriad approvals of the 33-man job were fobbed off on Kennedy by the pro-invasion group as approvals of a much bigger project, the Bay of Pigs invasion.

Another kind of evidence that the Bay of Pigs invasion was engineered by conspiracy was developed by Robert Scheer and Murray Zeitlin in their 1963 book, *Cuba: Tragedy in Our Hemisphere*.[12] By the method of comparing translations of Castro speeches used in White House papers with translations appearing elsewhere in the world press as well as with official Cuban transcripts, Zeitlin and Scheer established that the CIA translator either was naive about the Spanish language or intentionally changed Castro's meaning. Uniformly, the CIA translations being presented to Schlesinger and the Kennedys for analysis made Castro sound harsher and more belligerent than he was, encouraging the picture of a tyrant governing against popular will. This played into a wider concert of Hunt-style disinformation being orchestrated from somewhere outside the Oval Office with the purpose of making the Oval Office, the Kennedy brothers, think Castro had an unstable popular base and would be overthrown by the Cuban people if the United States would show support.

Or as Fred J. Cook said in his review of Haynes Johnson's book:

> When Kennedy took office, he was confronted with what amounted to a fait accompli. The invasion plans were perfected; he was given to understand that they had been drafted under the direction of his predecessor, a man of awesome military reputation. During the election campaign, he had called for aggressive action to topple Castro. Now he was presented with the opportunity. If he turned back, he would have to pit his untested judgment against, presumably, that of Eisenhower and all the military experts. He was on the spot.[13]

Against the Nixon-Hunt impression of Castro, Kennedy himself projected an impression formed of quite different assumptions. In his 1960 work, *Strategy of Peace*, Kennedy wrote of Castro as follows:

Just as we recall our own revolutionary past in order to understand the spirit and the significance of the anti-colonialist uprising in Asia and Africa, we should now reread the life of Simon Bolivar, the great "Liberator" of South Africa...in order to comprehend the new contagion for liberty and reform now spreading south of our borders....Fidel Castro is part of the legacy of Bolivar, who led his men over the Andes Mountains, vowing "war to the death" against Spanish rule, saying. "Where a goat can pass, so can an army." Castro is also part of the frustration of that earlier revolution which won its war against Spain but left largely untouched the indigenous feudal order.[14]

There is obviously a collision of two worldviews in these disparate impressions of Castro. The cornerstone assumption of the liberalism that underlay Kennedy's Alianza reformism is that the people rebel when conditions are bad, and that the wise prince therefore sees to the improvement of the people's condition. The explicit message of the Alianza was that the modern empire's only way to fight revolution was through reform.

This is not to sentimentalize our picture of Kennedy. His reformist strategy was after all a strategy of imperialism. But we have at the same time no need to condemn him for the crimes of his political adversaries. He did not accept the assumption that America could ever take as its enemy a foreign population as a whole. The JFK theory of "special war" presupposed that the native population would mostly support the regime for whose protection the U.S. Special Forces had been deployed, and that the insurgent forces could be isolated from the general population. When experience proved these criteria could not be met, Kennedy's response was to disengage, Johnson's to escalate.

Besides the B-26s and the assassination question, friction within the CIA between the Nixon "activists" of the invasion, such as Hunt, and the Kennedy group expressed itself also in a dispute over the form the post-Castro Cuban government should take should the invasion actually succeed. Tad Szulc reports [15] that as the date of the invasion approached, in March, Hunt was summoned to the Washington CIA office from Guatemala to be told that Manuel Rey, a liberal anti-Castroite, was going to be placed on the Cuban Revolutionary Council, the exile group's political leadership committee. Hunt also objected strongly to being instructed to put land reform in the new Cuban constitution he was drafting. "With a touch of desperation," writes Szulc, "Hunt insisted that Rey was proposing 'Castroism without Fidel,'... Rey was 'a revisionist and an opportunist,'... But his objections were met with stunning silence from the senior CIA officers assembled in Bissell's office. They had their instructions from the White House. Hunt finally blurted out that he would rather withdraw from the operation than compromise on the issue. To his astonishment, no attempt was made to dissuade him from resigning.... This marked the end of Hunt's direct involvement with the Bay of Pigs invasion."

Nixon writes, "I flew to Washington from my home state of California.... I was scheduled to make a foreign-policy speech in Chicago the following week, and I had written Allen. Dulles to ask that he brief me on some of the latest developments. President Kennedy readily gave his approval; I had an appointment to meet with Dulles at six o'clock on the afternoon of the 19th." Dulles arrived an hour and a half late, demanded a drink and pronounced the final judgment: "Everything is lost. The Cuban invasion is a total failure."[16]
The Fiasco was on.

This outcome seemed to vindicate the argument made by such liberals as Bowles (at the time) and Halberstam (ten years later) to the effect that the invasion attempt would be "counterproductive," that it would increase Castro's prestige. Halberstam reports that Undersecretary of State Bowles, a blood Yankee liberal, stumbled onto the invasion plans as they were hatching and hurried to the office of Secretary of State Rusk to protest. His argument was that "the chances of success are not greater than one out of three. This makes it a highly risky operation. If it fails, Castro's prestige and strength will be greatly enhanced."[17]

. In some ways, this is what happened. Yet the argument seems cynical. Halberstam and Bowles are not actually anti-Castro; neither one actually wants to see Castro's "prestige" destroyed. Their argument about counterproductivity seems an easy way to get a desired result—hands off Cuba, in effect—without having to be explicit in the support of the Cuban people's right to revolution and without having to attack the assumption that the United States has the right to invade country *x* if only practical standards can be satisfied.

But what about the CIA's job on Mossadegh in 1953, Arbenz in 1954, the invasion of the Dominican Republic in 1965, the subversion of the Allende government in 1973? Equally ruthless acts, but *effective, successful*. On the Halberstam-Bowles argument, how do we state our objection now? How do we meet the anti-Castroites' rejoinder that the original invasion plan *would* have succeeded, and would *not* have increased Castro's prestige, if the new president had not interfered with the prearranged plan of operations and introduced enormous changes at the last minute. From the standpoint of practical results alone, we cannot tell why Bowles and Halberstam could not just as easily object, "Then why were the colors *not* shown? Where *were* the Marines?" A *logical* Bay of Pigs invasion existed, in other words; it existed in the minds of its advocates. In this *logical* Bay of Pigs invasion, the president of the United States was to have been a friend, not an enemy. Nixon would have made everything different—with Nixon in command the bombers would have flown, the assassins would have struck, the fleet would have steamed again into Havana harbor if necessary.

But the bad fortune of the Cuban invasion project was to overlap an executive changeover installing a Yankee reformist, a Yankee who talked tough on communism only to upstage Nixon on his best side and who played at coalition with Johnson mainly to help get control of the Senate out of the South. What came forth as the Fiasco, so-called by all parties, each with its own private irony, was not the product of a unified venture. It was rather the product of palace *conflict*. One side began by wanting no Bay of Pigs at all. The result was the Fiasco.

Vietnam is the same story writ larger. Once again the left blames Kennedy for invading. Once again the right blames him for not invading with enough strength to win. Our counter-thesis is also the same: that the Quagmire was made of the same inner stuff as the Fiasco. Or in the words of Colonel Prouty, "Very few would ever be party to striking first in any event. So the first strike takes place in deep secrecy. No one knows this hidden key fact."[18]

The elements of the growth of the Vietnam war are schematically the same as those of the Bay of Pigs: (1) Clandestine beginnings within limited objectives; (2) the small force gets pinned down and a regiment must be sent to extricate it; (3) the regiment gets pinned down, etc.

From a domestic political standpoint, the Special War period under Kennedy was the link between the commando-style espionage and political action taken under Eisenhower and the full-dress air, ground, and sea war waged under Johnson. But Special War was supposed to lead away from Strategic War, not toward it, much as the commando politics of the late Eisenhower period was supposed to avert the necessity of engagement in the higher strategic scale of nuclear big-power confrontation. Indeed, each phase of escalation is begun with a definition of aims and limits that looks every bit like a built-in guarantee against the frantic rescue missions that inflame the original problem, but the limit is always defined in terms of a strong initial expectation of positive success. The spy will achieve the objective. The commandos will achieve the objective. The Special Forces will achieve the objective. The infantry will achieve the objective. The air forces will achieve the objective. But at last the objective is lost altogether in what becomes the supervening need to rescue the very rescue capability itself.

What was the theory of Kennedy's Special Forces phase? Its chief theoretician, Walt Whitman Rostow, defined communism as "a disease of transition,"[19] a social breakdown to which a society is peculiarly susceptible as it experiences the process of modernization. Once across the line, Rostow philosophized, a society again becomes stable, as though industrial life is stable in its natural state, as though there is or has been stability in American or European life. But just at the crossing, there is the temptation to go Red, to break faith with the universals of natural rights and free enterprise of the monopolies and turn the problem of development over to international communism.

That is where the Special Forces come in. They are there to hold the future for U.S.-world capitalism across the line of Third World social transition. Protected thus from its own transient delirium, country *x* can lock into the world system of American technical (i.e., military) development assistance and corporate activity defined as the Free World by those who most prosper in its games. That was the basis of the Alliance for Progress, the Peace Corps, the Special Forces, and the Special War expedition to Vietnam.

Kennedy carried the Rostowian assumptions to their combined conclusion. With an Alliance for Progress reform program depicted as working away at the larger social-economic base of the problem, he positions a Special Forces capability to nip the bud of transitional diseases in the social margin. Nipped, these diseases do not grow into revolutions, revolutions do not seize the small states one by one and carry them off into the camp of the adversary, and the United States continues to dominate a generally happy and prosperous world sphere, meanwhile easing toward detente in Europe, which really counts. Country x will have been protected from transitional diseases by the American exertions and can float up into the modern world system on a bubble of American aid, mainly in the form of military assistance designed, above all, to secure the local ruling group and thus keep that kind of peace, ultimately to conglomerate with all the other country x's in the happy molecule whose master atom is the multinational corporation.

That was the system of Special Forces/Alianza world-making for which Kennedy died: the vision of the Round Table, the CFR, the liberals in the Rockefeller-Morgan-Mellon-Carnegie group. What cost Kennedy his life was his attempt to impose the limits of Camelot Atlanticism on a Frontier-minded defense and security elite. His sense of the Cuban and Vietnamese situations seems to have been much the same. In each case, from a practical political standpoint, his immediate adversary was not Cuban or Vietnamese communism so much as it was the American prowar power elite to which he was so beholden and exposed. Recall that Kennedy could assume the loyalty of none of the clandestine and/or armed services—not the FBI, certainly not the CIA, a thousand times not the Joint Chiefs of Staff.

This is why it is so important to see the Kennedy Administration's record *not* in terms of its outward rationality, for it has none, and *not* as the expression of Kennedy's will alone, for his will did not prevail, but in terms of the impassioned political in-fighting that in reality constituted its actual life. It is the relations of power *in America* that speak in Kennedy's apparent formula: If the Cuban exiles can make the invasion alone, let it be done, *but only if*. Or again: If the Vietnamese threat can be contained with a Special Forces-level commitment, and without disrupting North Atlantic relations, let it be done, *but only if*.[20]

How strong is the evidence that Kennedy intended a

Vietnam pullback? We have a few fragments, a chronology.

1.   In the summer of 1961, as an outgrowth of the bitter experience of the Bay of Pigs (says Prouty), the Kennedy circle promulgated two key National Security Agency memos, NSAM 55 and 57. The first, a "red-striped" memo on which Prouty was the JCS briefing officer, directed the Chiefs to take the command of the Vietnam operation away from the CIA and commence a policy of disengagement. The second, not yet released, emerges in Prouty's description as a vast philosophical document of comprehensive scope propounding a doctrine of nonintervention in Third World revolutions and a concept of severe limitation in future clandestine operations.[21]

2.   (Ret.) General James M. Gavin in 1968: "There has been much speculation about what President Kennedy would or would not have done in Vietnam had he lived. Having discussed military affairs with him often and in detail for 15 years, I know he was totally opposed to the introduction of combat troops in Southeast Asia. His public statements just before his murder support this view. Let us not lay on the dead the blame for our own failures."[22]

3.   Paul B. Fay, Jr., Navy Undersecretary under JFK: "If John F. Kennedy had lived, our military involvement in Vietnam would have been over by the end of 1964."[23]

4.   Kennedy remarked to his aide Kenneth O'Donnell in 1963: "In 1965, I'll become one of the most unpopular presidents in history. I'll be damned everywhere as a Communist appeaser. But now I don't care. If I tried to pull out completely now from Vietnam, we would have another Joe McCarthy red scare on our hands, but I can do it after I'm reelected. So we had better make damned sure I'm reelected."[24]

5.   Wayne Morse, however, maintained that Kennedy was changing his Vietnam policy at the very hour of Dallas: "There's a weak defense for John Kennedy," he told the *Boston Globe* in mid-1973. "He'd seen the error of his ways. I'm satisfied if he'd lived another year we'd have been out of

Vietnam. Ten days before his assassination, I went down to
the White House and handed him his education bills, which I
was handling on the Senate floor. I'd been making two to five
speeches a week against Kennedy on Vietnam. . . . I'd gone
into President Kennedy's office to discuss education bills,
but he said, 'Wayne, I want you to know you're absolutely
right in your criticism of my Vietnam policy. Keep this in
mind. I'm in the midst of an intensive study which
substantiates your position of Vietnam.'"[25]

6. We come to know this study through the Ellsberg
Papers as the McNamara study (see especially volume 8,
detailing in Arthur Schlesinger Jr.'s phrase "Kennedy's plans
to extricate the United States from the Vietnam War").[26] In
an interview in late 1973, Ellsberg said, "A very surprising
discovery to me in the fall of '67, as I began to study the
documents of '61 in connection with the McNamara study
project, was that the major decision Kennedy had made was
to *reject* the recommendation made to him by virtually
everyone that he send combat units to Vietnam. Kennedy
realized that most of the people in the country, whatever
their politics, would have said, 'If it takes combat troops, or
if it takes heavy bombing or nuclear weapons, it's obviously
not worth it for us. We won't succeed.'[27] Prouty supports this
view also from personal Pentagon and intelligence-
community experience and believes that Kennedy "gave a
hint of his plans for disengagement when he said [in
September 1963], speaking of the Vietnamese, 'In the final
analysis it is their war. They have to win it or lose it.'"[28]

7. September 1963: The Kennedy administration
launches a general program for disengagement while trying
to make it appear we have won the war without having
actually fought it. Taylor and McNamara go to Saigon and
come back saying they have seen the light at the end of the
tunnel. It is announced that the American mission is
beginning to draw to a successful end. It is a foreshadowing
of the Senator Aiken Plan of 1967: Announce a victory at a
press conference and march home as in triumph. General

Paul Harkins, commander of the Military Assistance Command in Saigon, tells the troops: "Victory in the sense it would apply to this kind of war is just months away and the reduction of American advisers can begin any time now."[29] At that point U.S. "advisers" stood at 16,732.

8. October 2, 1963: McNamara takes to the steps of the White House to tell the press of plans to withdraw one thousand U.S. troops from Vietnam before the year is out.[30]

9. November 1-2: the Diem regime, hopelessly tied to a policy of no negotiations with the Viet Cong, is overthrown, then Diem and his brother Nhu are mysteriously assassinated. General "Big" Minh's regime, incubated in Bangkok exile for exactly this purpose, takes over shortly and proclaims its intention of negotiating a settlement and a coalition government with the Viet Cong. It is no secret that Kennedy was behind the coup and the coming of Big Minh, although there is a question as to whether he was also behind the assassinations of Diem and Nhu. Kennedy had professed public disfavor with their rule and had declared Diem "out of touch with the people." He sanctioned the Minh takeover and approved of its pronegotiations policy. But what do we make out of Howard Hunt's furtive work in the files of the State Department, busy with scissors and paste to create his own little "Pentagon Papers" convicting Kennedy of the murders of Diem and Nhu? Was he helping the truth or plying his disinformation trade?

10. November 15: In spite of confusion in Saigon resulting from the coup, "a U.S. military spokesman carried on the McNamara-Taylor-Harkins line," as recorded in the GOP's 1967 Vietnam study, "and promised 1,000 American military men would be withdrawn from Vietnam beginning on December 3."[31]

11. November 22: Dallas. Within days of taking over, Johnson issues National Security Agency Memorandum 273, reversing the Kennedy policy of withdrawal and inaugurating the period of build-up leading toward conventional war. [32]

12.   Early December: The first of the one thousand U.S. troops ordered home begin withdrawal from Vietnam. [33] Johnson's new orders have not reached the field.

13.   March-April 1964: Joint Chiefs draw up and submit to Johnson a list of ninety-four potential targets for bombing in Vietnam.[34]

14:   May: The new government in Saigon calls on the United States to bomb the North. Johnson declines to rule it out.

15.   June: There is a big war powwow of LBJ and JCS in Honolulu. Johnson resists pressure for a congressional resolution and decides to step up war effort. General William Westmoreland takes command of U.S. forces in Vietnam. Ambassador Lodge resigns and is replaced by Taylor.[35]

16.   July: South Vietnamese commandos, i.e., CIA/Special Forces units, raid two North Vietnamese islands in the Gulf of Tonkin. [36]

17.   August: On intelligence patrol in the Gulf of Tonkin, U.S. destroyers *Maddox* and *Turner Joy* report being attacked by North Vietnamese torpedo boats. Circumstances of the attack remain unclear. Doubt remains as to whether the incidents were real or staged. In the posturing at which he was so adept, in his imitations of passion, Johnson terrified all but Morse and Gruening of the Pacific Northwest and got the Senate to give him the Tonkin Gulf resolution, opening the way for major escalation.

18.   November: The Viet Cong hit Bien Hoa air base in the South and the Joint Chiefs grow heated in their demand for heavy U.S. retaliation. Johnson wins the 1964 election on a "peace" platform vs. Goldwater's (and later Nixon's) air-war line; Johnson's was the biggest "peace mandate" ever until Nixon's of '72.

19.   December: Johnson approves a plan for air attacks on North Vietnam, "reprisal air strikes for 30 days, then graduated air warfare against North backed by possible deployment of ground combat troops."[37]

20.   February 1965: The Viet Cong attack U.S. military

advisers' compound at Pleiku. In "retaliation" Johnson orders the first air strikes against the North. The air war is on.

21. April 1965: The First March on Washington to Protest the War in Vietnam is held by Students for a Democratic Society; twenty to twenty-five thousand hear SDS and SNCC speakers call for a mass antiwar movement.

Double-faulting on the invasions of Cuba and Vietnam was not Kennedy's only failure in the eyes of chauvinism, but that was without doubt the major problem. Cuba and Vietnam bracket Frontier Camelot as the ends of a coffin. But in between, there was much more for the Cowboy conscience to find deplorable in Kennedy's administration. Making no attempt to be inclusive, and leaving aside the much-observed differences of style and manners between the Kennedy group and the Johnson group, I cite the following examples as making the case that from the Cowboy standpoint Kennedy was as bad as he could be.

1. Kennedy's 1962 Geneva Accords on Laos made concessions to the Communists and led to the pullout of eight hundred U.S. military advisers.

2. Kennedy intervened through the UN and, with direct U.S. assistance, supported Congolese nationalism against Belgian-backed secessionists.

3. Kennedy cut off foreign and military aid to seven Latin American countries, most sensationally Haiti, on grounds that repressive strongman government was incompatible with the aims of hemispheric reform.

4. He struggled with Big Steel and Detroit Iron to hold down prices. Faced with an inflation rate of 4 percent, minuscule by the standards of the seventies, Kennedy actually wanted to impose a provisional price freeze and won labor's agreement to the most limited settlements since World War II on the promise that industry would hold the line on prices. When Big Steel took it all back, Kennedy fought (unsuccessfully) for a court-ordered price rollback. It brings to mind the observation of Indira Gandhi that

Kennedy "died because he lost the support of his peers"—
i.e., the support of the Yankee financial powers animating
the vast reaches of the iron and steel industry. For contrast,
when steel raised its prices five dollars a ton in 1967, Johnson
merely said that steel executives "knew his feelings" and that
price controls "could not be ruled out" in the future. Johnson
allowed another steel price raise to pass without comment in
1968.

5. JFK proposed elimination of the oil-depletion
allowance in January 1963. This by itself could easily have
screwed to the sticking point the courage of the American oil
cartel as a whole, and most particularly its mainly
Southwestern components, the so-called Independents
(distinct from the mainly Yankee "Majors"). The oil-
depletion allowance was and remains the whole basis of
Southwestern oil's special power and glory. Kennedy had
already aroused Texan ire in 1961 by attempting to collect a
federal tax on state business transactions, a tax no Texan
could remember having ever seen collected. Now came the
attack on the depletion allowance. Oil industry spokesmen
angrily predicted a 30 percent drop in earnings if Kennedy's
proposed tax reforms won out.[38]

6. JFK encouraged the civil-rights movement openly.
He introduced his civil rights bill in June 1963 in concert with
Martin Luther King's giant march on Washington. The
temperature of Congress rose ten degrees and the whole
Camelot legislative program was blocked by the civil-rights
debate.

7. The New Frontiersman attack on Johnson as a
personality began in 1961 and intensified toward Dallas,
focusing in the Kennedy brothers' pressure on Johnson's
Bobby Baker softspot. The feud between Johnson and
Robert Kennedy was unrivaled. What was at stake was not
simply Johnson's political career but the whole question of
Texas power and its political relationship to Eastern power.
When Johnson's man Connally was dispatched in October
1963 to convince Kennedy that he must come politicking

soon in Texas, Connally's argument was that the Texas Democratic party was in a growing state of disaffection from the national party under the reign of the Kennedys and that fences had to be mended or Texas might bolt the party in '64.

8. Robert Kennedy's Justice Department campaign against Jimmy Hoffa, within a wider Frontier Camelot campaign to bust the larger Teamster-Syndicate connection, threatened to expose and destroy a major and basic sphere of Syndicate activity, the Teamster Pension Fund complex.

9. On the first of April, 1963, Kennedy announced that all U.S. raids on Cuba would stop. On April 4, Detective Sgt. C. H. Sapp of the Miami Police Intelligence Unit reported to Assistant Chief of Police A. W. Anderson the following:

> For the past three days the Intelligence Unit has been receiving information concerning the feelings and proposed actions of the Cuban refugee colony in Miami. Since President Kennedy made the news release that the United States Government would stop all raiding parties going against Castro's government, the Cuban people feel that the United States Government has turned against them.... All violence hitherto directed toward Castro's Cuba will now be directed toward various governmental agencies in the United States.[39]

10. In September 1963, even as he was taking the first perceptible steps toward a Vietnam pullback, Kennedy ordered the FBI to raid secret CIA guerrilla training camps and staging bases in Florida and Louisiana. Dave Ferrie, linked by New Orleans District Attorney James Garrison to Clay Shaw and the CIA, was involved in the operation of the Louisiana camps. The camps were situated on land owned by a gambling associate of Jack Ruby's, Bill McLaney. The McLaney brothers, cogs in the Lansky Syndicate,[40] were among the big losers when the Cuban revolution ejected the Syndicate and its casinos from the island. Frank Fiorini

(aka Sturgis) of the Watergate burglary was also connected to the base Kennedy closed at No Name Key. Sturgis was visible at Dallas two months later and was actually questioned by the FBI in connection with the Assassination.[41]

11.   Constant and passionate struggle to win the hearts and minds of the Joint Chiefs of Staff was a leading existential feature of the actual life of Frontier Camelot. Camelot-Pentagon differences were multitudinous and many-layered, from theories of war to theories of peace, and they were heatedly joined, as indicated for example by Halberstam's report that on the question of nuclear disarmament, "McNamara virtually locked [the Joint Chiefs] in a room for a week to fight it out with them."[42]

12.   But more gut-basic still was Kennedy's assault on the sanctity of the defense budget. His administration drew up three defense budgets. The 1962 budget was $51.6 billion. In 1963 it went down to $50.8 billion. In 1964 it went down again to $49.9 billion. As of Watergate, after almost a decade of Cowboy rule, it had grown again to about twice that size.

Long-time no-conspiracy buff Garry Wills makes an opposite deduction about Kennedy's politics, which he characterizes as a more genteel but otherwise conventional militarism, by focusing on a different fact: "On the very day he died [that morning while in Fort Worth], Kennedy boasted publicly that he had 'increased our special counter-insurgency forces in Vietnam by 600 percent.'" Wills seems in no position to add (as late as 1973?) that "counterinsurgency" was Frontier Camelot's euphemism for cheaper defense and a nonnuclear world strategy. Is it not mischievous in serious polemic to decontextualize remarks made in a heightened context? Wills understands that Kennedy's whole purpose in being in Texas that day to begin with, answering Connally's imperative summons, was to persuade neo-Confederate elements in the Texas Democratic party that his administration had not been lax in the defense and national security areas in spite of the signing on October 7 just past of his limited test-ban treaty, in spite of his closing of the anti-Castro staging bases in Florida and Louisiana, and in spite of his successive annual cuts in the defense budget from $51 to $50 to $49 billion.

But was it not clear enough in the contemporary dialogue itself, without "analysis"? Kennedy says, "Yesterday a shaft of light cut into the darkness. Negotiations were concluded in Moscow on a treaty to ban all nuclear tests in the atmosphere, in outer space, and under water." And the voice of the Joint Chiefs says, "True security lies in unlimited nuclear superiority." Kennedy says, "There is the necessity for revolution in Latin America." And the JCS says it is "anxious concerning our future security." Kennedy says of the South Vietnamese, "We are prepared to continue to assist them, but I don't think that the war can be won unless the people support the effort." And the JCS says it is "not sure it's necessarily a good thing to cut down on tensions." One does not even have to believe that Khrushchev was telling us the truth, or that he knew the truth to tell, when he said in his putative memoirs that he got a message from Robert Kennedy at the height of the 1962 Missile Crisis saying, "We are under very severe stress. In fact we are under pressure from our military to use force against Cuba. . . . If the situation continues much longer, the President is not sure that the military will not overthrow him and seize power. The American army could get out of control."[44] Whether that threat specifically existed or not, the political outlines of that confrontation surely implied it.

The mystery which Nixon resigned to protect, and which the Ford pardon sought to "shut and seal," appears to center on some as-yet-unknown intertwining of Nixon's and Kennedy's fates as adversaries in the great misadventure of the Bay of Pigs. To get at what this mystery might be, we find we have to go beyond the conventional Cold War picture of the Bay of Pigs operation. Instead of seeing the invasion simply as a U.S.-vs.-Cuba conflict and "the policy of the

Kennedy administration," we see it as the product of a conflict internal to the policy apparatus pitting a liberal-minded Yankee president against conservative-minded stalwarts of the defense and security bureaucracies.

The motive of the Cowboy-Nixon side in this conflict was its desire to push through with Cuban plans laid lovingly in the last days of Eisenhower. (Vice-President Johnson also supported the Bay of Pigs "activists.") The motive of the Yankee-Kennedy side was its desire to avoid being drawn into a war against Castro's Cuba. The pro-invasion side was strong enough to break out, overcome, and be satisfied, just as the anti-invasion side was strong enough only to take the sting out of the invasion, not to stop it.

The result, the Cuban Fiasco, set the model for the Vietnam Quagmire, which followed exactly the same logical course, except in giant steps.

The period before Kennedy's assassination is thus a period of accumulating polarizations throughout the universe of the White House policy apparatus. The Massachusetts-Texas electoral coalition that squeaked into the White House in 1960 had by 1963 proved itself nonfunctional and self-destructive as a governing coalition. It is one measure of the power relativities of this coalition's crisis that the assassination of the president seemed to resolve it.

Whatever we decide about the evidence of the assassination, whether we walk away from Warren and the Warren critics believing in a right-wing conspiracy or a Castroite conspiracy or a left-wing lone assassin, we all will still acknowledge one monumental and central fact about the Dallas killing: It got rid of one policy and put another in its place. In the richness of his hypocrisy, Johnson successfully pretended to carry on the torch of domestic Kennedy reform and wholly mystified the question of war and peace in Vietnam by saying sometimes that Kennedy had actually been a hawk like him and other times that he, Johnson, was actually a dove like Kennedy. With Goldwater as an easy rightward foil, Johnson was able to represent his strategy of graduated ground, air, and naval escalation as the *peace strategy* and thus to campaign on all the arguments usually at the disposal of a peace candidate. Yet as the Ellsberg Papers later showed (and as the poet Brecht long before foretold), even as he beat his breast for *peace* in the ancient public dumbshow, Johnson was secretly signing the marching orders. In this case it was the detailed, day-by-day, target-by-target JCS plans for the bombardment of the North that would be launched, as though spontaneously against unexpected provocation (the VC attack on Pleiku), in February 1965, the elections safely past.

As for "the whole Bay of Pigs thing," Johnson was shortly taking care of that, too, in the secret project launched by his Great Society in 1964 called "Second Naval Guerrilla." This project, as reported notably by Szulc, began as a let's-do-it-right-this-time remake of the Bay of Pigs invasion in which U.S. troops would have been used and in which the assassination of Castro would have been attempted with presidential backing.[45] It was to have been carried out sometime in 1965 after Johnson's safe reelection, just as with Vietnam escalation. As Szulc observes, "it was an incredibly wild scheme because the resolution of the 1962 Cuban Missile Crisis, which brought the United States and the Soviet Union to the brink of nuclear confrontation, was based in part on Washington's promise to let Castro be."[46] The reason the "Second Naval Guerrilla" was never carried out is that the early 1965 rebellion in the Dominican Republic made it necessary to land in Santo Domingo the troops that had been made ready for Havana.

So Dallas was a turning point in any case, no matter who murdered Kennedy, no matter what the motive. Dallas brought to a close a period of Yankee dominance in the councils of state policy that stretched back essentially unbroken to the Civil War. Johnson easily attached to his own presidential coalition the bulk of Yankee forces willing to accept his reassurance that a military victory in Vietnam would soon be secured and that the advantages of it would be real. But the now splintered and demoralized detentist group found itself suddenly under the heel of precisely the man they had just been spitting on. Old New Frontierists hung on under Johnson, some on the strength of the argument that if they left those who came after would be worse or (as Halberstam suggests) out of a blend of naivete and arrogance that made them think they could find a solution; others because they thought their positions in the policy apparatus gave them power to hold the line of the Kennedy vision in spite of Johnson; others because Johnson seemed an improvement after all. For a long moment, there was even the heady fancy that by one of the ironies of politics, the death of the liberal prince and the ascendancy of the conservative would now make it still *more* possible to make peace in the world, *more* possible to bring about lasting changes for social and economic justice because (a) now everyone felt sorry for Kennedy and wanted to pay tribute to him and his social ideas, and because (b) now Johnson would be pulling all his people in, would actually bring the Solid South into the national civil-rights and peace coalition. Was there some uneasiness about that? But surely Johnson could be contained by the Yankess who controlled the bureaucracy around him? Outsiders are left wondering when, or if, the illusions finally wore through (for McNamara, say), or if any of the philosophers of Frontier Camelot ever asked if Kennedy died for Cuba and Vietnam in vain.

The illusion of the Cowboy-Yankee coalition proved ultimately the last illusion of Frontier Camelot, possibly because it was at bottom less an illusion than a gamble taken in the absence of alternatives. In any case, the consequences of that failure stretch out over the next decade like the ground path of a tornado. Here we anticipate our story of this failure enough to note briefly the long curve of it ahead: how the installation of Johnson in 1963 was in effect a transfer of presidential power from Yankee to Cowboy national ruling elites; how Yankee powers regrouped and challenged Cowboy rule with the bloodless power play of early 1968 which forced Johnson to abdicate, to start the peace negotiations in Paris, to stop the bombing of the North, and to open the way for the triumphal reform campaign of Robert Kennedy; how Johnson's overthrow in March was followed by the conspiratorial assassination of King in April, then of Robert Kennedy in June; and how against a backdrop of general world tumult (Paris, Mexico City, Greece, Prague) all forces converged on the complex climax of the Democratic party in Chicago and the eventual triumph of Nixon, which sent the country slanting fiercely toward Watergate.

We do not yet know if or how Nixon might have been directly involved in any of this after leaving the office of vice-president, or if he was part of any secret group manipulating Eisenhower through control of information flowing through the National Security Council. But we have developed a more specific sense of the heart of this mystery when we come to see the Cuban invasion as a result of a conflict in which Nixon acted strongly against Camelot policy by way of an invasion group which we know for a fact included Hunt, Sturgis, the Watergate Cubans, yeasty parts of the CIA, Howard Hughes through his man Robert Maheu (to whom we return), and the Lansky Syndicate through John Roselli, whom Maheu reached on behalf of the CIA. What could be the organizational form of the ad hoc clandestine government which such details imply? Finding this, we would find the answer to the mystery of Ford's pardon and Nixon's crime.

Now our reconstruction comes to the turning point of Dallas. It is time to confront the question that foregoing analysis of a divided Camelot suggests, namely: If we see that the JFK assassination was a coup d'etat *in effect*, is there any reason to suppose it was such a thing *by design*?

4

Dealey Plaza

According to the Warren Commission, Lee Harvey Oswald
was a chronic malcontent and loner who in 1959 broke off
his career in the U.S. Marines with an irregular discharge in
order to defect to the Soviet Union, to which he may have
supplied valuable military secrets. He married in Russia,
tried to settle down to a Communist domesticity with a job in
an electronics factory in Minsk, but reconsidered after two
years and decided to come home. He returned in mid-1962
with his wife Marina and their two children, stayed briefly in
New Orleans then settled in Dallas-Fort Worth.

He clung to his Marxist beliefs in spite of his evidently
unhappy experience in Russia and became indeed an
activist, setting up the New Orleans chapter of a pro-Castro
group called the Fair Play for Cuba Committee—a chapter
of which he remained, however, the only member. Early in
1963, he may have fired a shot at retired General Edwin
Walker, a hardline rightwinger. Strangely for one of his
apparent views, he tried later to join up with Prio's Cuban
Revolutionary Council, the major anti-Castro grouping
among the militant Cuban exiles camped those days in
Miami and New Orleans and still seething over the Bay of
Pigs. But then Earl Warren finds him back in character a few

days later passing out pro-Castro leaflets (a courageous act in the New Orleans of that period), then going to Mexico City in September in an (unsuccessful) effort to get a visa to visit Cuba. On November 22, in Dallas, at 12:31 P.M. at Dealey Plaza, according to Warren, he shot and killed the president and shot and severely wounded Texas Governor John Connally in the presidential limousine; then less than an hour later, in another part of town, desperate to escape, he shot and killed Dallas patrolman J. D. Tippit.

He was captured soon after by a police squadron alerted to a gate-crasher at the Texas Theater. He was interrogated for six hours off the record by Dallas officers, who charged him early with the murder of Tippit, then later with the Dealey Plaza shootings. Unlike the standard political assassin qua lone nut, who characteristically boasts of his deed and claims it before history, Oswald took an unashamedly frightened stance, begged someone to come forward to help him, and said from the beginning that he was being made a patsy and could prove it.

On the Sunday morning after that Friday, Oswald was to be transferred from the city jail to the county jail, where it was said he would be more secure. The millions absorbed in television scenes of the funeral procession were rudely switched to Dallas for the on-camera murder of Oswald by Jack Ruby in the very basement of the Dallas jail. Ruby was a Dallas nightclub operator who said he was motivated by sorrow for the plight of the widow, who would have to come to Dallas for the trial of Oswald, a further ordeal he wished to spare her. As a result of his act, the case against Oswald was effectively closed. Ruby's extensive ties to the Dallas police, organized crime, and the Dallas oligarchy were briefly noted by Warren, but not explored. Like Oswald, Ruby was painted as another lone nut.

Ruby died in prison in 1967, protesting in a voice constantly breaking into hysteria that the real truth about Dallas was still not known.

* * *

As will emerge from point to point in the following critique of the Warren theory of Dealey Plaza, the early objections to his theory have only been fortified over the years of debate by new discoveries and insights. More than a dozen years later, the classic critique of Warren retains its original form and power. The first-generation critics, notably Sylvia Meagher, Harold Weisberg, Josiah Thompson, Mark Lane, Edward Epstein, and Penn Jones, have not been surpassed.

This attests to their good sense, but it also points up the *magnitude* of the Warren theory's main faults. There they stand for all who look to see—the problems of the bullet and the rifle, the medical indications, the sloppy, not to say prejudiced character of the deliberation over the evidence, the concealment of doubts, etc.

The newcomer to the detailed evidence is often surprised to find the Warren *Report's* flaws so apparent. For example, Connally never gave up his conviction that he was hit by a different bullet from the one that went through Kennedy's neck. If that is true, then (as we see in detail below) any lone-gunman theory tied to Oswald is ruled out absolutely, no subtlety to it. Yet Connally is today, as he always has been, a *supporter* of the Warren theory. Asked to reconcile the two beliefs, he answers that he knows he was not hit by the first Kennedy shot, but that the Warren commissioners were "good patriots" whose word could not be doubted. The main support for the Warren no-conspiracy theory was Warren's reputation.

Contemporary critique is not so dazzled by Warren's moral genius. We do not for a moment doubt his passionate desire to do the right thing. We insist, however, that in the complex moral predicament into which the assassination of Kennedy plunged Warren (and Warren liberalism), it was entirely possible that Warren lost his way and did know what the right thing was. Then he could not resist taking the path others were expecting him to take, the path of the lone-assassin pretense.

We criticize the Warren theory of Dallas in any case on purely factual terms, concentrating on (1) the physical details of the shootings of Kennedy and Connally, (2) the identity of Oswald, and (3) the testimony of Ruby. Then we take up (4) the politics of the evident Warren cover-up. Finally we attempt (5) an alternative reconstruction of the crime.

The Shootings

Oswald had been a stock handler at the depository since October. At lunchtime on Friday, November 22—according to Warren—he was alone in the southeast corner window of the sixth floor with a 6.5-mm bolt-action Mannlicher-Carcano rifle in his hands, an early World War II weapon which, according to Warren, he had purchased only a few months before from Klein's Mail-Order Sporting Goods for $12.79, and which he had brought to work that morning wrapped as curtain rods.

At 12:30 the lead cars in the motorcade from Love Field appeared below him at the corner of Main and Houston (see map), turned up Houston directly toward him, then turned again to pass in front of him down Elm toward the triple underpass. Then the presidential limousine followed. J. Edgar Hoover once observed that Oswald's easiest shot came as his target was approaching him up Houston. He waited until the car had made the turn and was several hundred feet down Elm. According to Warren, he then fired three shots at the president's back within a period not longer than 5.6 seconds.

Of the first two shots, according to Warren, one or the other struck Kennedy high up on the back, deviated the first

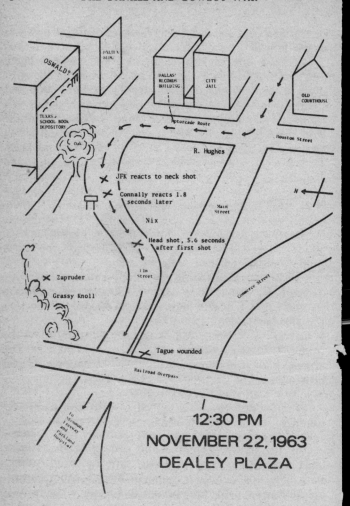

OSWALD?

DALLAS BLDG

DALLAS RECORDS BUILDING

CITY JAIL

OLD COURTHOUSE

TEXAS SCHOOL BOOK DEPOSITORY

Motorcade Route

Houston Street

Oak

R. Hughes

X JFK reacts to neck shot

X Connally reacts 1.8 seconds later

Main Street

Nix

X Head shot, 5.6 seconds after first shot

Elm Street

Commerce Street

N

X Zapruder

Grassy Knoll

X Tague wounded

Railroad Overpass

To Stemmons Freeway and Parkland Hospital

12:30 PM
NOVEMBER 22, 1963
DEALEY PLAZA

of several times from its original flight path, ranged upwards and leftwards through his body, exited at his neck, nicked the left side of the knot in the necktie, deviated again downwards and to the right, struck Connally in the back over the right armpit, tore through the governor's body, and came out just inside the right nipple, leaving a gaping exit wound. It then deviated again to strike his right hand at the wrist, smashing the wrist bone into seven fragments. It exited the wrist and plunged into the left thigh just above the knee. Then it worked its way out of Connally's thigh on to the stretcher at Parkland Hospital, where it was found by a hospital attendant and turned over to the Dallas police. This bullet found on the stretcher, Commission Exhibit 399, is the totality of the hard evidence tying Oswald's Mannlicher-Carcano rifle to the crime, just as the rifle itself is the only hard evidence tying the crime to Oswald. Everything else is circumstantial. But we are getting ahead.

The other of the first two shots missed altogether and hit the curb far ahead of the car. A fragment of curbstone chipped off by the bullet superficially wounded the cheek of a bystander, James Tague.

Oswald's third shot, said Warren, hit Kennedy above the front right temple and blew off that portion of his head. The limousine had been slowing until then. At that point it sped off for Parkland Hospital.

The physical and logical inadequacies of this reconstruction may be grouped into three areas:

   (1)   the magic bullet;
   (2)   the magic rifle; and
   (3)   indications of a front shot.

   1.   *The magic bullet* (Commission Exhibit 399), according to Warren, made four wounds in two men, then turned up on a stretcher in the hospital in what ballistics experts call a "pristine" condition. There are several reasons for thinking this bullet did not do what it is said to have done.

Its pristine condition is the simplest of these reasons and

in any other situation would easily be conclusive all by itself. One can simply see from the Warren photos that the bullet is all but undamaged.[1] It never hit anything harder than a bale of cotton; it had nothing to do with these wounds.

As if indeed to force us to see this, Warren prints the photograph of CE399 alongside an identical bullet fired by the FBI through the wrist of a cadaver.[2] As all can see, the test bullet came through severely distorted; the whole upper body of the bullet was flattened by impact with the wristbone, one of the denser bones in the body. The only explanation offered by Warren for CE399's pristine condition was that it must have tumbled upon smashing through Connally's ribs and hit his wrist flying backwards, that is, with the blunt end to the fore—as though a blunt-end impact would not lead to a still more radical shape deformation and still greater weight loss.

Second, as we have noted, Connally was convinced that the bullet that hit him and the bullet that hit Kennedy in the neck were two separate bullets, not the same CE399. Warren Commission Attorney Arlen Specter, the author of the single-bullet theory, examined Connally before the commission on April 21, 1964. The exchange on this point went as follows:

MR. SPECTER: In your view, which bullet caused the injury to your chest, Governor Connally

GOVERNOR CONNALLY: The second one.

MR. SPECTER: And what is your reason for that conclusion, sir?

GOVERNOR CONNALLY: Well, in my judgment, it just couldn't conceivably have been the first one because I heard the sound of the shot. In the first place, I don't know anything about the velocity of this particular bullet [2000 fps], but any rifle has a velocity that exceeds the speed of sound [6-700 fps], and when I heard the sound of that first shot, that bullet had already reached where I was, or it had reached that far, and after I heard that shot, I had time to turn to my right, and start to turn to my left before I felt anything.

It is not conceivable to me that I could have been hit by the first bullet, and then I felt the blow from something which was obviously a bullet, which I assumed was a bullet, and I never heard the second shot, didn't hear it. I didn't hear but two shots. I think I heard the first shot and the third shot.

MR. SPECTER: Do you have any idea as to why you did not hear the second shot?

GOVERNOR CONNALLY: Well, first, again I assume the bullet was travelling faster than sound. I was hit by the bullet prior to the time the sound reached me, and I was in either a state of shock or the impact was such that the sound didn't even register on me, but I was never conscious of hearing the second shot at all.

Obviously, at least the major wound that I took in the shoulder through the chest couldn't have been anything but the second shot. Obviously, it couldn't have been the third, because when the third shot was fired I was in a reclining position, and heard it, saw it and the effects of it, rather—I didn't see it, I saw the effects of it—so it obviously could not have been the third, and couldn't have been the first, in my judgment.[3]

Third, the famous Zapruder film shows that as much as a full second after Kennedy was shot in the neck, Connally remained apparently unwounded. When he did react, there was nothing ambiguous about it. His hair shot up. His mouth dropped. Then he seemed to be hit a second time. He slumped immediately to his left into his wife's lap.

The Warren lawyers explain away the time lapse as a "delayed reaction," even though the specific pathology of Connally's wounds, notably the breaking of the ribs and the wrist, make such a theory implausible on its face, and even though the commission had heard expert medical testimony against the delayed-reaction explanation. (Connally is

visibly holding his Stetson in the hand with the shattered
wrist many Z-frames after Kennedy has first been hit.)

Fourth, the commission produced out of its own inquiries
the most technically conclusive evidence against the magic-
bullet theory, although the significance of this evidence may
have been concealed from the commission by the FBI, which
arranged for the test to be conducted for the commission by
the Atomic Energy Commission. This test, neutron-
activation analysis, or NAA, involves the same technique
that two Swedish scientists used to prove in 1961 that
Napoleon had actually been murdered by gradual arsenic
poisoning. The method is to bombard the specimen material
with neutrons and then measure the emissions thus
produced. The operating premise is that any difference in
atomic structure of two materials, however slight, will be
observable in these emissions. This is why Allegheny County
coroner Cyril Wecht describes NAA as "one of the most
powerful and sophisticated forensic science methods ever
developed."[4]

In the current case, NAA was used to compare fragments
of a bullet taken from Connally's wrist (and elsewhere) with
material taken from the nose of CE399. If the fragments and
the slivers are from the same bullet, they will give off
precisely the same emissions under neutron activation.

Until the success of Harold Weisberg's Freedom-of-
Information Act suit in 1974, it was not known for a fact that
NAA had been performed. Hoover reported that it had been,
but knowingly or not, he concealed the significance of it in a
letter to Warren's chief counsel Rankin dated July 8, 1964.
By that time, Specter's draft of chapter 3 of the *Report*,
setting forth the single-bullet theory, had already been
submitted to Rankin. As Wecht observes, Hoover's
language "has to be read in its entirety to be appreciated," so
I follow him in repeating the letter in full:

As previously reported to the Commission, certain
small lead metal fragments uncovered in connection

with this matter were analyzed spectrographically to determine whether they could be associated with one or more of the lead bullet fragments and no significant differences were found within the sensitivity of the spectrographic method.

Because of the higher sensitivity of the neutron activation analysis, certain of the small lead fragments were then subjected to neutron activation analyses and comparisons with larger bullet fragments. The items analyzed included the following: C1—bullet from stretcher; C2—fragment from front seat cushion; C4 and C5—metal fragments from President Kennedy's head; C9—metal fragment from the arm of Governor Connally; C16—metal fragments from rear floor board carpet of the car.

While minor variations in composition were found by this method, these were not considered sufficient to permit positively differentiating among the larger bullet fragments and thus positively determining from which of the larger bullet fragments any given small lead fragment may have come.

Sincerely yours,
[s] J. Edgar Hoover[5]

The boiling obfuscations of that last paragraph show us Hoover at his best. There is no way for the technically uninformed to know that in the NAA test *any* difference is "sufficient." If one could strip down Hoover's subordinate clause to its grammatical essentials, one would have the heart of the matter right enough: "Variations...were found." Therefore the fragments from Connally's wrist and CE399 were not of the same bullet. Which should have been obvious to grown men to start with from looking at bullet CE399 with their two eyes open.

2.   *The magic rifle* is Oswald's 6.5-mm Mannlicher-

Carcano. Like its companion bullet CE399, it rates the status of magic because it too shows so little sign of having been able to do what, for Warren theory purposes, it must have done.

The weapon Oswald is supposed to have selected for his great moment was a bolt-action Italian army rifle mass produced in the early 1940s. It was not a serious sharpshooting weapon when it was made and two decades of aging could not have improved it.

The telescopic sight was fitted for a left-handed marksman. Oswald was right-handed.

The scope was misaligned so badly that the FBI had to adjust the mounting apparatus before it could test-fire the rifle.

But the deeper problem would still exist even if the rifle had been straight-shooting and fitted with a properly mounted and adjusted scope, because the deeper problem is that the maximum number of shots Oswald could have taken with that rifle in five-and-half-seconds was three, and three shots are too few to explain all the damage that was done that moment to people and things in Dealey Plaza.

Add to this the fact that Oswald was rated only a poor marksman in the Marines and that, in one expert's words, "The feat attributed to Oswald at Dallas was impossible for any one but a world champion marksman using a high-precision semiautomatic rifle mounted on a carriage and equipped with an aim corrector, and who had practiced at moving targets in similar set-ups."[6]

The most impressive defense of the Mannlicher and Oswald's ability to use it in the way claimed by Warren that anyone has seen so far was produced by CBS News in the first of its four-part special called *The American Assassins*, aired in most cities around Thanksgiving 1975. The first part was devoted to the physical analysis of the JFK case. Setting out to settle the dispute about the rifle's capabilities once and for all, CBS erected in the countryside a target-sled and platform arrangement simulating the geometry and dis-

tances of the shot from the southeast corner of the sixth floor
of the Book Depository, then brought 11 expert riflemen—
from the military, from the police, from the firearms
industry—to give it a crack: Here goes the sled at the speed
and along the path of the limousine. You have 5.6 seconds to
squeeze off three shots and score with two of them. After
practice, two of the eleven experts were able to do what
Oswald is said to have done, two hits out of three shots in 5.6
seconds. CBS does not pause to say how many total series
were fired by these eleven, or how many times the two who
did it once could do it again. They are impatient to state their
interpretation of this result. The reasoning now goes: Since a
small percentage of expert riflemen could do it, it was
possible. Since it was possible, it was possible for Oswald.
Therefore he must have done it. CBS knew that Oswald had
never practiced from that position or elevation, that he had
not even been on a target range for at least two months, and
that all his ex-Marine comrades regarded him as a poor shot.
CBS is forced to make the argument, read from the
teleprompter by an unblinking Dan Rather, that Oswald had
scored, "after all, in the second highest category of marks-
men in an outfit, the United States Marines, that prides
itself on its marksmanship." Whoever wrote that had to
know that when Oswald was in the Marines, there were only
three categories, that you were already in the third of these if
you could heft the rifle to your shoulder, and that the
minimum score required to enter "the second highest
category" was 190, and that Oswald's score was 191. CBS
knew this. It is all in the Warren hearings. It is all nicely
accessible in Sylvia Meagher's work, which CBS says it
consulted (see her *Accessories After the Fact*, pp 108-109).
Misunderstanding or differences of interpretation can
always be understood, but does this treatment of the rifle's
capabilities, the demands of the shot, and Oswald's skill with
the weapon fall within that dispensation? Do these look like
honest mistakes?

But the worst problem is that for all its testing and

proving, CBS is not even addressing the real issue with the
rifle. The problem that leads people to doubt that Oswald
did what Warren said he did with that rifle is that the shot
that first hit Kennedy and the shot that first hit Connally
came only 1.8 seconds apart, as is easily determined by
analysis of the Zapruder film, and not even the fastest of the
CBS team of experts was able to reload and refire the
Mannlicher anywhere near that fast.

3.   Among several *indications of a front shot*, the
backward snap of Kennedy's head and body visible in the
Zapruder film at frame 313 is without doubt the most
gruesome and most convincing piece of evidence against the
lone-Oswald theory. Indeed, not taking Zapruder into
advance account may ultimately prove the big mistake the
assassination cabal made.

With his brand-new 8-mm Bell and Howell camera,
Abraham Zapruder was standing part way up the grassy
knoll that borders Elm on the north and runs up to the
railroad tracks (see map). He looked to his left (east) to pick
up the motorcade as it turned from Houston left onto Elm,
and panned with the Kennedy limousine as it passed in front
of him. Kennedy disappeared momentarily behind the
Stemmons Freeway sign. He was shot first at precisely that
one moment offstage to Zapruder's camera. When he
reappeared a fraction of a second later, his hands were
already going to his throat. Then in about a second and a
half Connally was going over too.

Just when the episode seems finished comes that endless-
seeming moment before the fatal headshot. Zapruder had
steadied his camera again. The limousine is actually slowing
down. Four-one-thousand, five-one-thousand. Kennedy is
straight in front of us. Then his head explodes in a plume of
pink mist and he is driven violently into the back of the
carseat.

Members of the Assassination Information Bureau,
including myself, presented the Zapruder film and other

photographic evidence to the editorial board of the *Boston Globe* at the meeting at the *Globe* offices on April 23, 1975. Two days later *Globe* Executive Editor Robert Healey published a long editorial in which he summed up the board's general reaction to the Zapruder film as follows:

> It is this particular piece of film, with stop action and with individual still frames, that is being shown around the nation and which has convinced some, at least, that Oswald could not have fired all the shots that killed President Kennedy.... This visual presentation is far more convincing than all the books and all the magazine articles that have ever been advanced. They make a simple and convincing case that President Kennedy had to be killed by bullets fired from two directions and thus by more than one person. And no words can make the case better than the Zapruder film. It is as simple as that.[7]

It was not as simple as that to CBS, of course, or its carefully selected array of medical and ballistics experts.

Warren defenders, among them CBS prominently, have searched over the years for a plausible explanation of the backward movement of Kennedy's head. How could a shot fired from behind the President have driven him backward?

An early theory was that the car lurched forward at just that moment, but that was abandoned when it was pointed out (from Zapruder) that the limousine continued to slow down until Secret Service agent Clint Hill got to the back of the car and climbed on. It did not speed up until Jackie Kennedy had crawled out on the rear deck to pick up a piece of her husband's skull.

Then it was explained that "a neuromuscular spasm" was to blame, but that lost favor when resort to Zapruder's film showed Kennedy's body not stiffened but rather hitting the back seat (in Robert Groden's phrase) "like a rag doll." Then came the theory that the bullet hit the back of the head with such force that it caused the brain to explode, that in exploding, the brain blew out the front of the head, and that, as a "jet effect" of this explosion, the head was driven backwards. This novel explanation suffers unfairly from the painfulness of explaining it, but its main problem is that the technical premise has never been demonstrated outside its creator's backyard.

CBS was satisfied with none of these explanations and preferred, again through an unblinking Rather, to offer an altogether new explanation for the backward motion. "Jackie pushed him!" (??) Yes, in her shock, she pushed him away. Again we turn to the film. Can we see it? Does she push? Is there the least sign of a pushing motion on her part? We go frame by frame again and again through the horrible sequence of images from Z-300 or so through 313 and on to 330. What could be clearer? He is knocked backwards out of her hands by a violent force. She is like a statue as he moves. CBS people can see that as readily as you and I. Then why do they say Jackie pushed him?

There are other indications that shots were fired from the front. Here are a few of these.

Another film of the assassination moment, this one taken by Orville Nix from the south side of Elm. He was on the inner mall of the plaza panning with the limousine from right to left (see map). In much poorer quality exposures and with eye-level crowd interference, we nevertheless see everything in the Nix film we see in the Zapruder film, except from the other side—the president thrown backwards. We see Zapruder filming this. We also see the whole crowd on that side of the street reacting spontaneously as though they hear gunfire from the area of the grassy knoll and the railroad bridge.

Two thirds of the ninety witnesses whom Warren asked said the firing came from the grassy knoll area.

Two Parkland Hospital doctors, the first to reach and examine Kennedy upon his arrival at emergency, thought the hole in Kennedy's neck was a wound of entrance, not exit. A complete autopsy might have determined this one way or another, but the throat wound was never explored by the autopsy surgeons.

A Dallas policeman named Joe Smith, one of several policemen who hurried to the grassy knoll area and the shoulder of the railroad bridge in the belief that the gunfire had come from there, said he was summoned by a woman crying: "They are shooting the President from the bushes." When he got to the knoll he found a man. He told the FBI, "I pulled my gun from my holster and I thought, 'This is silly, I don't know who I am looking for,' and I put it back. Just as I did, he showed me he was a Secret Service agent." Secret Service records, which in this respect are careful, show that no Secret Serviceman was assigned that area. No Secret Service agent afterward identified himself as the person confronted by Smith.[8]

Oswald

First we examine the evidence linking Oswald with the crimes he was accused of, then we examine arguments on behalf of his outright innocence of any direct role whatsoever in the Dealey Plaza shootings. This will lead us to a reconsideration of his identity—the Warren story that he was pro-Communist and pro-Castro—and to a challenge of this story based on his discernible background with U.S. intelligence.

The Case against Oswald

Here is the chain of evidence that convicts Oswald: The wounds to Kennedy and Connally are caused by CE399. The bullet CE399 was fired from the Mannlicher-Carcano found in the depository at the sixth-floor window. The

Mannlicher-Carcano had been purchased from a mail-order gun supplier a few weeks before in the name of one A. Hidell. Oswald was carrying papers identifying him as Hidell at the time of his arrest.

The astonishing thing is that this is the entirety of the case against Oswald. Besides that chain of associations, the rest of the evidence comes down to an eyewitness who could not repeat his identification of Oswald at a police line-up and a photograph of the alleged assassin published to the whole world on the cover of *Life* which contained as plain as the nose on Oswald's face the ocular proof of its totally bogus character.

First take up the links of this chain one by one.

1.   The bullet's link to the wounds: We have already seen how conjectural this link is. It simply does not appear that CE399 was fired into anything harder than a bale of cotton. No test, whether old technology or new, has ever established that any of the fragments found in Kennedy, in Connally, or on the floor of the car came from CE399.

2.   The bullet's link to the rifle: This is the Warren theory's strong point. There is no doubt that CE399 was fired from a 6.5-mm Mannlicher-Carcano.

3.   The rifle's link to Oswald: As we have noted, Oswald did not own this rifle in his own name. He used the name A. Hidell to buy it through the mail, said the Dallas police, who claimed they found papers on him identifying him as that person. The Alek Hidell whom Oswald supposedly pretended to be is reckoned by Warren to be the same A. Hidell who left off the Mannlicher-Carcano at a Dallas gunshop several weeks before the shooting to have the sight mounted.

The problems with this link are several. First, the gunshop tag showing that the weapon had been scopesighted was discounted by the commission itself as unverifiable and suspect because at the time "Hidell" brought it into the gunshop, Oswald was supposed to be in Mexico City.[9] Second and most important, Warren's only source for this Hidell information was the Dallas police, and the Dallas police cannot be relied on in this matter. Even one of the Commission's members. Assistant Council (now Judge) Burt W. Griffin, has discredited the role of the Dallas police in the investigation, telling reporter Robert Kaiser in 1975, "I don't think some agencies were candid with us. I never thought the Dallas police were telling us the entire truth. Neither was the FBI."[10]

This is not to say that the rifle could not be Oswald's. The Dallas police are not reliable in this case, but one may still not claim that they always lied in it, or presume that since it was the police who found the Hidell papers on Oswald, then the Hidell papers must be attributed to them as part of the frame-up; or that since it was the police who discovered the rifle at the depository window with its three spent shells neatly in a row against the wall and the cartridge jammed in the firing chamber, it must be the police who set the scene.[11] It would be playing games to deny that there is a certain temptation toward saying the cops did it because who else could get away with it. But there may be other answers to our questions going beyond current anticipations and fantasies. It would be better to wait for a real investigation, if only because of the likelihood that there are *several* cover stories hiding the truth of Dallas, of which the lone-Oswald cover story is only the most thinly transparent. Once the necessity for *some* conspiracy hypothesis is clearly and widely acknowledged, only then will the real arguments erupt. What *kind* of conspiracy? Left or right? Foreign or domestic? Private or public?

We are already seeing the Castro-plot theory recirculated. On the CBS News for April 24, 1975, Walter Cronkite screened for the first time some footage from his September 1969 interview with Lyndon Johnson which had formerly been suppressed to comply with a government request based on the usual standard of national security. CBS now revealed this footage, said Cronkite, because a columnist had lately given the secret away. Actually, it had been out of the bag since Leo Janos's reminiscence of Johnson's final

days published in the *Atlantic Monthly* of July 1973, in
which Janos quotes Johnson as saying that while he could
"accept that Oswald pulled the trigger" he could not be sure
the Commission had got to the bottom of it, and his hunch
was that Oswald might have been linked to pro-Castro
Cubans out for revenge for the Bay of Pigs.

So we have the first-degree cover story that Oswald was
alone; now we have the second-degree cover story that
Oswald was Castro's agent. There are likely to be other
stories increasingly difficult to challenge and explore from
afar: The CIA did it. The FBI did it. The Secret Service did it.
The Pentagon did it. The Dallas cops did it. The White
Citizens Council did it. The Syndicate did it. The Texas
oligarchy did it.

We have every citizenly need and right to voice our
intuitions in this matter; we also have a citizenly right to
force the question politically on the basis of the flimsiness of
the official case against Oswald, not on the basis of a
necessarily speculative interpretation. No new interpretation
could possibly be elaborated and defended in the absence of
subpoena powers and a strong national commitment to find
the truth. The issue is not whether I or someone else can tell
you who killed JFK. The issue at the moment is whether or
not the government has been telling or concealing the truth.

Next take the *Life* magazine cover photo of Oswald which
appeared on February 21, 1964. People will find it easy to
locate. They will see for themselves what might have been
obvious at once to the whole world, and certainly to the
photo lovers who put *Life* and the Warren *Report* together,
namely, that this a a doctored photo, and more than that, it is
a crudely doctored photo, and doctored more than once, by
different hands, at different times.   •

At first glance, we see simply Oswald in his battle gear,
more encumbered-seeming than menacing. In his left hand
with the butt against his thigh is (possibly) the weapon of the
sixth floor. In his right hand he shows us some literature of

the Socialist Workers Party (the FBI's favorite radical whipping boy; see Hoover's antileft "cointelpros"). On his right hip is the pistol with which he is supposed to have slain patrolman Tippit.

But if we notice the shadows on Oswald's face and the shadows his body casts, at once we see that they fall at obviously different angles. The shadow under his nose falls straight down, as though the sun were in front of him. All the other shadows in the photo, including the shadow of his body, fall off sharply to his right behind him, as though the sun were to his left. Then we notice how the entire body is standing seemingly at a gravity-defying angle.

A still closer look at Oswald's face shows another give-away: the chin is not Oswald's sharp cleft chin but a broad, round, blunt chin bearing no resemblance to Oswald's at all. The horizontal line separating the face of Oswald from the rest of the body is also perfectly apparent once one looks.

Where did this bogus photo come from? It was said to have been found among Oswald's effects by the Dallas police, who also produced another photo of Oswald armed, similarly doctored, taken with the same camera as the first. No other pictures in the collection had been taken by that camera, nor was that camera found among Oswald's things.

But we said it was doctored more than once. The second time was in the photolab of the Time-Life building, where someone unknown, but with the authority to do so, told an illustrator to paint a telescopic sight on the rifle shown in the photo, something the rifle had when the police presented it to the world after the killing but not when this picture was taken.[12] What could have possessed *Time*'s editors, that they would tamper in the least respect with this critical piece of evidence?

But there was to come a third and much worse tampering, again by the specialists of Time, Inc. In its issue of November 24, 1975, once more sallying forth to lay all doubts of the lone-Oswald theory to rest, *Time* reprinted this photo—rather, an artfully selected portion of it. For as though to solve the problem of the contradictory shadows, *Time* cut off the picture at Oswald's knees, so there was simply no shadow on the ground to see. And as though to solve the problem of the tilting figure, *Time* rotated the whole photo a few degrees to the right, aligning the figure vertically, then recropping to straighten the sides and lightly airbrushing the background of fence and houses to obscure the fact that now the background was tilting crazily to the right.

What kind of journalism is this? The only possible innocuous explanation is ignorance, and how could ignorance unaided have hit all these hidden bases so squarely? The layout man at *Time* is not an expert on Dealey Plaza, but surely the writers and editor of that story cannot claim such an excuse. How do we avoid drawing an inference of intentional deception?

To top it off, with the same article, *Time* printed a diagram of Dealey Plaza which totally mislocated the famous grassy knoll. As every schoolchild to the debate about JFK's death learns on the first day in class, "grassy knoll" is a term used exclusively to refer to the area north of Elm up an incline towards the triple overpass (see map, p. 85, where it is shown correctly located), that is, the area to Zapruder's right. But in the *Time* drawing, the grassy knoll is shown at Zapruder's left, just next to the depository.

Could this be another accidental slip? Certainly it is not trivial. The whole debate about JFK's assassination hinges on the shots which Warren's critics say came from this area, the grassy knoll. What gives so much concrete power to this claim is the massive congruity between the president's reaction to the headshot and the response of the crowd: he is thrown backwards, and they, after a moment of shock, surge up the knoll in the direction they thought the shots were coming from. This area, of course, is totally separated from Oswald's supposed perch in the depository at Zapruder's left.

But on the other hand—as evidently occurred to someone—if the grassy knoll were *next* to the depository instead of at the other end of the plaza from it, then the immensity of this problem for the Warren reconstruction of the crime would be lost on the newcomer to the dispute. The newcomer will look at *Time*'s diagram and justly conclude that, since the grassy knoll and the depository are *next* to each other, the conflict among the witnesses about the origin of the shots must not be so important.

The Case for Oswald as Patsy

Over and above the weakness of the case against him, Oswald has a handful of interesting positive arguments in his defense. One of these is that he may be visible (in the ubiquitous Altgens photo) in the crowd inside the depository entranceway at the very instant of the shooting. Another is that he was seen by a Dallas policeman and his boss at the depository, standing calmly in the lunch room on the second floor, a maximum of a minute and a half after the shootings. Confronted by a policeman with a drawn pistol within a minute and a half after shooting the president of the United States and the governor of Texas—supposedly—and supposedly having run down four flights of stairs in the meantime, Oswald showed not the least discomposure. Said another depository employee, "I had no thoughts . . . of him having any connection with it all because he was very calm."[13]

A different kind of evidence was introduced in 1975 with the so-called Psychological Stress Evaluator, PSE, an instrumental technique that came into being through CIA efforts to improve the standard lie-detector test.[14] Its technical premise is that the frequency patterns of normal, relaxed speech disappear under stress. A person can show stress and be telling the truth at the same time, say ex-CIA officer George O'Toole and other advocates of the PSE, but if there is no sign of stress, that is a positive indication of truthfulness. "Stress is a necessary but not sufficient condition of lying," says O'Toole, "but the absence of stress is a sufficient condition of truthfulness." The device has the added interest of being usable with any voice record, even on low-quality telephone tapes. Its inventors, says O'Toole, originally intended it as an additional channel in their conventional polygraph setup, but found in use that "the new variable was so reliable and accurate a measure of psychological stress there was really no need to measure the other polygraph variables."

Two acoustic tape recordings of Oswald's voice denying his guilt are preserved, recorded during his stay in the Dallas jail between Friday and Sunday. O'Toole found one in the CBS archive. It contains the following exchange between Oswald and the press at midnight Friday in the basement of the jail, Oswald shackled between two policemen.

OSWALD: I positively know nothing about this situation here. I would like to have legal representation.

REPORTER: [Unintelligible.]

OSWALD: Well, I was questioned by a judge. However, I protested at that time that I was not allowed legal representation during that very short and sweet hearing. I really don't know what this situation is about. Nobody has told me anything, except that I'm accused of murdering a policeman. I know nothing more than that. I do request someone to come forward to give me legal assistance.

REPORTER: Did you kill the President?

OSWALD: No, I have not been charged with that. In fact, nobody has said that to me yet. The first thing I heard about it was when the newspaper reporters in the hall asked me that question.

O'Toole tracked down the second specimen in the private collection of a conspiratorialist of Dallas, Al Chapman, in a Columbia Records audio documentary attack on Warren's critics put out in 1966. Oswald speaks once on this record.

O'Toole conjectures the recording was made while Oswald was being led along the crowded third-floor corridor of the police station that Friday night.

> OSWALD: These people have given me a hearing without legal representation or anything.
> REPORTER: Did you shoot the President?
> OSWALD: I didn't shoot anybody, no sir.

In both specimens, says O'Toole, Oswald shows low stress. The second, categorical denial "contains almost no stress at all." O'Toole finds in this proof, "that Oswald was telling the truth, that he was not the assassin." He has support in this judgment so far from several leading technical specialists and practitioners in the PSE field, [15] although at the time of the publication of his book *The Assassination Tapes* in spring 1975, he says he had not sought expert endorsement. The only criticism of his findings so far is the criticism of the PSE method itself. Presumably this means that if the method is sound, then we have an acoustical companion piece to the Zapruder film. As the film shows us that others had to be shooting at Kennedy, the tape shows us that Oswald was not.

Oswald's Identity

Oswald joined the Marines in 1957 and after basic training was sent to Atsugi, Japan, where one of the CIA's larger outfront bases was located, a staging area at that time for covert operations into the Chinese mainland and for U-2 overflights.

In September 1959, two months before normal mustering out, Oswald suddenly applied for a hardship discharge to take care of his mother, who had been slightly injured at work ten months before. Mother Oswald was supported by her regular doctor and an Industrial Accident Board when she denied that this or any other accident cost her any wage-earning capacity or that it was the real motive of her son's hasty discharge. According to researcher Peter Dale Scott, "...the swift handling of Oswald's release suggests that it was a cover: Oswald was being 'sheep dipped' [prior to] assignment to a covert intelligence role."[16] Scott points out that his immediate application for a passport for travel to Europe suggests that the role concerned his "defection" to the Soviet Union.

The commission was of course not interested in such speculation and decided to take the word of two CIA and five FBI officials that, in the *Report*'s words (p. 327), "there was no, absolutely no type of informant or undercover relationship between an agency of the U.S. Government and Lee Harvey Oswald," even though in its secret session of January 27, 1964, the commission heard its own member say that the CIA and the FBI both would deny a connection with Oswald even if one existed.

From the moment of Oswald's arrest, the story circulated to the effect that he indeed did enjoy such an FBI relationship. This story was finally passed on to the Warren Commission as a formal charge by Texas Attorney General Waggoner Carr. Carr said he had learned from reliable informants (who turned out to be on the Dallas district attorney's staff) that Oswald got two hundred dollars every month from the FBI as an informer and that his FBI number was 179. On January 27, 1964, the commission went into a secret session to deliberate on this. The record of that meeting would not be released for ten years. The transcript shows Chief Counsel J. Lee Rankin defining the problem and the task: "We do have a dirty rumor that is very bad for the Commission...and it is very damaging for the agencies that are involved in it and it must be wiped out insofar as it is possible to do so by this Commission."

But as spy-wise Commissioner Allen Dulles was quick to point out, even if Oswald was an agent for Hoover, it would never be possible to prove it because Hoover would deny it and there would be no way to prove him wrong. "I think under any circumstances," said Dulles, "...Mr. Hoover would certainly say he didn't have anything to do with this fellow.... If he says no, I didn't have anything to do with it, you can't prove what the facts are." Would Dulles lie in the same situation, asked the commissioners. Yes, said Dulles, and so would any other officer of the CIA. Whereupon the commission goes on to ask two CIA and five FBI officers if Oswald was secretly connected with their outfits, and records their answer that he was not as the basis of their official conclusion on the matter.

Discharged in record time from a CIA-related detachment of the Marines on a seemingly fabricated need to take care of a mother who was not infirm, Oswald stayed home a total of three days, then set off for the Soviet Union by way of France, England and Finland with a $1500 ticket purchased out of a $203 bank balance (never explained).

By 1960 he was in Moscow to stage a scene at the U.S. Embassy. First he renounced his American citizenship, then declared that he was about to give the Russians valuable military secrets. He was then shipped off by the Russians to a factory job in Minsk. There he met and married Marina Pruskova, the niece of a top Soviet intelligence official in the Ministry of the Interior.

He decided in 1962 that he now wanted to come back to the States. In spite of his former scene at the Embassy and the radar secrets and failure to recant, the State Department speedily gave him a new passport and an allotment of several hundred dollars for the expenses of the return trip with Marina.

The Oswalds were met in the United States by Spas T. Raikin, whom Warren identifies as an official of Travellers Aid. Warren knew, of course, but decided not to add that Raikin was also the former secretary general of the American Friends of the Anti-Bolshevik Bloc of Nations, a group with extensive ties to intelligence agencies in the Far East and Europe, including the Gehlen-Vlassov operation (chapter 2) and the CIA.

The presumed leftwinger Oswald and his Red wife Marina immediately were taken into the bosom of the two most militantly anti-Communist communities in the United States, the White Russians of Dallas and the Cuban exiles of New Orleans and Miami. They were befriended by George de Mohrenschildt, an officer of the World War II Gehlen-Vlassov operation.

In April 1963, the Oswalds moved to New Orleans. According to former CIA official Victor Marchetti, Oswald at that time came into contact with Clay Shaw, now identified positively (by Marchetti) as a CIA officer. Shaw was also close to David Ferrie, an instructor at the guerrilla training camps at which, at this point, militant anti-Castro exiles and possibly breakaway elements of the CIA were preparing raids if not new invasions of Cuba. This was the month in which Kennedy for the first time publicly acknowledged the existence of these bases and ordered them closed. The world does not now know what Oswald's relationship to the CIA's Shaw was, only that it existed (this by the testimony of nine witnesses). It was while this intimate association with the CIA was alight, however, that Oswald became the one-man New Orleans chapter of the Fair Play for Cuba Committee, supposedly a pro-Castro organization.

The pro-Castro leaflets Oswald once distributed for this committee were stamped with the address, "544 Camp Street." The commission found no evidence that Oswald kept an office there, but it did find the office of an anti-Castro group, the Cuban Revolutionary Council. We now know the Cuban Revolutionary Council was a CIA creation put together by Howard Hunt, and the 544 Camp Street was a major headquarters of anti-Castro activity throughout that period.

In August 1963, while passing out his pro-Castro leaflets (something he did twice), Oswald got into a scuffle with some anti-Castro Cubans and was arrested by the New Orleans police. The first and only thing he said at the police department was that he wanted to speak to the FBI, a novel request for a leftwinger of that place, period, and predicament. The agent appeared and Oswald got off quickly with a ten-dollar fine.

In September 1963 Oswald supposedly took a bus from New Orleans to Mexico City. His purpose is said to have been to obtain a Cuban travel visa. On October 1, the CIA cabled the State Department and the Office of Naval Intelligence to tell of information from "a reliable and sensitive source" that one Lee *Henry* Oswald had entered the Soviet Embassy. When the National Archives released a previously classfied memo from Helms to the commission dated March 24, 1964, another piece fell into the puzzle: "On 22 and 23 November," said Helms "immediately following the assassination of President Kennedy, three cabled reports were received from [deleted] in Mexico City relative to photographs of an unidentified man who visited the Cuban and Soviet Embassies in that city during October and November 1963" (Commission Document 674, National Archives).

The original description of this Oswald in the CIA report ran like this: "The American was described as approximately 35 years old, with an athletic build, about six feet tall, with a receding hairline." Oswald was 24, about 5′8″ and 160 pounds. Who was pretending to be Oswald at the Russian and Cuban embassies in Mexico City a month before this same Oswald allegedly was to shoot the president?

There is evidence actually of several Oswalds in circulation at this time. There is in the first place the presumptive original himself installed since late October in the depository. There is the thirty-five-year old Oswald in Mexico City freshening up the Red spoor at the Cuban and Soviet missions. There is the Oswald or Oswalds who move around Dallas just before the hit planting unforgettable memories of a man about to become an assassin: the Oswald of the firing range who fires cross-range into other people's targets and then belligerently starts a loud argument in which he carefully and loudly repeats his name; the Oswald of the used-car lot who sneers at Texas and the American flag and drives recklessly, though Oswald had no driver's license and did not know how to drive; the Oswald who visited exile Sylvia Odio a few weeks before the assassination in the company of two anti-Castro militants at a time when the *real* Oswald (or is it the other way around?) is supposed to be in Mexico City. Who are all these Oswalds?

In another crucial Freedom of Information suit, Harold Weisberg forced the government to make and release the transcript of a theretofore untranscribed stenographer's tape of another secret meeting of the Warren Commission on January 22, 1964. The transcript indicates that Congressman Gerald Ford suspected Oswald of being an informant for the FBI. Ford participated in a discussion concerning Oswald's repeated use of post office boxes, an operating method characteristic of undercover FBI informants, and remarked on Oswald's informer-like behavior in playing both sides of the wrangle between the Communists who identify with Stalin and the Communists who identify with Trotsky. "He was playing ball," said Ford of Oswald, "writing letters, to both elements of the Communist Party. I mean, he's playing ball with the Trotskyites and the others. This was a strange circumstance to me."

In that same meeting, Chief Counsel Rankin told the commissioners the FBI was behaving in an unusual way in the Oswald investigation and seemed to be attempting to close the case without checking out numerous leads into Oswald's activities. On the final page of the thirteen-page transcript, Allen Dulles summed up his reaction to the idea of an Oswald connection to the FBI by saying, "I think this record ought to be destroyed."[17]

Ruby

Rose Cherami at forty was employed as a stripper at Jack Ruby's Dallas nightclub, the Carousel, at the time of Kennedy's murder.[18] She was a narcotics addict with an arrest record two-and-a-half pages long from jails in San Antonio, Amarillo, Dallas, Shreveport, Angola, Houston, New Orleans, Austin, Galveston, Los Angeles, Tucson, Deming, Albuquerque, Oklahoma City, Montogomery, Jackson, and South Gretna, mostly on vagrancy and narcotics charges, though the charge filed in Jackson was "criminally insane."

On November 20, 1963, she and two unidentified men were driving through Louisiana on a dope run—so she later said—for Jack Ruby. An argument turned violent. The men threw her out of the moving car and abandoned her on a state highway outside Eunice.

She was found hurt and dazed by Lt. Francis Fruge of the Louisiana State Patrol. Fruge took her for treatment to a hospital, then brought her back to jail and held her on a suspected narcotics connection. Her withdrawal symptoms grew violent. She stripped off her clothing and slashed her ankles. Fruge committed her to the Jackson Mental Hospital, where she was confined until November 26.

During her confinement, after the Kennedy assassination but before Ruby killed Oswald, she told the house psychiatrist at Jackson, Dr. Victor J. Weiss, Jr. (in the words of Frank Meloche), "that she knew both Ruby and Oswald and had seen them sitting together on occasions at Ruby's club."

"Information was also received," says Meloche, "that several nurses employed at Jackson Mental Hospital who were watching television along with Rose Cherami the day Kennedy was assassinated stated that during the telecast moments before Kennedy was shot Rose Cherami stated to them, 'This is when it is going to happen,' and at that moment Kennedy was assassinated. Information states that these nurses had told several people of this incident."

On November 26 Rose Cherami was returned to prison in Eunice for questioning. She gave Lt. Fruge information about a narcotics ring operating between Louisiana and Houston. Lt. Fruge told Meloche this turned out to be "true and good information."

She was then flown to Houston for further questioning on this narcotics angle. "While in flight," said Meloche,

Rose Cherami picked up a newspaper with headlines of Ruby killing Oswald and further on down in the newspaper it stated where Ruby denied ever knowing or seeing Oswald in his life. Rose Cherami laughed and stated to Lt. Fruge that Ruby and Oswald were very good friends. They had been in the Club (Ruby's) together and also stated that Ruby and Oswald had been bed partners. Upon arrival at Houston she again repeated this story to Captain Morgan. When asked to talk to the federal authorities about this, she refused and stated that she did not want to get involved in this mess.

Meloche and Fruge tried to track Rose Cherami down in 1967 in connection with Garrison's case but found that in September of 1965 she had been killed in a peculiar auto accident outside Big Sandy, Texas. Reads Fruge's report:

The accident was reported to Officer Andrews by the operator of the car after he had taken the subject to the hospital. Andrews stated that the operator related that the victim was apparently lying on the roadway with her head and upper part of her body resting on the traffic lane, and although he had attempted to avoid running over her, he ran over the top part of her skull, causing fatal injuries. An investigation of the physical evidence at the scene of the accident was unable to contradict this statement. Officer Andrews stated that due to the unusual circumstances, namely time, location, injuries received and lack of prominent physical evidence, he attempted to establish a relationship between the operator of the vehicle and the victim to determine if any foul play was involved. This resulted negative. It should be noted that Hwy #155 is a farm to market road, running parallel to US Hwys #271 and #80. It is our opinion, from experience, that if a subject was hitch-hiking, as this report wants to indicate, that this *does not* run true to form. It is our opinion that the subject would have been on one of the U.S. Highways. Andrews stated that although he had some doubt as to the authenticity of the information received, due to the fact that the relatives of the victim did not pursue the investigation, he closed it as accidental death.

We wish to further state that fingerprint identification shows that deceased subject, Melba Christine Marcades, is the same person as subject Rose Cherami, who was in custody, by us, from November 21, 1963, through November 28, 1963, at which time she stated that she once worked for Jack Ruby as a stripper, which was verified, and that Ruby and Lee Harvey Oswald were definitely associated and known to be, as she stated, "bed partners." She further referred to Ruby as alias "Pinky."

The fate of Julia Ann Mercer, another Ruby witness, was much better but still bad. As she deposed in New Orleans in January 1968 to Garrison:

On the morning of the President's assassination, in the vicinity of 11:00 o'clock, I was driving west on Elm Street toward the Triple Underpass. There was a green pickup truck parked on the right-hand side of the road, with its two right wheels up on the curb. I was delayed by traffic congestion long enough to observe a man remove from the back of the truck a rifle wrapped in paper.

Because of the delay caused by traffic I happened to see the face of the driver of the truck quite clearly. While I was stopped there he looked at me twice. This man was, as I later recognized from the papers, Jack Ruby.

The next morning FBI agents showed me photographs. This was on Saturday—the day after the assassination and the day before Ruby shot Oswald. The FBI then showed me some photographs to choose from. One of the men I picked out was Jack Ruby. When one of the FBI agents turned the picture over I saw Ruby's name on the back....

The next morning I was looking at television with my family and when I saw Ruby shoot Oswald, I said, "That was the man I saw in the truck." From the view the television screen gave of Ruby—especially when they showed it again slowly—I recognized him as the man who was at the wheel of the truck on Friday and as the man whose picture the FBI showed me on Saturday.

But what happened to her information in the hands of the FBI is just another of the countless reasons serious investigators of the JFK death are driven to the conclusion that the FBI was in some way creatively involved in whatever foul play happened in Dallas. Her testimony was turned completely upside down in the FBI report filed by Special Agent Louis Kelley. Kelley reported that she "was shown a group of photographs which included a photograph of Jack Ruby. Mercer could not identify any of the photographs as being identical with the person she had observed.... She was then shown a photograph of Ruby, and she advised the person in the truck had a rather large round face similar to Ruby's, but she could not identify him as the person."

Four years later, Garrison showed Julia Mercer a copy of this FBI report. "This is not an accurate statement," she deposed, "because I did pick out Ruby's picture. Also, this report does not mention the fact that the FBI showed me Ruby's picture on November 23rd, the day before he shot Lee Oswald."

I have also been shown a separate FBI report . . . [which states] that I only felt able to identify the man with the gun and not the driver. Contrary to this indication, I had no doubts about what the driver's face looked like. This was on the same day they showed me Ruby's picture, among others, and the day when I picked him and three similar pictures as looking like the driver of the truck. I do not know whether the other three pictures shown me were other men who looked like Ruby or whether they were three other pictures of Jack Ruby. But they definitely showed me Jack Ruby and I definitely picked him out as looking like the driver.

Another funny thing. The FBI report of November 23 says that Mercer described a sign on the door of the green truck made up of the words "air conditioning" in a crescent design. Half the force was sent looking for a green Ford pickup with a sign like that on its door. "This is not true," deposed Mercer to Garrison. "Every time I was interviewed—and at least two of the interviews were by the FBI—I stated that there was no sign of any kind on the side of the truck. The words 'air conditioning' were not painted on the truck, nor were any other words. It was a plain green truck without any printing on it and I made this clear from the outset."

She goes on to depose that her signature as it appears on a document put out as her affidavit by the Dallas County Sheriff's Department is a forgery; that a notary public has signed this document, whereas there was no notary present at her interviews; that like the FBI statement, the sheriff's affidavit also has her describing the nonexistent sign. "That is not the way it was at all," she deposed to Garrison: "The truck was plain and had no letters whatsoever painted on it."

And her coda: "That 'affidavit' also has me stating, with regard to the driver, that 'I could not see him too clearly.' That is not true. I saw the driver very clearly. I looked right in his face and he looked at me twice. It was Jack Ruby.

"I was not asked to testify before the Warren Commission."

The Warren *Report* tells us that "Ruby was unquestionably familiar, if not friendly, with some Chicago criminals" (p. 790). A partial list of Ruby's organized-crime connections, *as they were known to the Warren Commision*, would include:

Lewis McWillie, a "gambler and murderer" who had managed the Lansky Syndicate's Tropicana in Havana before 1959 and by 1963 was an executive at the Thunderbird in Las Vegas, another prime Lansky holding. Ruby traveled to Cuba with McWillie, received two phone calls from him from Cuba, and shipped him a pistol, all in 1959.[19]

Dave Yaras, an intimate of Ruby's from Chicago childhood days, a Syndicate mobster operating out of Chicago and Miami.[20] Yaras told the Warren Commission that Ruby was also close to:

Lenny Patrick, another Chicago-based hood also known to Ruby's sister Eva as a friend of her brother's. Yaras and Patrick are both prominently identified in congressional crime hearings as important figures in the Chicago Syndicate.[21]

Paul Roland Jones, Paul "Needlenose" Labriola, Marcus Lipsky, Jimmy Wienberg, Danny Lardino, and *Jack Knappi*, the Chicago Syndicate group that moved into Dallas in 1947 (the year Ruby moved to Dallas).[22] Jones, an opium smuggler in the forties, told the Warren Commission that "if Ruby killed Lee Harvey Oswald on orders, the man to talk to would be Joe Savella [properly *Civello*]," then head of Syndicate operations in Dallas. *Chicago Daily News* crime reporter Jack Wilner also told the commission that Ruby was involved in 1947 in the Chicago Syndicate takeover of Dallas gambling. "The Commission finds it difficult to accept this report," said Warren. [23]

Robert "Barney" Baker, a Teamster hood convicted by RFK. His phone number was in Ruby's address book.[24]

Milt Jaffe, also in Ruby's address book, a point holder in the Stardust of Las Vegas with Cleveland Syndicate heavy Moe Dalitz.[25]

At the age of fifteen Ruby already belonged to a gang of Chicago youths who ran messages for *Al Capone*. This gang produced such other notables as Frank "The Enforcer" Nitti, Capone's successor as head of the Chicago Syndicate, and his associate, Charles "Cherry Nose" Gioe, busted in 1943 with John Roselli who is later associated with the CIA-Syndicate scheme to assassinate Castro.[26]

Peter Dale Scott (whose citations I gratefully borrow here) has identified three independent reports to the Warren Commission strongly suggesting that Ruby was "in fact a pay-off or liaison man between organized crime and the Dallas police department (over half of whose policemen Ruby knew personally)."

1.   In 1956, the Los Angeles FBI advised the Dallas FBI that Mr. and Mrs. James Breen, "acting . . . as informants for the Federal Narcotics Bureau," had become involved with "a large narcotics setup operating between Mexico, Texas and the East. . . . In some fashion, James [Breen] got the okay to operate through Jack Ruby of Dallas."[27] In 1964, reinterviewed by the Chicago FBI, Mrs. Breen confirmed her 1956 story.[28]

2.   After the assassination, a prisoner in an Alabama jail told the FBI that a year previous to the assassination, when he had tried to set up a numbers game in Dallas, he was advised "that in order to operate in Dallas it was necessary to have the clearance of Jack Ruby . . . who had the fix with the county authorities."[29]

3.   Again after the assassination, another prisoner in Los

Angeles, Harry Hall, contacted the Secret Service (who vouched for his reliability) with the information that in his days as a Dallas gambler he had turned over 40 percent of his profits to Ruby, who "was supposed to have influence with the police."[30]

The Warren Commission's conclusion was that "the evidence does not establish a significant link between Ruby and organized crime."[31]

The commission also failed to investigate a communication received on June 9, 1964, only two days after Ruby's testimony, from J. Edgar Hoover, in which Hoover disclosed that Ruby may have been an FBI informant for several months in 1959.[32] Nor did it seek to reconcile its picture of Ruby as a small time psychotic with evidence that Ruby was on good terms with such powerful Texas millionaires as H. L. Hunt, his son Lamar (whose office Ruby visited the day before the assassination),[33] Billy Byars, and Clint Murchison, a power behind Johnson and involved heavily in the Bobby Baker scandal.[34]

All the examinations in the twenty-six volumes of the Warren Commission *Hearings* begin with conventional courtroom punctilio, except for that of the second lone assassin of Dallas. In Ruby's act, the hero himself is the first to break the silence.[35]

"Without a lie detector on my testimony," he blurts out of nowhere, "my verbal statements to you, how do you know if I am tell[ing] the truth?"

His lawyer Joe Tonahill jumps: "Don't worry about that, Jack."

Ruby persists: "Just a minute, gentlemen."

Warren turns: "You wanted to ask something, Mr. Ruby?"

Ruby: "I would like to be able to get a lie detector test or truth serum of what motivated me to do what I did at that particular time, and it seems as you get further into something, even though you know what you did, it operates against you somehow, brainwashes you, that you are weak in what you want to tell the truth about, and what you want to say which is the truth."

I offer here that Ruby's tortured phrase, "you are weak in what you want to tell the truth about," is monumentally expressive of the situation in which he found himself. *He was too weak to tell the truth that he wanted to tell*. But we must come the long way around to this in order to see it.

We pick Ruby's testimony up a few sentences later as he continues struggling to explain why he wants a lie-detector test.

As it started to trial—I don't know if you realize my reasoning, how I happened to be involved—I was carried away tremendously emotionally, and all the time I tried to ask Mr. [Melvin] Belli [his first lawyer], I wanted to get up and say the truth regarding the steps that led me to do what I have got involved in, but since I have a spotty background in the nightclub business, I should have been the last person to ever want to do something that I had been involved in.

In other words, I was carried away tremendously.

You want to ask me questions?

Yes, Mr. Ruby, I would have said. Take this last sentence, "since I have a spotty background in the nightclub business, I should have been the last person to ever want to do something that I had been involved in." Can you straighten that out? Are you trying to say that since you have a Syndicate-linked background, it doesn't make sense for you to have killed Kennedy's assassin in order to protect the beloved widow from the mortifications of a trial? Is that what you are trying to say through your clenched teeth?

But Warren said no such thing. Instead he said, "You tell us what you want, and then we will ask you some questions."

And Ruby says, "Am I boring you?"

The more closely one reads the some hundred pages of

Ruby's testimony to Warren (the second two-thirds of which are spoken from a polygraph harness to the FBI's top interrogator), the harder it is to avoid seeing something very brave in Ruby. The exasperated pugnacity of that "Am I boring you?" for example, couldn't be better: Warren, he is saying, if you want to understand me, you are going to have to pay close attention to what I say. It would seem a fair enough proposition from a key witness to the chief commissioner of a big public probe. But of the seven august commissioners only two were present, Warren and the ubiquitous Gerald Ford, and they were not overly inclined to probe. And Warren had not even wanted to talk to Ruby. Ruby had to fight his lawyers and send the messages to Warren through his family. The hearing took place with a handful of lawyers hostile to Ruby present, plus the court recorder, and a Dallas policeman at the door. They were all in the interrogation room of the Dallas County Jail at Houston and Main looking out on Dealey Plaza. It was 11:45 A.M., June 7, 1964. The Warren Commission *Report* was at this point virtually complete. For that reason in itself, perhaps, the commission members were disinclined to pursue distant echoes in Ruby's difficult but suggestive language.

Against the commission's passivity, what Ruby most wants to tell them is that he wants a lie detector test. The reason for this, he says, is that the story he is telling about why he shot Oswald in inherently implausible. How can the commission believe he is telling the truth if he is not put in a polygraph harness? But why is his story inherently implausible? We will come across that, too, in his own words.

We skip through a half-dozen pages of meandering but tense discussion of Ruby's activities on November 22, 1963, mainly bearing on an anti-JFK ad placed in one of the Dallas papers. Then at last Ruby comes to the events of that night. He tells Warren how he remembered that it had been a hard day for his friends, the police (he was on personal terms with virtually the entire force), and how he decided to take them a snack:

RUBY. . . . I had the sandwiches with me and some soda pop and various things, and Russ Knight opened the door and we went upstairs.

(Mr. Alen Specter, a staff counsel, entered the room.)

WARREN: This is another man on my staff, Mr. Specter. Would you mind if he came in?

(Chief Justice Warren introduced the men around the room.)

RUBY: Is there any way to get me to Washington?

WARREN: I beg your pardon?

RUBY: Is there any way of you getting me to Washington?

WARREN: I don't know of any. I will be glad to talk to your counsel about what the situation is, Mr. Ruby, when we get an opportunity to talk. [Ruby has been intermittently begging a chance to talk to Warren alone.]

RUBY: I don't think I will get a fair representation with my counsel, Joe Tonahill. I don't think so. I would like to request that I go to Washington and you take all the tests that I have to take. It is very important.

TONAHILL: Jack, will you tell him why you don't think you will get a fair representation?

RUBY: Because I have been over this for the longest time to get the lie detector test. Somebody has been holding it back from me.

WARREN: Mr. Ruby, I might say to you that the lateness of this thing is not due to your counsel. . . . It was our own delay due to the pressures we had on us at the time.

Ruby carefully summarizes his story up to this point, starts into a skirmish with Tonahill, then abruptly, "throwing pad on table," as the commission stenographer notes (a stage direction preserved), he returns abruptly to his main idea and desire, to get out of Dallas somehow.

> RUBY: . . . Gentlemen, unless you get me to Washington, you can't get a fair shake out of me. If you understand my way of talking, you have got to bring me to Washington to get the tests. Do I sound dramatic? Off the beam?
>
> WARREN: No; you are speaking very, very rationally, and I am really surprised that you can remember as much as you have remembered up to the present time. You have given it to us in great detail.
>
> RUBY: Unless you can get me to Washington, and I am not a crackpot, I have all my senses—I don't want to evade any crime I am guilty of. But Mr. Moore, have I spoken this way when we have talked?
>
> MOORE: Yes. [Elmer W. Moore is a Secret Service agent.]
>
> RUBY: Unless you get me to Washington immediately, I am afraid after what Mr. Tonahill has written there . . .

An argument ensues with Tonahill, Tonahill trying to stop him from saying things a prosecutor could use to show he had prior intention of killing Oswald. Unmindful of Ruby's apparent belief that his best interest lay in getting the truth out, Tonahill as defense attorney wants at least to be able to argue that the killing was an unpremeditated act, motivated by an errant burst of emotion. Ruby had the same complaint against Belli, his first lawyer. Belli could only think in lawyerly terms, that is, in terms of conviction and acquittal. Ruby, on the other hand, wanted to tell his story to a lie detector. Why?

Exasperated with Tonahill, he turns back to Warren: "Well, it is too bad, Chief Warren, that you didn't get me to your headquarters six months ago."

We skip a few pages of intense but repetitive discussion on the question of premeditation and the lie-detector and truth-serum tests Ruby wants to take, with Ruby hurling obscure shafts to Tonahill, such as "it is a greater premeditation than you know is true," which sends Tonahill up the wall. "I don't say it is premeditation," says the lawyer, "I never have. I don't think it is." And Ruby, discounting a certain story helpful to the spontaneous-act-of-passion theory: "You would like to have built it up for my defense, but that is not it. I am here to tell the truth."

The question turns to why Ruby was not dealt with earlier and Warren promises a no-delay lie-detector test. Ruby pushes for speed and discovers that Warren is leaving in the morning. And at that point, Dallas County Sheriff J. E. (Bill) Decker, unbidden enters the dialogue.

RUBY: Are you staying overnight here, Chief Warren?

WARREN: No; I have to be back, because we have an early session of Court tomorrow morning.

RUBY: Is there any way of getting the polygraph here?

DECKER: May I make a suggestion? Jack, listen, you and I have had a lot of dealings. Do you want my officers removed from the room while you talk to this Commission?

RUBY: That wouldn't prove any truth.

DECKER: These people came several thousand miles to interview you. You have wanted to tell me your story and I have refused to let you tell me. Now be a man with a bunch of men that have come a long way to give an opportunity to—

RUBY: I wish the President were right here now. It is a terrible ordeal, I tell you that. . . . [He subsides for a moment to his pat narrative, then turns back to Decker.] Bill, will you do that for me that you asked a minute ago? You said you wanted to leave the room.

DECKER: I will have everyone leave the room, including myself, if you want to talk about it. You name it, and out we will go.

RUBY: All right.

DECKER: You want all of us outside?

RUBY: Yes.

DECKER: I will leave Tonahill and Moore. I am not going to have Joe leave.

RUBY: If you were not going to have Joe leave—

DECKER: Moore, his body is responsible to you. His body is responsible to you.

RUBY: Bill, I am not accomplishing anything if they are here, and Joe Tonahill is here. You asked me anybody I wanted out.

DECKER: Jack, this is your attorney. This is your lawyer.

RUBY: He is not my lawyer.

(Sheriff Decker and law enforcement officers left room.)

Gentlemen, if you want to hear any further testimony, you will have to get me to Washington soon, because it has something to do with you, Chief Warren. Do I sound sober enough to tell you this?

WARREN: Yes; go right ahead.

RUBY: I want to tell the truth, and I can't tell it here. I can't tell it here. Does that make sense to you?

WARREN: Well, let's not talk about sense. But I really can't see why you can't tell this Commission.

RUBY: But this isn't the place for me to tell what I want to tell.

MOORE: The Commission is looking into the entire matter, and you are part of it, should be.

RUBY: Chief Warren, your life is in danger in this city, do you know that?

WARREN: No; I don't know that. If that is the thing that you don't want to talk about, you can tell me, if you wish, when this is all over, just between you and me.

RUBY: No; I would like to talk to you in private.

WARREN: You may do that when you finish your story. You may tell me that phase of it.

RUBY: I bet you haven't had a witness like me in your whole investigation, is that correct?

WARREN: There are many witnesses whose memory has not been as good as yours. I tell you that, honestly.

RUBY: My reluctance to talk—you haven't had any witness in telling the story, in finding so many problems.

WARREN: You have a greater problem than any witness we have had.

RUBY: I have a lot of reasons for having those problems.

WARREN: I know that, and we want to respect your rights, whatever they may be. And I only want to hear what you are willing to tell us, because I realize that you still have a great problem before you, and I am not trying to press you....

RUBY: When are you going back to Washington?

WARREN: I am going back very shortly after we finish this hearing—I am going to have some lunch.

RUBY: Can I make a statement?

WARREN: Yes.

RUBY: If you request me to go back to Washington with you right now, that couldn't be done, could it?

WARREN: No; it could not be done. It could not be done. There are a good many things involved in that, Mr. Ruby.

RUBY: What are they?

WARREN: Well, the public attention that it would attract, and the people who would be around. We have no place for you to be safe when we take you out, and we are not law enforcement officers, and it isn't our responsibility to go into anything of that kind. And certainly it couldn't be done on a moment's notice this way.

RUBY: Gentlemen, my life is in danger here. Not with

my guilty plea of execution [i.e., not because of killing Oswald]. Do I sound sober enough to you as I say this?

WARREN: You do. You sound entirely sober.

RUBY: From the moment I started my testimony, have I sounded as though, with the exception of becoming emotional, haven't I sounded as though I made sense, what I was speaking about?

WARREN: You have indeed. I understand everything you have said. If I haven't, it is my fault.

RUBY: Then I follow this up. I may not live tomorrow to give any further testimony. The reason why I add this to this, since you assure me that I have been speaking sense by then, I might be speaking sense by following what I have said, and the only thing I want to get out to the public, and I can't say it here, is with authenticity, with sincerity of the truth of everything and why my act was committed, but it can't be said here.

It can be said, it's got to be said amongst people of the highest authority that would give me the benefit of doubt. And following that, immediately give me the lie-detector test after I do make the statement.

Chairman Warren, if you felt that your life was in danger at the moment, how would you feel? Wouldn't you be reluctant to go on speaking, even though you request me to do so?

WARREN: I think I might have some reluctance if I was in your position, yes; I think I would. I think I would figure it out very carefully as to whether it would endanger me or not. If you think that anything that I am doing or anything that I am asking you is endangering you in any way, shape, or form, I want you to feel absolutely free to say that the interview is over. [A prize specimen of Warren integrity: If telling us the truth in Dallas would hurt you, cost you your life, we'd rather you just left it unsaid than go to the trouble of getting you to a place where you could feel safe to say it.]

RUBY: What happens then? I didn't accomplish anything.

WARREN: No, nothing has been accomplished.

RUBY: Well, then you won't follow up with anything further?

WARREN: There wouldn't be anything to follow up if you hadn't completed your statement.

RUBY: You said you have the power to do what you want to do, is that correct?

WARREN: Exactly.

RUBY: Without any limitations?

WARREN: Within the purview of the Executive Order which established the Commission. . . .

RUBY: But you don't have a right to take a prisoner back with you when you want to?

WARREN: No; we have the power to subpoena witnesses to Washington if we want to do it, but we have taken the testimony of 200 or 300 people, I would imagine, here in Dallas without going to Washington.

RUBY: Yes; but those people aren't Jack Ruby.

WARREN: No; they weren't.

RUBY: They weren't.

WARREN: Now I want you to feel that we are not here to take any advantage of you, because I know that you are in a delicate position, and unless you had indicated not only through your lawyers but also through your sister, who wrote a letter addressed either to me or to Mr. Rankin saying that you wanted to testify before the Commission, unless she had told us that, I wouldn't have bothered you. . . .

RUBY: The thing is, that with your power that you have, Chief Justice Warren, and all these gentlemen, too much time has gone by for me to give you any benefit of what I may say now.

Warren protests that it is not so. Ruby names his family, says they are all threatened; and for a moment he seems to give up and revert to the basic story of his motive, the unpremeditated-murder story, namely, that he saw in that Sunday morning's newspaper "the most heartbreaking letter to Caroline Kennedy...and alongside that letter a small comment in the newspaper that...stated that Mrs. Kennedy might have to come back for the trial of Lee Harvey Oswald. That caused me to go like I did; that caused me to go like I did." Then continuing in this new tone, Ruby goes almost singsong: "...I never spoke to anyone about attempting to do anything. No subversive organization gave me any idea. No underworld person made any effort to contact me. It all happened that Sunday morning."

So Sunday morning he drives downtown on an errand taking him to the Western Union office near the ramp of the county jail, where Oswald was being moved that morning. The errand had to do with a call he received that morning from "a little girl—she wanted some money—that worked for me" at the Carousel. The next day was payday, but he had closed the club.

It was ten o'clock when he got downtown. He tells us he noticed the crowd at the jail but assumed Oswald had already been moved. He carried out his errand at the Western Union office, "sent the money order, whatever it was," and walked the short distance to the ramp. "I didn't sneak in," he says, "I didn't linger in there. I didn't crouch or hide behind anyone, unless the television camera can make it seem that way. There was an officer talking—I don't know what rank he had—talking to a Sam Pease in a car parked up on the curb." Thus he underscores the fact that the police saw him and let him pass freely into the closed-off ramp area. Then to the killing: "I think I used the words, 'You killed my President, you rat.' The next thing I knew I was down on the floor."

In the murkiest passages of his testimony, Ruby then proceeds to tell (as he calls it) "a slipshod story" in which he insinuates at least a part of the background information he feels he cannot directly give out. We will not try unraveling it here because it would take a lot of unraveling and we are interested in the coming climax of the Warren-Ruby

confrontation. But in his slipshod story, Ruby develops a
quite detailed and potentially verifiable picture of his
underworld past, but as though to deny that it existed. For
example, he names as a "very close" friend one Lewis J.
McWillie as typical of "Catholics" Ruby knew who would be
especially "heartbroken" over Kennedy's murder. Which is a
joke. "Catholic" McWillie was even then a prominent
Syndicate gambler with big interests in pre-revolutionary
Cuba. "He was a key man over the Tropicana down there,"
says Ruby. "That was during our good times. Was in
harmony with our enemy of the present time." In August
1959, Ruby tells Warren, McWillie paid his plane fare down
to Havana. "I was with him constantly," Ruby says, strongly
suggesting a professional relationship if only because
McWillie was such an important Syndicate executive, and as
of August 1959, the Syndicate had concern for the future of
its Havana games.

Ruby also mentions another important racketeer with
whom he had had an association, but in a strangely
concealing way, as though he were preparing for subsequent
denials. "As a matter of fact," he says, "I even called a Mr.—
hold it before I say it—headed the American Federation of
Labor—I can't think—in the state of Texas—Miller."
Warren says, "I don't know." Then Ruby gets it: "Is there a
Deutsch I. Maylor? I called a Mr. Maylor here in Texas to
see if he could help me out" in an obscure situation involving
nightclub competition, i.e., Syndicate vice arrangements,
some years before. This person, whom Ruby first calls Miller
and then, ever so deliberately, changes into Deutsch I.
Maylor, is actually Dusty Miller, head of the Teamsters
Southern Conference. Peter Dale Scott made this identification first, but blamed the Warren stenographer for the
distortion of *Dusty Miller* into *Deutsch I. Maylor*, even
though Ruby had just shown that he could prounounce
Miller perfectly well and the stenographer had shown that he
could spell it. I think it is a precious detail in the
reconstruction of Ruby, and I submit to common sense

whether *Deutsch I. Maylor* could have been anything other
than an intentional and purposeful distortion on Ruby's
part. *He is hiding something in order to reveal it*. Chief
Council Rankin forces the testimony back to other
questions, but Ruby tirelessly weaves in his stories of Cuban
gambling and bigtime crime, his relationship to McWillie
and other Syndicate people like Dave Yaras and Mike
McLaney, and his general awareness of Syndicate networks.

When Rankin asks him point blank, "Did you know
Officer Tippit?" he responds with another intriguingly
indirect and suggestive answer, thus: "I knew there was three
Tippits on the force. The only one I knew used to work for
special services." This last refers to the Dallas Police
Department's Special Services Bureau. The SSB was
working closely with the FBI and was responsible, as Scott
indicates, for both the world of subversives and the world of
organized crime, the worlds of the cover-story Oswald and
the underlying Ruby. (Scott adds that another responsibility
of the SSB was taking care of intelligence preparations for
visiting VIPs like the president.) Ruby says he is "certain" his
Tippit and the dead Tippit are not the same, but then
perhaps the "wrong" Tippit was the dead one after all, and
the "right" Tippit was this other one that Ruby did indeed
know, the Tippit of the SSB whom Vice-Chief Gilmore
elsewhere testified was "a close friend" of Ruby's and visited
his club "every night they are open."

The above came out when Warren confronted Ruby with
the story with which Mark Lane had already confronted the
commission some time earlier, that shortly before the
assassination Ruby had been seen at a booth in his nightclub
with Officer Tippit and "a rich oil man" otherwise not
identified. Above is Ruby's denial of any such Tippit
relationship, that is to say, his nondenial of it ("I knew there
was three Tippits," etc.). On the score of the "rich oil man,"
he only volunteers it might have been the man who then
owned the Stork Club, William Howard. Warren observes
that Lane's informant had not given Lane permission to

reveal this story. It was before them after all as groundless hearsay. They had decided nevertheless to put it to Ruby in the bigness of their intellectual curiosity. They had now put it to him. He had now answered it. "So we will leave that matter as it is," which elicited from Ruby another of his remarkable improvisations: "No, I am as innocent regarding any conspiracy as any of you gentlemen in the room. . . ."

Warren grows restless and turns to Ford and the lawyers. "Congressmen, do you have anything further?"

Ruby, one imagines quickly, says: "You can get more out of me. Let's not break up too soon."

And Ford, perhaps startled, comes up with a good question: "When you got to Havana, who met you in Havana?" This gives Ruby an opportunity he obviously relishes to spin a little thicker web of insinuations that his Havana relationship to Syndicate executive McWillie was a serious one. But Warren again tires: "Would you mind telling us anything you have on your mind?" Ruby falters, then starts a line that suddenly swerves to the heart of the matter: "If I cannot get these tests you give [the truth tests], it is pretty haphazard to tell you the things I should tell you."

Rankin decides he must test the slack:

RANKIN: It isn't entirely clear how you feel that your family and you yourself are threatened by your telling what you have to the Commission. How do you come to the conclusion that they might be killed? Will you tell us a little bit more about that, if you can?

RUBY: Well, assuming that, as I stated before, some persons are accusing me falsely of being part of the plot—naturally, in all the time from over six months ago, my family has been so interested in helping me.

RANKIN: By that, you mean a party to the plot of Oswald?

RUBY: That I was a party to a plot to silence Oswald.

In other words, this is the inference which he has all along been begging them to make. The commission does not respond. The stenographer moves Ruby to a new paragraph. He stumbles through several hundred murky words on the impact of the affair on his family and notes that he has the sympathy of a good many people for killing the President's assassin. But he says, "That sympathy isn't going to help me, because the people that have the power here, they have a different verdict. [Get this:] They already have me as the accused assassin of our beloved President." The commission must have given him a blank look as this new idea tried to register: *Ruby shot Kennedy?* Ruby says, "Now if I sound screwy telling you this, then I must be screwy."

Warren rallies his senses and moves into the breech:

WARREN: Mr. Ruby, I think you are entitled to a statement to this effect, because you have been frank with us and have told us your story.

I think I can say to you that there has been no witness before this Commission out of the hundreds we have questioned who has claimed to have any personal knowledge that you were a party to any conspiracy to kill our President.

RUBY: Yes, but you don't know this area here. [They squabble about the point. Warren really wants to evade this.]

WARREN: Well, I will make this additional statement to you, that if any witness should testify before the Commission that you were, to their knowledge, a party to any conspiracy to assassinate the President, I assure you that we will give you the opportunity to deny it and to take any tests that you may desire to so disprove it.

But how does he know that this is what Ruby is talking about, or that Ruby would necessarily want to "deny and disprove" it? And above all, why should Warren be so blazingly *uninterested* in this man? Ruby maybe said it all back in the first minute: "Am I boring you?"

It is the beginning of summer, the report is in, the presses are about to cook, the awful part of this thing in Dallas is about to be wrapped up, and now this hangnail, Ruby, with his weird way of talking, his ominous and portentous airs, his impenetrable, melodramatic double-meanings:

RUBY: . . . And I wish that our beloved President, Lyndon Johnson, would have delved deeper into the situation, hear me, not to accept just circumstantial facts about my guilt or innocence, and would have questioned to find out the truth about me before he relinquished certain powers to these certain people. . . . Consequently, a whole new form of government is going to take over our country, and I know I won't live to see you another time. Do I sound sort of screwy in telling you these things?

WARREN: No; I think that is what you believe or you wouldn't tell it under your oath.

RUBY: But it is a very serious situation. I guess it is too late to stop it, isn't it? . . .

Ruby seems to struggle against his insight later, but I think that at just this point in the text he is about to see into the heart of darkness. He is coming to think that, indeed, it is too late, because not only are the Dallas police and the Dallas sheriff in on it, but so is the Chief Justice of the Supreme Court. And unknown to everyone but Ruby and the ones actually in on it, as a consequence of this, "a whole new form of government is going to take over our country."

FORD: Are there any questions that ought to be asked to help clarify the situation that you described?

RUBY: There is only one thing. If you don't take me back to Washington tonight to give me a chance to prove to the President that I am not guilty, then you will see the most tragic, then you will see the most tragic thing that will ever happen. . . .

* * *

And again:

RUBY: ... Now maybe something can be saved. It may not be too late, whatever happens, if our President, Lyndon Johnson, knew the truth from me.

But if I am eliminated, there won't be any way of knowing.

Right now, when I leave your presence now, I am the only one that can bring out the truth to our President, who believes in righteousness and justice.

But he has been told, I am certain, that I was part of a plot to assassinate the President. [!]

I know your hands are tied; you are helpless.

WARREN: Mr. Ruby, I think I can say this to you, that if he has been told any such thing, there is no indication of any kind that he believes it.

RUBY: I am sorry, Chief Justice Warren, I thought I would be very effective in telling you what I have said here. But in all fairness to everyone, maybe all I want to do is beg that if they found out I was telling the truth, maybe they can succeed in what their motives are, but maybe my people won't be tortured and mutilated. [That is, Ruby begs forgiveness from the assassination conspiracy, having failed in his effort to rat on it through double meanings tossed into Warren's ear.]

WARREN: Well, you may be sure that my President and his whole Commission will do anything that is necessary to see that your people are not tortured.

RUBY: No.

WARREN: You may be sure of that.

RUBY: No. The only way you can do it is if he knows the truth, that I am telling the truth, and why I was down in that basement Sunday morning, and maybe some sense of decency will come out and they can still fulfill their plan, as I stated before, without my people going through torture and mutilation.

WARREN: The President will know everything that you have said, everything that you have said.

RUBY: But I won't be around, Chief Justice. I won't be around to verify [!] those things you are going to tell the President.

TONAHILL: [Who never left the room] Who do you think is going to eliminate you, Jack?

RUBY: I have been used for a purpose, and there will be a certain tragic occurrence happening if you don't take my testimony and somehow vindicate me so my people don't suffer because of what I have done.

WARREN: But we have taken your testimony. We have it here. It will be in permanent form for the President of the United States and for the Congress of the United States, and for the courts of the United States, and for the people of the entire world.

It is there. It will be recorded for all to see. That is the purpose of our coming here today. We feel that you are entitled to have your story told.

RUBY: You have lost me though. You have lost me, Chief Justice Warren.

WARREN: Lost you in what sense?

RUBY: I won't be around for you to come and question again.

WARREN: Well, it is very hard for me to believe that. I am sure that everybody would want to protect you to the very limit.

RUBY: All I want is a lie-detector test, and you refuse to give it to me.

Because as it stands now—and the truth serum, and any other—Pentothal—how do you pronounce it, whatever it is. And they will not give it to me, because I want to tell the truth.

And then I want to leave this world.

Warren again promises the test, and soon, and then again starts trying to wrap things up. But again Ruby asks for

more: "Hold on another minute." Warren says, "All right."
Ruby says, "How do you know if the facts I stated about
everything I said, statements with reference to, are the truth
or not?" Ruby's overburdened syntax is finally crumbling.
Ford and Warren repeat their promise of protection and
speedy tests and again seem half out of their chairs.

> RUBY: How are we going to communicate and so on?
> WARREN: We will communicate directly with you.
> RUBY: You have a lost cause, Earl Warren. You
> don't stand a chance. They feel about you like they do
> about me, Chief Justice Warren.
> I shouldn't hurt your feelings in telling you that.

Remarking that he knows he has his enemies, Warren
adjourns the session. It has consumed three hours and five
minutes.

Ruby got his lie-detector test six weeks later, not exactly
right away in the Warren scheme of all deliberate speed.
Against all standard procedures, the test was a marathon,
some eight hours long with only short breaks.[36] Other people
were in the room, some of whom Ruby insisted were his
enemies (for example, his lawyer, Joe Tonahill). Little
wonder that the chief FBI expert in lie-detection polygraphy,
Bell P. Herndon, who gave the test, testified later that its
results were too ambiguous to support any conclusive
interpretation.

Yet Ruby's session with the lie-detector is as rich with
suggestive details as the session before Warren and Ford. We
are anxious to press on to a statement of our conception of
Dallas, but the person of Ruby has been ignored too long,
and the special volatility of the JFK issue as a whole just now
begs for special awareness of the importance of Ruby's role.
*Ruby's gangland situation makes him a direct link between
the Bay of Pigs and Dallas.*
The text of this interview must be read in its entirety to be
appreciated, something we cannot begin to do here. We must

be satisfied with the key points from the interview itself. Then we go to the sequel, the psychiatrist's on-the-spot analysis of what Ruby was up to in his "psychotic delusional" state, and the examiner's explanation of the ambiguity of the test.

The basic problem of the lie-detector test surfaces as soon as Ruby comes into the Dallas City Jail interrogation room at 2:23 P.M., July 18, 1964. His lawyers and family have taken the position that he must not give the prosecuting attorney (William Alexander, present in the room) a way to prove his murder of Oswald was a premeditated act. His lawyers want to argue that it was total coincidence that he drifted into the basement of the jail just as Oswald was being moved, and that it was only when he happened thus to see Oswald before him that he was overwhelmed by the idea of taking out the pistol, which he was packing by another coincidence, and shooting him down on the spot, without stopping to think about it.

But the story Ruby seems careless in telling is that his motive began to form early that morning when he saw a press item about Caroline Kennedy in the Sunday paper and realized that the widow would have to return to Dallas for the trial of Oswald. Ostensibly to show that Jews like himself (so runs his story) could act in a patriotic and brave way, he seized the time. It is true that Ruby never says he started planning to kill Oswald that morning before he went downtown. He says clearly he went downtown to send money to a stripper who complained that morning by phone from Fort Worth that she needed money since Ruby had closed the Carousel for three days including the regular payday. He went down to the Western Union office to send her a money order, then went in a very straight line over to the jail, eased down the ramp, was confronted at once with Oswald, and stepped into the experience that killed the two of them.

The polygraph testimony opens with Ruby offstage, his

lawyers laying what ground they can to keep the results of the lie-detector test closed up. The Warren people are sympathetic to that. Assistant Counsel Spector loses no opportunity to make it clear that the test is not happening because of any desire of the commission's; its members have never entertained the least doubt of Ruby's basic story.

Ruby is not long on stage before this comes up. He at once moves to make his position plain, lawyers or no lawyers. "I want to supersede the attorney...in stating that I want everything to come out immediately, as soon as possible, and whoever wants to know the results—what the results are—I want it to be known, regardless of which way it turns."

A little later he tries unsuccessfully to get one of his lawyers out of the room:

> RUBY: Did you get your pants sewed up, Joe?
>
> TONAHILL: It went through to my leg.
>
> RUBY: That was a pretty rough brawl we had, wasn't it, Joe?
>
> TONAHILL: Yes.
>
> RUBY: Joe, I'd appreciate it if you weren't in the room. Can I ask you to leave, Joe?
>
> TONAHILL: I'll be glad to leave, if you want me to, Jack.
>
> RUBY: As a matter of fact, I prefer Bill Alexander to you, you're supposed to be my friend.
>
> TONAHILL: Let the record show that Mr. Ruby says he prefers Bill Alexander being here during this investigation, who is the assistant district attorney who asked that a jury give him the death sentence, to myself, who asked the jury to acquit him, his attorney.
>
> HERNDON: May we proceed?

And they do, and no one leaves the room. From this point on, no doubt, it is absurd to think the polygraph could prove anything whatsoever. The atmosphere is demonstrably too unsettling; conditions are too uncontrolled from the standpoint of forensic polygraphy to support any meaningful interpretation of Ruby's responses. The test is being run purely to satisfy Ruby, and no one shows any intention of treating it as a serious probe for a difficult truth.

Finally comes the test proper, the long, emotionally grueling examination covering exactly those aspects of the event that Ruby specified, touching on such issues as the Cuban connection, the Syndicate connection, the Communist angle, and his intentions toward Oswald. Herndon first walks Ruby through each test series, adjusts the questions to make sure they are exactly the questions Ruby wants to answer and that he understands them completely, then goes through them again with the polygraph switched on. The sixty-six pages of testimony are shot through with haunting and suggestive exchanges, such as the following, as Herndon reads through the question that comes closest to the heart of the premeditation issue:

HERNDON: Did you tell anyone you were thinking of shooting Oswald before you did it?

RUBY: No.

HERNDON: Is that question all right, do you understand it?

RUBY: Yes—I take that back. Sunday morning—I want to elaborate on that—before I left my apartment—it evidently didn't register with the person [he may mean his roommate, George Senator] because of the way I said it. In other words, the whole basis of this whole thing was that Mrs. Kennedy would have to come back for trial.

Whereupon Tonahill's partner, Fowler, stages a demonstration to stop Ruby from saying such a thing with his prosecutor present.

For purposes of our summary, Ruby's key statement in

this lie-detector testimony is the following. It comes toward the end, when he is tired and seems to feel the situation slipping away.

> RUBY: Let me put it this way: Here I run a nightclub. I run a nightclub, and on Friday this tragic event happens, and I get carried away more so than anyone else. Why? Why was I so sick mentally or so carried away?
>
> I immediately replace my newspaper ads so that I would be closed for those 3 days. This is the ironic part of it, that wouldn't it be a tremendous hoax, or certain people would probably believe it that way, that here's a fellow that didn't vote for the President, closes his clubs for 3 days, made a trip to Cuba, relayed a message from a person—from Ray Brantley—look at circumstantially how guilty I am. If you want to put these things together. Then, I happen to be down there [the ramp], which is a million to one shot, that I should happen to be down there at that particular second when this man comes out of whatever it was, an elevator or whatever it was. All these things. Plus the fact of the post office box and other rumors that they saw us together at the club. How can we give me the clearance that the ads I put in were authentic, my sincerity, my feeling of emotionalism were sincere; that that Sunday morning I got carried away after reading the article, a letter addressed to Caroline and then this little article that stated Mrs. Kennedy might be requested to come back and face the ordeal of the trial.
>
> Also, if there was a conspiracy, then this little girl that called me on the phone in Fort Worth then is part of the conspiracy. Do you follow me?[37]

If I follow Ruby, he is giving us here a perfectly serious lead—who was "this little Fort Worth girl?"—as well as a powerful list of reasons why he should *not* be taken at his word about killing Oswald out of love for Kennedy and sympathy for the widow. (a) He was not a Kennedy man. (b) It was verifiable that he was in Cuba on Syndicate business just before the Revolution took power, and that he relayed an important Syndicate business message in 1959, i.e., Ruby was on the exact opposite side of the fence from the anti-Syndicate Kennedys. (c) It was a million-to-one shot that he should have been on the ramp just as Oswald appeared. (d) There are traces of a prior Ruby-Oswald-Tippit relationship, or of some such thickening of the story underneath. But this excited no great interest in the commission or Assistant Counsel Specter, who believed already that these were innocuous coincidences and acceptable doubts.

Three minutes after Ruby left the room, at 9:10, the commission reconvened to question Dr. William Robert Beavers, a psychiatrist who had been examining Ruby, on his reaction to Ruby's behavior under the long questioning.

Specter was trying to get Beavers to say that Ruby was out of his mind, and technically at least Beavers does that. He says that when he first examined Ruby late in April, "he had briefly what I call a psychotic depression, that is, he had evidence of auditory hallucinations and a poorly defined but definite delusional system which waxed and waned during the time of the interview, and he had evidence of a severe degree of depression...."

Asked if he has now a different view in light of the interrogation just concluded, Beavers answers, "Yes, I do. I think that as I have seen him, the depressive element has diminished, and that the delusional system has become much less open and obvious...."[38]

What struck him as indicative of Ruby's unsoundness of mind was "the relationship he has with his attorneys [Tonahill and Fowler]. There are certain kinds of actions and behavior in these two relationships which fit better in my opinion with the continuation of a covert delusional system concerning threats to his race, his family, based on his presumed activity in a conspiracy, than it would with rational realistic appreciation of the factors in his environment."[39]

A few lines later, Beavers backs a little closer to it: "... It seemed to me, because he was fairly certain in his answers during the trial run, and then following this during the actual run of the polygraph, there was so much hesitation and uncertainty which resulted in no answers, that we were seeing a good deal of internal struggle as to just what was reality."[40]

Then speculating on the possible reason for this "hesitation and uncertainty," Beavers almost puts his finger on it: "It possibly could have been his trying to protect in some way an answer from the polygraph."

Protect? Meaning to conceal? This Ruby who has given us a hundred tips that he is concealing something which he does not wish to conceal? And who could have concealed everything by simply not demanding this test at the top of his voice against the wishes of all the other parties?

Maybe on the contrary, *Ruby was trying to say something*. As he said when Herndon asked him why he closed his eyes in answering the questions, "I'm trying to be more emphatic with the truth when I close my eyes—more than the truth."[41]

The more Beavers goes on, the more he dissolves his own original picture of Ruby as a depressive-delusional psychotic. "In the greater proportion of the time that he answered the questions," he says, "I felt that he was aware of the questions and that he understood them, and that he was giving answers based on an apprehension of reality." And again: "In short, he seemed to behave like a man with a well-fixed delusional system in which whole areas of his thinking and his behavior are not strongly interfered with by the delusion."[42]

That is, Beavers thought Ruby was sane in all respects except his belief that there had been a conspiracy in Dallas. But now Ruby's hated attorney Joe Tonahill comes on

and poses a preposterous but fascinating question. First he
sums up what they have all seen about Ruby's attitude
toward himself and Alexander, the prosecuting attorney in
his murder trial. Tonahill notes that Ruby has been
consistently antagonistic to himself and yet has shown
"tremendous faith and confidence in Mr. Alexander." Now
comes the question: "Have you an opinion as to what goes on
with reference to Ruby's mental illness that causes him to put
faith in Mr. Alexander and no faith in me?"

Beavers first accepts the premise of that question, i.e., that
Tonahill's view of Ruby's best interests is correct, and that if
Ruby's view does not coincide with this view, then Ruby
must be crazy. But then Beavers starts to go beyond that
assumption and comes as close as anyone I know of to the
conception of Ruby I am working out here. Like Icarus he
soars and then falls:

> . . . in fact there is a considerable body of people, the
> district attorney's office and district attorneys included,
> who do feel that he is part of a conspiracy, and that in
> fact either past, present and/or future actions toward
> loved ones and toward members of his race are going to
> be taken against these people because of this presumed
> conspiracy. If this were the case, then it would make
> extremely good sense that he would want Mr.
> Alexander here, and he would want him here very
> definitely, because . . . he is much more concerned with
> getting the truth out so that a whole host of terrible
> things won't happen.[43]

Ten days later Specter interviewed Herndon on the
interpretation of Ruby's polygraph. Herndon took note of
the others who had been present in the room, acknowledged
the irregularity of that and of the length of the test, and said
outright that during the latter part of the test Ruby's fatigue
had probably "desensitized" his reactions. Within that limit,
Herndon's general conclusion was, "if in fact Ruby was

mentally competent and sane, that there was no indication of deception with regard to the specific relevant pertinent questions of this investigation."[44]

But then even under the incurious questioning of Specter, Herndon seemed to cast doubt on his own judgment, or more exactly, on the polygraph's ability to support a solid interpretation of any kind.

For example, he says that Ruby's negative answer to the question, "Did you assist Oswald in the assassination? could be interpreted [as suggesting] that there was no physiological response to the stimulus of the question," and yet when Specter asks him what he means by "could be interpreted," it develops that the polygraph showed "a slight impact of the GSR" (galvanic skin response) to that question.[45] Or again, to the question, "Between the assassination and the shooting, did anybody you know tell you they knew Oswald?" Herndon says Ruby answered with "a noticeable change in the pneumograph pattern," but waves it off as owing to "the relatively long length of this particular question."[46] Then consider Herndon's explanation of Ruby's response pattern to one of the most significant sequences of questions:

HERNDON: This particular series, 3a [Exhibit 4], was what would be called a modified peak of tension series [i.e., all questions are "significant" and not interspersed with insignificant ones]. Ruby was carefully instructed prior to the series that four relevant questions were going to be asked in a consecutive order.

Question No. 3: "Did you first decide to shoot Oswald on Friday night?" He responded "No."

Question No. 4: "Did you first decide to shoot Oswald Saturday morning?" He responded "No."

Question No. 5: "Did you first decide to shoot Oswald Saturday night?" He responded "No."

Question No. 6: "Did you first decide to shoot Oswald Sunday morning?" He responded "Yes."

These are the only relevant questions in this series. A review of the chart with regard to his responses in this series reveals that Ruby's blood pressure continually rose from the question No. 3 until it reached a peak just as question No. 6 was asked. In addition it was noted that there was a rather noticeable change in his breathing pattern as question No. 6 was approached. There is a slight impact in the GSR tracing as question No 6 is approached. This would mean to me in interpreting the chart that Ruby reached a peak of tension as the question No. 6 was about to be asked in which he responded "Yes" to "Did you first decide to shoot Oswald Sunday morning?" This particular type of series cannot be interpreted with regard to whether or not there was any deception, but it does indicate that Ruby built up a physiological peak of tension to the time of Sunday morning with regard to his shooting Oswald.

SPECTER: Is there any correlation between the building up of a peak of tension and the accurate answer to the series?

HERNDON: In normal usage of polygraph technique where a peak of tension is used, if the series is effective, the party will usually respond to a particular item which happens to be the most pertinent with regard to the offense. In this case it appears that Ruby projected his entire thoughts and built up a physiological peak of tension to the point of Sunday morning.

SPECTER: Are there any other significant readings on Exhibit No. 4?

HERNDON: There is no other significant reading on series 4.[47]

Decoded and straightened out, what Ruby was trying to say to Warren comes down to the following main points:

Because of threats against his family emanating from the Dallas Police Department primarily, he could not tell his story in Dallas or indeed to anyone not powerful enough to secure his family once he did talk.

Failing in his plan to escape to Washington with Warren, Ruby opts for the shrewd but naive strategy of telling his lie to a lie detector. But thanks to Herndon, that didn't work either.

His story is a long way yet from reconstruction, but he give us leads and fragments, the most spectacular of which is a whole rich set of suggestions tying him variously into high-level Syndicate figures operating in pre-revolutionary Cuba, and as we know today, involved later in attempts against the Castro government in covert operations connected with elements of the CIA and stemming from the Bay of Pigs, operations which Kennedy used force to extirpate two months before his death. This makes the Ruby case totally of a piece with the over-all affair of the Bay of Pigs/Dallas reactions. The world of Ruby, of the Carousel, and of the Dallas cops was also the world of the Bay of Pigs and of the secret staging bases outside Miami and New Orleans.

Ruby asks us as directly as he can to entertain the hypothesis that he was a member of the JFK assassination cabal, that his purpose in liquidating Oswald was to satisfy the cabal's need to keep the patsy from standing trial, and that something happened to him in the Dallas jail between the time he killed Oswald and the time he began demanding to come before Warren, something to change his mind. Of course I do not press this speculation, but I do say that it better fits the few facts we have than the Warren theory that Ruby too was just another lone nut of Dallas. Thanks to the providential bust at Watergate, we are now too ferociously educated about our government to dismiss as inherently crazy Ruby's fear of covert reprisals from the police or his warnings that "a whole new form of government" was being installed as a result of Dallas.

For this is indeed the direction in which our current discoveries and insights about the assassination and its cover-up are propelling us, namely, that what happened in

Dealey Plaza was a *coup d'etat*. The motive of this coup no one could have grasped at the time without access to the innermost closets of the group that engineered it. As Johnson began shouldering Yankee advisers aside (see the Pentagon Papers), meanwhile mystifying his relationship to Kennedy to make himself seem merely the continuation of Kennedy by other means, it was hard for many to see the coming of a radically new war policy in Vietnam, though the big war was very soon upon us (two hundred thousand troops by the time of the first national March on Washington against the war in April 1965). As we have noted, Johnson also set in motion plans to carry out a for-good invasion of Cuba, the so-called Second Naval Guerrilla, abandoned only because of the outbreak of the Dominican revolt in early 1965 and Johnson's decision to suppress it with the invasion forces assembled originally for Cuba. Now we see these under-the-table moves quite clearly and see them as radical *departures* from Frontier Camelot policy lines, not as the *continuations* which Johnson and Nixon and all the other chauvinists found it convenient to pretend they were. The Johnson administration was not the fulfillment of Kennedy policy; it was its defeat and reversal.

Among the witnesses who testified to Warren, few more than Ruby make us feel the presence of these momentous themes. He is garbled, murky, incomplete, and as his friend and roommate George Senator says, apolitical in any conventional sense. Yet something about what happened to him after killing Oswald makes him more fully in touch with the situation's underlying realities than anyone else who testified—or who listened from the bench.

In November 1965, nationally-syndicated columnist Dorothy Kilgallen advised a few close friends, including Mark Lane, that she was developing a lead that would "blow the JFK assassination case wide open." Twice before Kilgallen had achieved major scoops on this case, both times in connection with Jack Ruby. First, she published Jack

Ruby's secret testimony to the Warren Commission months before the Warren *Report* came out. Second, she interviewed Ruby privately in the judge's chamber during Ruby's murder trial. Before she could make good on her promise, she died of an overdose of alcohol and barbiturates, ruled an accidental death. Her JFK-case notes never turned up.

Sick with cancer (he claimed he was being poisoned), Ruby died in his cell of a stroke in 1967.[48]

The Warren Cover-up

The more familiar one grows with the material evidence available to the Warren Commission, the harder it is to see the Warren Commission's failure to find the truth as a result of mere blundering or philosophical prejudice against "conspiracy theories." That prejudice was no doubt present and operating; it seems a standard attachment to that vintage (as well as current) liberal sensibility. But there is too much here for Warren to have ignored it all by mistake or prejudice alone: the Zapruder film, the problems of the single-bullet theory, the implications of Oswald's intelligence background, Ruby's promise to tell some whole new story if he could be got out of Dallas. And as we now know, thanks to Judge Griffin, the scent of police and FBI obstructionism had reached the commissioners and their staff even at the time.

Is it thinkable that Warren himself was complicit in a cover-up of the truth? May we think such a thing of this paragon? Was it not mainly his reputation that made the lone-Oswald story go down (as in the case of Connally)?

I think we are compelled to look at Warren's reactions from the beginning all the way through the investigation in terms of what we can now divine of the cover-up, because nothing is clear if not that Warren played a key role. The cover-up could in no way have succeeded had Warren wanted to find and publish the truth.

But what could motivate a man of such unimpeachable reputation to support a cover story, an obstruction of justice, a lie beyond any lie yet told in American political life, all for the sake of the conspirators' skin?

I too agree that Warren's integrity is not to be doubted. It was evidently in some respects quite strong. But what if your strong integrity, for example, is confronted with a choice it is not familiar with, a problem mere integrity might not know how to solve? What if the choice is not between truth and falsehood but between falsehood and oblivion? What does "a patriot of unimpeachable integrity" do if the choice is between covering up a murder and sending a whole world to the brink of war?

Recall that Warren resisted the commission appointment to begin with and had to have his arm twisted by Johnson in a lengthy private session before agreeing to take the job, a session from which he emerged in tears everyone presumed were motivated by his love of the dead chief, but which might as easily have been motivated by something else. Warren himself suggested thereafter a different interpretation when he spoke so ominously of "national security" considerations bound up with the assassination, and then sealed up certain documents and evidence for seventy-five years (until 2039).[49]

The cover story of Dallas appears to be many-layered. It has the internal structure of boxes within boxes. We struggle to get past the lone-Oswald theory and to assert (against all kind of psychological and pseudophilosophical as well as political defenses) the strict technical need for a conspiracy theory of some kind, that is, for a reconstruction of the crime on the premise that there was a minimum of two gunmen. The simple-minded inclination of faithful citizens is to think that this need, once established in public debate, must necessarily lead to the truth. On the contrary, the disintegration of the lone-assassin cover story only introduces us to the really difficult part of the controversy, the question of who did it if Oswald did not, or who was with him if he was not alone. And in this second phase of the controversy, the need will be to pierce the second layer of the Dallas cover, namely, the story that Oswald was a Castroite agent whose purpose was to avenge the Cuban revolution against Kennedy for the Bay of Pigs and the CIA's attempts on Castro's life.

This was the apparent theory of Lyndon Johnson and other right-wingers who from time to time have hinted they were never altogether convinced by the Warren conclusion. For example, Jesse Curry, Dallas police chief at the time of the assassination, said in 1969 (celebrating the coming of Nixon?) that he himself had doubts about the lone-Oswald idea, leaving out the fact that he and his department ran a big part of the investigation themselves and were responsible for much of the deception that crippled the investigation at its base. "We don't have any proof that Oswald fired the rifle," he said. "No one has been able to put him in that building with the gun in his hand."[50]

Another Texan, Lyndon Johnson in retirement, let fall a few side thoughts on the assassination to Walter Cronkite in the famous September 1969 interview and then to *Time* writer Leo Janos somewhat later. Janos published his report on Johnson's last days in the *Atlantic Monthly* for July 1973. The relevant passage runs as follows:

> During coffee, the talk turned to President Kennedy, and Johnson expressed his belief that the assassination in Dallas had been part of a conspiracy. "I never believed that Oswald acted alone, although I can accept that he pulled the trigger." Johnson said that when he had taken office he found that "we had been operating a damned Murder Inc. in the Caribbean." A year or so before Kennedy's death a CIA-backed assassination team had been picked up in Havana. Johnson speculated that Dallas had been a retaliation for this thwarted attempt, although he couldn't prove it. "After the Warren Commission reported in, I asked Ramsey

Clark [then Attorney General] to quietly look into the whole thing. Only two weeks later he reported back that he couldn't find anything new." Disgust tinged Johnson's voice as the conversation came to an end. "I thought I had appointed Tom Clark's son—I was wrong."

Then on April 25, 1975, CBS released a formerly unreleased segment of Cronkite's September 1969 interview with Johnson containing the same views quoted by Janos, but a little less explicitly put. Cronkite asks Johnson if he thought there was an "international connection" in the Kennedy murder, and Johnson puckers his eyes, stares at Cronkite, waits a moment, then says he cannot "completely discount" it. "However," he goes on, "I don't think we ought to discuss suspicions because there's not any hard evidence that Oswald was directed by a foreign government. Or that his sympathies for other governments could have spurred him on in the effort. But he was quite a mysterious fellow and he did have connections that bore examination on the extent of the influence of those connections on him, and I think history will deal with much more than we are able to now." The Warren people "did the best they could. . . . But I don't think that they, or me or anyone else is always absolutely sure of everything that might have motivated Oswald or others that could have been involved."[51]

The Oswald connections that Johnson wants us to think about (remember both he and Police Chief Curry are expressing these doubts about Warren at the springtide of Nixon power, 1969) are the connections implied by his defection to Soviet Russia and his membership in the Fair Play for Cuba Committee. We have seen that these are peculiar connections—whether Johnson knew it or not, by the way, and whether Warren knew it or not. Oswald is much more substantially linked into the U.S. than into the USSR or Cuban intelligence systems from the days of his training in the Russian language at the CIAU-2 base at Atsugi, clear through the Russian adventure, and back to the New Orleans-Dallas shuttle in the bosom of the Great White Russian Czarist exile community and the veterans of Fiasco.

The public record does not tell us what to make of Oswald and his game, but it does suggest that he was no more a left-winger than a loner, and that his apparent attachments included both the CIA and the FBI. He may have been simply an FBI informer bullied into the assassination job by an FBI agent threatening his wife's awkward status, as O'Toole speculates. He may have been a CIA operative *covering* as an FBI informer, for such is the way of the clandestine sphere, and one cannot often be sure where the spiral of deception finally closes and the spy's absolute political identity becomes manifest. Howard Hunt, in the motto to his post-Watergate autobiography, would muse that the spy can have no loyalty more final than his loyalty to himself because to do his work he must be able to accommodate all masters. Perhaps Oswald too would be the last to know for what or for whom he was working on the bottom line.

But what did we all believe in 1964 about the integrity of our upper government? What did we believe about spies, clandestinism, *real politik*, about intrigue as a method of decision-making and murder as an instrument of policy? In 1964 we could not yet even see through the fraud we call "the Gulf of Tonkin incident." We may look back in some chagrin to recall that the "event" that aroused the Senate to give Johnson the legal wherewithal to make big war in Vietnam was conceived, planned, and staged exactly to do just that— *by forces we still cannot name*. We see the whole story of the Vietnam war as one unbroken cover-up designed to deceive not "the enemy" but us, the people of the land, the ones who paid the costs of war.

But what could Warren have been able to believe in 1964? Hearing of a conspiracy to assassinate Kennedy and reviewing the most prominent features of Oswald's vita under the pressure of Johnson's Red-conspiracy interpretation, Warren might easily have been persuaded that there had indeed been a conspiracy of Castroite Reds behind Oswald. There could even be a Russian presence in the affair (Oswald's defection, the secrets given over, Marina the niece of a highly placed Soviet intelligence official, the possibility of brainwashing, etc.). If such a thing ever got out, the United States would find itself publicly confronting, ready or not, the most classic of all causes of war, the murder of the head of state by a hostile foreign power.

Moreover, since Castro's Cuba had enjoyed the protection of the Soviet Union ever since the Missile Crisis, how could an armed clash with Cuba be confined to the Caribbean? Given that Russian and American A-bombs had been pressed so hotly up against each other the preceding October, how could Warren countenance pursuing an investigation that might press them up against each other more hotly still?

Perhaps the question of Warren's motivation can never be settled. Presuming it will be established that he and his commission's verdicts were wrong, and that Oswald really was a patsy, one can form answers to the question, "How could Warren have done it?" less awesome than the theory I have just sketched out. Maybe it was that he didn't know, that the evidence seemed less clear then than it does a decade later, that he was misled by the police, CIA and FBI, that he was in a hurry to get the onerous task out of the way, or that his liberal ideology blinded him to indications of conspiracy. I have no desire to rule out such alternatives. What I do claim, however, is that close study of the evidence available to Warren through his commission's own investigation will raise to any open mind the question of whether or not Warren turned aside from the Zapruder film, the absurdities of the single-bullet theory, and the mysteries of Oswald's identity and Ruby's motive *on purpose*, with an *intention* to hide the truth, not to protect the guilty, but because he had been persuaded that the truth, let out, could lead to a nuclear war.

Alternative Models of 11/22/63

One cannot discuss Dealey Plaza conspiracy theories without taking up an early and persisting specimen, the John Birch Society theory that the assassination cabal originates within the orbits of the Council of Foreign Relations, the Bilderberg Group, the secret Round Tables, the inner power sphere of the Rockefeller-Morgan-Rothschild world system. The JBS would say it was Yankee power that killed JFK, as I would say it was Cowboy power. Yankees are as capable as other types of turning against their own, and it seems self-evident from the problem remaining before us that they were quite capable of abandoning the pursuit of his killers as soon as it was convenient to do so and going along with the Johnson program of progress through war. Kennedy was far to the left within the coalition through which he sought to govern, even in his own base and constituency. By fall of 1963, he had probably "lost the support of his peers," in Indira Gandhi's phrase. But it is naive of the JBS to think Yankee power could have succeeded in covering up such a thing in an important Cowboy capital like Dallas.

Then did the CIA do it?

This is likely to be the most appealing cover-up of all, now that the CIA has lost so much of its former charm. "The CIA did it."[52] But as I argue here and there in this book, and especially in the essay on McCord (chapter 8), this could easily be a meaningless shibboleth. The interior of the CIA appears strongly *polycentric*; there are ideological nooks and crannies within it. What the Intelligence side sees is not always what the Operations side reacts to. Indeed, it is former CIA agents like George O'Toole, Phillip Agee, Victor Marchetti, Jon Marks, and others who are currently contributing so much impulse to the campaign for a new JFK investigation and uniformly they are of Intelligence, not Operations.

We can easily get lost below this level. The names of the organizations that enter the expert discussions at this point are no longer so familiar. Now we come upon stranger beasts the likes of Permindex, Six Star, Intertel, Interpol, the Great Southwest Corporation...the Illuminati. But on the evidence as we have it, the plot of Dealey Plaza could not have succeeded without the specific collusion of *elements* of the Dallas Police Department, the FBI, the CIA, and various branches of military intelligence.

But this does *not* teach us to conclude that the FBI did it, or the CIA did it, and so on. The very multitude and magnitude of public institutions apparently implicated in the crime and/or its cover-up actually suggest a different and not so overwhelming picture of "the cabal," namely, that these institutions were drawn in by pieces from the bottom rather than as entities from the top; drawn in by an ideologically, politically, and morally corrupt renegade agentry rather than ordered in by commands flowing routinely downward through the bureaucratic hierarchy. We can still risk assuming, that is, without flying in the face of all reason, that the cabal is not inclusive, its dominion not universal throughout our political system, that there is a residual, basic loyalty to the Constitution and our tradition-al democratic and republican values flowing through the national defense and security institutions. This is not to say that such loyalty is not put to the night in every storm, only that it is not totally stupid to assume that it may still in some little part survive—in DOD, CIA, FBI, etc. We might assume that these institutions have merely been penetrated, not commandeered, in much the same way that our typical big-city constabulary has been penetrated by organized crime but (possibly) not totally conquered by it.

Yet there is nothing so very reassuring, is there, about the analogy to mobster penetration of the police. The crisis of "law and order" is directly rooted in the larger crisis of the infestation of metropolitan police by organized crime, and around that penetration, a vast surrounding bruise of bureaucratic corruption and demoralization spreading to the population through every institutional pore. The general criminalization of the police is obviously horrifying enough, but in theory that disease is at least confined to "local" structures and checked (if never thrown back) by action at a higher power level. We do not feel quite so powerless before a corrupt municipal police force as before a corrupt federal government (and military), simply because the scale of the former is not so overwhelming. *How could we possibly confront the corruption and criminality of the state itself?*

If one holds out a theoretical hope that the American state might still be an instrument of its own salvation, and is not irreversibly a tool of big crime, big business, big militarism and right-wing treason, that is not to say that the following picture of Dallas is so very much more hopeful. Only that there is a little more time in it.

In our review of Frontier Camelot, we have observed an intensely inflamed line of conflict running between the Kennedy side and the Johnson side of the 1960 electoral coalition. We have traced out the line of this conflict chiefly with respect to the main foreign policy issues Kennedy had to face—Cuba and Vietnam. But we have also noted that this conflict is apparent in every phase of Frontier Camelot's life, in domestic policy as in foreign policy, in substance as in style.

I have proposed the Yankee-Cowboy model as a simple structure to situate the events in which this conflict unfolded. From this perspective, we identify Kennedy as a left-wing Yankee, adopted child and hero of the Eastern Establishment, and Nixon as a right-wing Cowboy. The game began in earnest in 1960 when Kennedy beat Nixon by the narrowest of margins through the expedient of allying himself with the most right-wing elements in the Democratic party around Johnson. (Cowboy Nixon's strategy was the mirror image of Kennedy's: his running mate was the Massachusetts Yankee Henry Cabot Lodge.) Then Kennedy scuttled a basic project of the Nixon-Johnson group, the Bay of Pigs invasion, pet project of the very Cowboys whose fierce-warrior rhetoric he had so cynically coopted for campaign purposes.

From the furies generated by that immediate internal conflict about Cuba and what we came to call "Third World Revolution," the line led only to one escalation after another, each new battle compounding prior differences, Kennedy all the while pressing the military budget down and finally trying to turn the FBI against the rebellious Bay of Pigs clique of the CIA.

The magnitude of this battle we can appreciate better from afar, after the fall of Saigon and the liberation of Ho City. The stakes in the fight over Cuba in 1961 were the underlying if not explicit stakes in every American fight that transpired thereafter to May Day 1975. Cowboy militarism, fired by the need to press outward against America's closing world frontiers and force an Open Door to the Third World, versus Yankee imperialism, fired by the need to expand the Atlantic system, to reform and consolidate the Western base and foundation of the empire. Those are always the contending inner forces.

The first great contemporary subplot of this conflict was laid in that complex American experience leading from the twenties and Prohibition forward to the thirties, the Depression, Repeal, and the slide toward World War II. The Prohibition-Repeal mechanism in particular was like a slingshot in terms of the economic and political impetus it imparted to organized crime. Repeal, to put it simply, legalized organized crime, and it did that by legalizing its main product, liquor, and then more diffusely, by opening up the general kingdom of vice as a sector of the larger national economy.

Then came Operation Underworld, another big step forward in the wedding of crime and the state. The Lansky Syndicate's interests in Cuba became absolute during the early forties. Kennedy's decision not to commit the United States to countering the Cuban revolution was thus in practice, from the standpoint of the Syndicate, a reneging on the basic relationship instituted by Operation Underworld, just as from the standpoint of the hard right it was a violation of the unifying principle of the domestic Cold War coalition, the only real basis of internal American unity since the end of World War II.

Then came another thickening. The Gehlen apparatus was incorporated within the womb and bowels of the American foreign intelligence system; this was probably the ballgame by itself. Everything after this, on top of Operation Underworld, was probably just a consequence of this merger. How can a naive, trusting, democratic republic give its secrets to crime and its innermost ear to the spirit of central European fascism and expect *not* to see its Constitution polluted, its traditions abused, and its consciousness of the surrounding world manipulated ultimately out of all realistic shape? It now seems only natural and logical that things would go toward Dallas from Misery Meadow, toward Watergate from the burning of the *Normandie*.

In Frontier Camelot the Cowboy/Yankee contradictions are all present, all agitated, all at full spin and drive. First the Bay of Pigs showdown, then the Missile Crisis showdown, then the big-steel showdown, then the disarmament showdown, then the oil-depletion showdown, then the civil-rights showdown, then the astounding showdown between the FBI and the CIA in the swamps of Lake Pontchartrain, the Everglades, and No Name Key.

Then on top of that, in September 1963, came Kennedy's first clear restraint of further escalation of the Vietnam war. He began to move toward disengagement and a negotiated agreement with yet another new Communist regime. From the standpoint of the Cowboy and indeed of the mainstream American political imagination of the early sixties, what was not imperiled by such reckless and sudden departures from the standard anticommunism of the fifties? If there was ever to be a time when old-minded patriotism must kill the king, was 1963 not the time?

So the motive of the Syndicate couples with the motive of the Nazi-Czarist intelligence clique, of American anticommunism, of the military elite, of the independent oilmen, of reaction, of racism: Everything in America that wants and likes and believes in guns and the supremacy of force over value was at hair-trigger against Kennedy when he resolved that he would no more lead the country into a big land war in Vietnam than in to a full-scale over-the-beach operation in Cuba.

That was September, that indubitable and final clarification of Kennedy's intentions. In October, the Texas Democratic party sent Connally up to see Kennedy about coming down to mend fences in Texas as soon as possible. The patsy was in place at the Depository. The "Wanted For Treason" posters were printed. The Vietnam war was about to take place.

So who was Oswald? Now even Ford admits he doesn't know. The campaign to re-open the investigation of Dealey Plaza succeeded at least to that extent. The likes of Time, Inc., and CBS and Ford will cling to the theory that Oswald killed Kennedy, but by the time of the CBS special of Thanksgiving 1975, even they had been compelled to admit that the loner theory of Oswald had not withstood a decade of criticism. But now they want to say that Oswald must have been a Castro agent.

This move was anticipated by The Assassination Information Bureau in its January 1975 conference at Boston University, "The Politics of Conspiracy," when it called for a larger effort to understand Oswald from the standpoint of his bureaucratic and personal associations. The no-conspiracy position is going to collapse, we predicted, and when that happens, and suddenly everyone is an assassination buff or a conspiracy freak, then the great claim of the cover-up artists will be that Oswald was part of a leftwing conspiracy answering to Cuban or Russian discipline.

This repeats completely the bias of the Warren Commission in its original work. Always for them the word "conspiracy" actually meant "international Communist conspiracy," such that the alternative to the lone-assassin concept was axiomatically the next thing to war. The idea that a conspiracy to murder Kennedy might as well be domestic as foreign and as well rightwing as leftwing certainly occurred, but if it was given any serious thought, we have yet to see the record of it. Now again, still in the time of Ford, the same bias is imposed: Probably there was no conspiracy, and if there was a conspiracy, probably it was the work of the Castroites or the KGB.[53]

After the Thanksgiving 1975 CBS specials on JFK and Ford's positive reaction to them, the AIB at once raised its tiny voice to say that the questions of the assassination itself had by no means been resolved by CBS's self-commissioned board of inquiry (as if CBS had a mandate to resolve this dispute!), and that nobody was going to get anywhere at all with the question, "Who was Oswald?" by starting out convinced that Oswald killed Kennedy. That was where Warren had started. Any new investigation starting from the same assumption will come to the same or worse confusion. As it always was, and as it will remain until an open investigation is carried out by some group (such as a federal grand jury?) capable of commanding the public trust, the key question is still, "Who killed JFK?" Oswald is not yet proved guilty.

But at the same time, the question of Oswald's identity obviously remains one of the outstanding submysteries of the larger drama and contains within it many of the decisive threads. If it is explored without a presupposition of Oswald's guilt, it can prove a rewarding—a startling, an astonishing—area of study. For my part, I would have no desire to try to anticipate the outcome of such a study were it not for the insistence with which Warren defenders press the unfounded picture of Oswald as the lone assassin upon the public consciousness. Be reminded that it is a *theory* that Oswald did it, not a fact—a minority theory to boot. However speculative it must be, then, the presentation of a different theory of Oswald seems justified if only to counter the impression that Oswald, whatever else, must have been a leftwinger.

From his involvement in top-secret CIA intelligence work (the U-2 flights) at a big CIA base (Atsugi), we surmise that Oswald became a CIA workman while he was still a Marine. From the peculiarities of his defection in 1959 and his turn-around and return in 1962—how precipitous the going, how smooth the coming back—we surmise that he was in the Soviet Union on CIA business for which the role of Marxist defector was only cover. When he came back to the United States, he was met by one CIA operative (Raikin), taken under the wing of another CIA operative (de Mohren-schildt), and accepted in the two most militantly reactionary communities in the United States at the time (the White Russians and the exile Cubans).

Assuming Oswald might have been a CIA man, what possible mission could have brought him to this scene?

Think back to the Bay of Pigs Fiasco and recall the anger of Cuban exile reaction to Kennedy's last-minute shortening of the invasion effort and his refusal at the crisis of the beachhead to stand by implied promises of support. We know now that a group around Howard Hunt and Richard Nixon was sentimentally and politically at one with the anti-Castro Cubans in their sense of outrage with Kennedy and their desire to force the issue.

A militant faction of this group broke regular discipline in the period after the Fiasco, the period in which Kennedy fired Warren commissioner-to-be Allen Dulles, installed John McCone in his place, and threatened "to smash the CIA into a thousand pieces and scatter it to the winds." This breakaway component operated independently of official control and carried out, with the exile Cubans, its own program of "pin-prick" raids along the Cuban coast. These attacks were staged from bases inside the United States.

This group existed. It was organized. It was being funded. It was getting large supplies of weapons. It was mounting illegal operations from within the continental interior. Yet Kennedy could not find it. And particularly after the October 1962 Missile Crisis, he *had* to find it, because he had to shut it down; for now he had promised the Russians that the United States would respect the integrity of the Castro government. How do you look for such a group?

You get a trusted agent with the right background and capabilities. You dress up your agent to look like one of the other side's agents. You get your agent circulating in the flight patterns of the suspect communities.

Obviously we are still far from being able to say for sure what Oswald's identity and role really were. But to my mind, the hypothesis that best fits the available facts about him is that he was a loyal CIA man sent out to help locate the renegade Bay of Pigs group, contact it, penetrate it, and determine its organization, backing and plans. The now-famous Oswald letter to the Dallas FBI of November 19, 1963, which the FBI first destroyed and then lied about, and which it now says contained a threat to blow up its Dallas office, was just as likely a warning from Oswald that he had discovered a plot against the President's life set to be sprung that Friday in Dallas. Oswald and his control could not guess the FBI communications were not secure, or that Oswald himself was all the while being groomed for the role of patsy.

5

1968

The Gold-Outflow Crisis

The gold-outflow crisis of January-February showed the
Yankees how vulnerable the Vietnam war of the Cowboy
administration had made the American economy and all
those economies that depended on it. There were sophisticated ways to mystify the fact, and they were used, but most of
the world had no trouble grasping the main thrust of events.
The larger economic system of the Western world as a whole
was suffering from another great malaise which in some way
or another was connected to the Vietnam war. Interpretation
was, as it remains, of course, open to the usual ideological
variations, and as there were those who decided Vietnam was
getting too expensive to win and those who decided it was
getting too expensive to lose, the new realization about the
actual magnitude of the cost did not in itself settle a thing,
except that the fight would grow more intense.

The Tet Offensive

This was another event both fatally unambiguous and ultimately mystifying. All parties to the dispute would continue to agree that Tet was a major event, full of military meanings and political consequences—whatever they might turn out to be. For who in 1968 could see how the war was going to turn out? Cowboys thought the main thing about Tet was that the opposing forces, in an all-units, all-out attack, had been beaten back from their objectives, mauled and spent beyond powers of recovery, *provided* that the United States and friendlies would now seize the time. Yankees tended to think, on the contrary, that Tet's main teaching was that it was indeed the strategy of military escalation itself that had failed. If you could field a half-million men in Vietnam and commit the strategic squadrons at such length and such intensity and still get a Tet offensive unannounced, then something was wrong with the strategy and/or the assumptions upon which it was founded. The economy was meanwhile bleeding away, main arteries open and gushing. West Europe was blanching. If the Americans lost grip, what would become of the rest? The correct strategy must then be to cut Vietnam losses and bid to hold the line in Thailand, where conditions were better.

Precisely according to their material interests and their historical perspectives, Yankee consciousness affirmed the priority of the Atlantic basin while Cowboy consciousness affirmed the priority of the Pacific rim. Formerly these images had been harmonized in the conduct of a two-front, two-ocean, two-theater war, a great Atlantic and Pacific effort joined and supported equally by all descendants of Civil War foes. This World War II coalition endured in the strategy of two-front Cold War in which Red Russia traded places with Nazi Germany and Red China with Fascist Japan, a friend for a foe and a foe for a friend. With the Tet offensive, people started pulling back from the coalition. Naturally enough, the ones who were the first to pull back were the ones who had the least to win from staying in and winning and the most to lose from staying in and losing, the Yankees.

Historian Geoffrey Barraclough of Oxford and Brandeis writes of this moment "that the war in Vietnam, and the mounting inflation that ensued, undermined the international system built up since 1947, and in particular weakened the position of the United States, the linchpin of the system."[1] He quotes C. Fred Bergsten of the Brookings Institution and the Kissinger fraternity: "After 1967, the rules and institutional bases of the old structure began to disintegrate."[2]

This sense of collapse prompts the Yankee rejection of Johnson. Barraclough observes, "In retrospect, it would seem probable that the operative cause [of Johnson's "retirement"] was less the much advertised student unrest than a revolt of big business and corporate finance, frightened by the damage Johnson's policies were inflicting on the U.S. economy and on its economic position abroad."[3] This "revolt of big business and corporate finance" is what I imagine was at the base of the movement afoot early in 1968 to get rid of Johnson: a Yankee revolt.

The Abdication of Johnson

The tell-tale sign that Johnson's March 31 stepdown was a result of a power play was the number of chieftains of the opposing tribe who played key roles in the ceremonies of transition, most notably and visibly the top-class Yankee gunslingers Clark Clifford, Averill Harriman, Cyrus Vance, and George Ball. Defense Secretary Clifford was the acting chief national executive presiding behind the scenes from his perch over the Defense Department because it was (and is) basically the Defense Department that the president of the United States is required to rule. Harriman and Vance set up the Paris peace talks. Vance defused the Pueblo incident.

Ball went to the UN. All the old boys were spinning and driving together.[4]

That Johnson's decision not to run in 1968 was somehow forced upon him is to my mind further indicated in such details as (a) the suddenness of his move, (b) his failure to pass power on to a designated heir the likes of John Connally, and (c) the extent to which the stepdown benefited his main blood enemies: the Kennedys and the Yankee Establishment. Johnson's abdication as well as his switch to a negotiated settlement line on Vietnam may be more clearly seen as outcomes of in internal power struggle much like the struggle we discerned in the record of Frontier Camelot. I am far from wanting to say that Johnson's downfall was in the least detached from the Tet Offensive, or the rise of the antiwar movement, or the degeneration of the Atlantic-system Free World economy under the burden of limitless Vietnam expenses. On the contrary, these large social motions, "contingencies" of world-historical scale, defined the terms of clandestine power struggle and determined the objectives of its participants: the Cowboy to win a war believed to be winnable except for domestic and internal dissension, the Yankee to break off a war believed to be unwinnable except through an internal police state, both sides fighting for control of the levers of military and state-police power through control of the presidency. Johnson's Ides of March was a less bloody Dallas, but it was a Dallas just the same: it came of a concerted effort of conspirators to install a new national policy by clandestine means. Its main difference from Dallas is that it finally did not succeed.

The Turn Toward Peace

Was the Eugene McCarthy campaign a stalking horse for Kennedy? By design or by flaw, it had that effect. It warmed the waters and perfumed the air for the Kennedy antiwar campaign. When Kennedy stepped out to soar he already knew where the wind was. So did the hunters.

What is it about the Kennedys' politics and situation that makes it possible for this Irish Catholic and decidedly nonestablishment family to form national electoral coalitions inclusive of big-city machines, academic liberals, and the Establishment? We have noted (chapter 2) how the Kennedy link with the WASP Establishment was formed in pre-World War II days when father Joseph and son John were at the Court of St. James: sympathies tendered the English aristocracy became the basis of American prestige. But what was the basis, for example, of John Kennedy's access to Johnson in 1960 or Robert Kennedy's to Daley in 1968?

However the Kennedy presidential coalition was formed, it was in the process of forming again in 1968 around Robert. We do not and cannot ever know whether he would have returned the crown to the East, but we should not forget that at the time of his assassination he had assembled a prowithdrawal coalition easily strong enough to dominate the Democratic party and carry off the nomination, and that owing to Johnson's early "retirement," he would have enjoyed the further advantage of not having to face an incumbent.

The Assassination of King

The problems with the lone-Ray theory are much the same as the problems with the lone-Oswald.[5] Four eyewitnesses to the April 4 killing, including two police detectives spying on King, said they saw the gunman in bushes on the ground, not in the second-story window in which Ray was said to have been perched. The angle of the mortal wound is consistent with a shot fired from the ground, inconsistent with a shot fired from the second story. For the alleged murder weapon, a rifle, to be aimed at the correct angle from the bathroom window alleged to have been Ray's nest, the butt would have had to project into the wall. Ray's travels after the assassination took him to Montreal and then Europe, though (like Oswald) he had no visible purse. He traveled under the aliases Eric S. Galt, Paul Bridgman, and George Ramon Sneyd, which turned out to be names of real people living in Montreal, all Ray's age, all Ray's build, all bearing an astonishing facial resemblance to Ray, including in one case identical scars. And so on.

Ray's first lawyer, Alabaman Arthur Hanes, convinced Ray to sell the rights to his story as the only way to raise funds for legal defense. The author thus retained came to pressure Hanes not to let Ray testify in court for fear of compromising the commercial prospects of the forthcoming book—according to Ray, who therefore dissolved the contract.

His next lawyer, Percy Foreman, connected to the H. L. Hunt empire, took the stance from the start that Ray's only reasonable tactic was to plead guilty, which he did only after he and his family strenuously resisted; all Foreman's lawyerly skills almost could not make them see the necessity of a guilty plea. (The guilty plea guaranteed, of course, against a serious trial and a serious investigation.) Foreman was at the same time involved in a big-money deal on the book rights to Ray's story, a deal whose only commercial premise obviously was that Ray would in fact be convicted as the real assassin of King. Foreman told the Ray family that he "didn't want Jimmy to testify because he'd talk about conspiracy." Strange reason, but it may ring a distant bell to learn that Foreman was also one of Jack Ruby's lawyers during the no-conspiracy period. Meanwhile, the only witness who positively connected Ray to the crime was a drunk, alleged to be on the Memphis police payrolls as an informant, whose wife testified that, at the time of the shooting, he "was drunk and saw nothing."

Ray's later assertion of innocence does not reject the possibility that he may have been unwittingly used: "I personally did not shoot Dr. King, but I may have been partly responsible." The evidence of conspiracy and cover-up has persuaded Coretta King among others that a new investigation is necessary: "I do not believe an impartial investigation has been held." As of early 1976, it had not been held because of the refusal of the Tennessee court to let Ray reverse his guilty plea.

The May Memos of Hoover

This is the battery of memos signed May 10 with which Hoover formally launched the FBI's so-called counter-insurgency intelligence program, called "Cointelpro," the explicit purpose of which was to crush the civil rights and antiwar movement, the New Left. We do not yet know all the details of Cointelpro, we do not know its full range; above all, we do not know its impact—except that there is no longer a New Left. But we have the large print up front and it is not hard to deduce the basic variations. Directing all offices to mount an attack on the "New Left movement and its key activists . . . who spout revolution and unlawfully challenge society to obtain their demands," Hoover wrote that "the purpose of this program is to expose, disrupt and otherwise neutralize the activities of the various New Left organizations, their leadership and adherents. It is imperative that the activities of these groups be followed on a continuous basis so we may take advantage of all opportunities for counterintelligence and also inspire action where circumstances warrant." He said, "consideration must be given to disrupting the organized anarchistic activity of these groups . . . the devious maneuvers and duplicity of whose activists . . . can paralyze institutions of learning, induction centers, cripple traffic, and tie the arms of law enforcement officials to the detriment of our society. . . . Law and order is mandatory for any civilization to survive."[6]

The Assassination of RFK

Besides the woman in the polka dot dress, there are the following mysteries in the RFK shooting:[7]

1. The Los Angeles coroner, Thomas T. Noguchi, insisted from the first that the shots fatal to Kennedy were fired from the rear, point blank to the back of his neck, not from Sirhan's position several feet in front of Kennedy. As in the JFK case, this problem of the direction of the lethal fire is basic.

2. The bullet taken from Kennedy's neck and the bullet taken from the body of newsman William Wiesel have never been matched to the same pistol.

3. The bullet removed from Kennedy has never been conclusively matched to the Iver Johnson .22 Cadet, the revolver the police took from Sirhan.

4. There is even a single-bullet theory. Since Sirhan's pistol held only eight bullets and seven were recovered from the bodies and there were three bullet holes in the ceiling, the L.A. police were inspired, Specter-like, to theorize that one of these bullets went up through a ceiling panel, ricocheted off the floor, bounced up and wounded a bystander in the head. In the summer of 1975, Kennedy aide and former Congressman Allard Lowenstein reported that the Los Angeles police had destroyed the ceiling panels.

5. The L.A. police might have laid the ballistics doubts to rest long since by simply test-firing the Sirhan pistol.[8] On one occasion they did carry out a test firing, but the results were odd. Yes, the police said, the test proved it against Sirhan, the bullet fired from his pistol into a watertank and recovered compared positively with the bullet removed from Kennedy. But closer inspection turned up the fact that the serial number of the pistol fired in this test was totally different from the serial number of Sirhan's pistol. This embarrassment doubtless reinforced the natural shyness of the police, and the ten volumes of evidence collected by the unit set up to investigate "Special Unit: Senator" are still secret.[9]

Whatever time teaches us to think about the origins of the RFK assassination, its *result* was the destruction of the Yankee effort at unhorsing the Cowboys in 1968. The nomination of McCarthy had always been impossible, and the ascendancy of Hubert Humphrey guaranteed against any basic new departures in U.S. foreign policy and Vietnam.

Then came Chicago against the background of Prague, Paris, Mexico City. Then the election of Nixon, the continuation of war and repression—the secret wars, Bach Mai, Kent State, Jackson State, Watergate.

III

Watergate

Watergate is a labyrinth we traverse in three directions in the following essays on Howard Hughes, Dorothy Hunt, and James McCord. My central claim is that the arrest of the Watergate burglars was the result of a set-up, that it was no more an accident that the Plumbers were caught than that they were in the offices of the Democratic National Committee to begin with, that there were actually two secret operations at Watergate, colliding invisibly as hunter and prey.

The issues joined in this incredible intrigue are the general issues of the struggle between Yankees and Cowboys. The essay on Hughes takes up the Yankee-/Cowboy theme at length and sets out to show in concrete detail how the larger forces thus indicated can be seen at work in the history of Hughes and his battles and wars, first against the East Coast banking combines around the Rockefellers, then against the international crime Syndicate under Lansky. We follow step-by-step the evolution of the general features of the Watergate confrontation.

The essay on Dorothy Hunt's death in an airplane crash argues that the crash was the result of sabotage with a Watergate-related motive, bearing on the crisis of the Howard Hunt/White House blackmail scheme. I do not know or pretend to know how or by whom this plane was brought down, any more than I know who killed the two Kennedys and King. But just as in those cases, the careful review of the material evidence indicates that we are once again in the presence of an official deception in a capital case.

The McCord essay then explores in detail the anomalies surrounding McCord's person and role in Watergate. The argument is that McCord did not blunder, that there was no slip-up to it when he left the telltale tape on the door, that he was actually an anti-Nixon double agent responsible to Yankee interests, pointman in another Yankee attempt at counter-coup—this one a success.

6

The Hughes Connection

Howard Hughes's name surfaced in the story of Watergate on May 20, 1973, when James McCord told the Ervin committee and its media audience of an abandoned 1972 White House plot to steal certain documents from the safe of editor Hank Greenspun's *Las Vegas Sun*. Greenspun was an ally of Robert Maheu, the top Hughes aide who connected the CIA and the Mafia in 1960, who came to prominence in the Hughes empire during the Las Vegas period, and who then lost out in the Las Vegas power struggle that violently reconfigured the Hughes empire late in 1970. McCord testified that his fellow Plumbers, Hunt and Liddy, were to have carried out the break-in and theft of the papers and that Hughes interests were to have supplied them with a getaway plane and a safe hideout in an unnamed Central American country.

What could the Greenspun documents have been? Why should both Hughes and Nixon have been interested enough in them to attempt a robbery?

Liddy said [testified McCord] that Attorney General John Mitchell had told him that Greenspun had in his possession blackmail type information involving a Democratic candidate for President, that Mitchell wanted that material, and Liddy said that this information was in some way racketeer-related, indicating that if this candidate became President, the racketeers or national crime syndicate could have a control or influence over him as President. My inclination at this point in time, speaking as of today, is to disbelieve the allegation against the Democratic candidate referred to above and to believe that there was in reality some other motive for wanting to get into Greenspun's safe.

For their own reasons, the senators were not tempted to follow that thread in their public examination of McCord. But the investigative staff took a few more steps, and some independent but related court cases came to term, and it thus became possible to build a reasonably solid speculation about the role Hughes and his empire played in the Watergate confrontation. It is still not possible for outsiders—i.e., ordinary citizens—to form more than a rough sense of the underlying truth, but the following provisional reconstruction may sharpen our impression of the quality of the Hughes mystery and show why we cannot be satisfied with the conventional sense that it belongs only to the realm of the eccentricities of the rich, not to the realm of world-historical politics.

Hughes unites in his single person all the major sides of Cowboy capitalism's current situation: its compromised relationship to organized crime, its servility towards militaristic authority, its last-ditch entrepreneurial desperation and bitterness, its gradual transformation into multicorporatized (i.e., monopolized) business structures in spite of all. Yet Hughes was *not* the ally of big crime, and he was *not* finally Nixon's friend.

Hughes Aloft

In 1935, when Bebe Rebozo was opening his first gas station in Miami and Richard Nixon was at Quaker school and Meyer Lansky was launching his Cuban projects and David Rockefeller was cutting his banker's teeth on Depression economics, Howard Hughes at thirty was flying a widely admired aircraft of his own conception, design, and fabrication, the Hughes H-1 Racer, to a world speed record of 352 miles per hour.[1] Two years later he set the coast-to-coast flying record of seven hours and twenty-eight minutes. In 1941 he flew around the world in a Hughes-modified Lockheed Lodestar, demonstrating the feasibility of a world air transportation network. Congress struck a medal for him in 1941 for his aviation exploits. He was a force behind the Lockheed Constellation, the first American high-speed passenger transport, replaced only by the big jets of the fifties. He was a force behind the big jets.

In World War II, as we noted in chapter 2, there was a great feeling of insecurity about the sea lanes. Industrialist Henry Kaiser suggested that the best way to beat the Nazi submarine menace would be to make giant airplanes that could take over the work of ships. Hughes found that idea congenial and got behind it. Shortly he and Kaiser had a contract calling for the delivery in 1944 of three monster flying boats designed to fly nonstop from Honolulu to Tokyo loaded with two batallions of armed infantry or equivalent.

By delivery date, the hull was barely begun and at least another year of work remained. In a foretaste of later troubles at Hughes Aircraft, the works manager quit, Hughes dawdled at replacing him, and twenty-one engineers resigned en masse protesting they were without leadership.

In February 1944, the contract was cancelled. Hughes flew to Washington to tell the War Production Board that his and Kaiser's HK-1 Hercules was not only the biggest airplane in the world, it was also a flying laboratory that would influence the direction of aviation development for decades. Would it not be foolish to waste the time and money already invested?

President Roosevelt was an admirer of Hughes. The contract was rewritten, cutting back from three planes to one.

Hughes returned to California, work resumed, FDR died, the war ended, Lansky founded the Strip, Nixon won his first election, and in 1947 Republican Senator Owen Brewster of Maine angrily exposed the fact that the U.S. government had paid Hughes $66 million for XF-11s and the HK-1 and had yet to receive a single airplane.

Hughes was not alone in this vulnerable position. The United States spent some $825 million for warplanes and some $6 billion for other weapons that were undelivered at the end of the war. Possibly Brewster recalled the impact of the Merchant-of-Death hearings at the end of World War I and sensed that Hughes's Hollywood playboyism would make him a soft target on profiteering. And Brewster knew that Hughes was connected in a potentially scandalous relationship with the late President's son, Col. Elliott Roosevelt.

Hughes had a Hollywood aide by the name of Johnny Meyer whose job was to pick up the tab for the entertainments that Hughes provided those who would do him favors. Meyer told the Brewster committee that between 1942 and 1945 he laid out about $160,000 of Hughes's money for entertainment of military and government officials. A large part of that, he said, provided for the entertainment of Col. Roosevelt.

Besides the connections of a good name, Col. Roosevelt had the additional advantage of being chief of the Requirements Division of the Army Air Force Reconnaissance Branch. He was treated with due respect when he visited Hughes's Culver City works in the summer of 1943 and by the way plunged into a brilliant public romance, leading to marriage, with actress Faye Emerson. Meyer said

Hughes provided the Roosevelt-Emerson party with race-track tickets, liquor, hotel rooms, lavish dinner parties, black market nylons, and a wedding party.

The calendar showed that it was in the welter of those heady days that Col. Roosevelt made the recommendation that won for Hughes a $48 million contract to produce the ultimately unproduced forerunner of the XF-11.

The colonel got out his piss and vinegar and charged into the committee room to defend his honor, but possibly helped Brewster make a larger point by denying "with all my heart and soul that Johnny Meyer ever got me a girl" and pushing hard the lame assurance that he never made "recommendations that would have in any way endangered the lives of the men under me."

Now what could Hughes do? Had he not told Meyer to pay out this money? Had he not plainly hustled for the favors of a man whose influence was worth tens of millions to him in war contracts? Had his bribes not been shamelessly accepted by this officer-son of the president? Had the probable purpose of the bribes not been realized? Had not the contracts been awarded on the president's approval? And then to top all, the planes had never even been delivered. Was it worse than wasteful? Was the XF-11 a straight rip-off? Was the Spruce Goose not an unflyable travesty from the start?

So Hughes came to the hearing tieless in an open shirt, sloppy work pants, and an old brown fedora to defend himself. He began by accepting and then brushing aside Brewster's charges about influence buying: "All the aircraft companies were doing the same thing," he said.

> I believe Meyer patterned his work after what he saw in other companies. I don't know whether it's a good system or not. But the system did obtain. And it certainly did not seem fair for all my competitors to entertain while I sat back and ignored the government and its officials. You, Senator, are a lawmaker, and if

you can pass a law that no one can entertain Army officers and you can enforce it, I'll be glad to abide by it. I never wanted to bother with it. If you can get others to do business that way, I'll be glad to do so, too.

Then he bore down. Influence was not even the real issue in the hearing, he said, no more than the issue was his guilt or innocence in the question of delivering the airplanes.

The hearings, said Hughes, were part of a well-heeled Wall Street conspiracy to force him out of control of TWA. Senator Brewster in particular was privy to this conspiracy, Hughes claimed. Brewster was acting as its agent in pushing these hearings on Hughes. Said Hughes to a startled committee:

If Senator Brewster really believed me guilty of obtaining war contracts by improper means, he would not be romancing me on the side, inviting me to lunch, and making appointments over the telephone to see me in California. I charge specifically that at a lunch in the Mayflower Hotel in Washington, D.C., last February, Senator Brewster in so many words told me that the hearings need not go on if I agreed to merge the TWA airline with Pan American Airways and go along with the bill for a single overseas airline.

And with that was launched an explicit and fateful confrontation between Yankee and Cowboy business forces.

Brewster was close to Juan Trippe, the president of Pan American Airways. Pan Am was (and is) controlled by a high-powered Wall Street banking consort around Rockefeller interests. Trippe's proposal was that the Congress legislate the merger of all of America's overseas airlines into a single giant carrier. The argument for this was of the essence of postwar Yankee consciousness. In the wake of the war and under the intense and numerous pressures of European reconstruction and the Cold War, European capitalism found it convenient to the point of necessity to organize government-industry cartels as a means of generating large amounts of finance capital quickly. In practical terms, that meant that America's several transoceanic airlines would have to compete against one big united West German fleet (Lufthansa), one big united British fleet (BOAC), and so on. How could we maintain our competitive position in international air transportation unless we too resorted to a national cartel?

Hughes could see through that. So the Yankee banks had taken a liking to his airline, had they? And wanted to melt it into their airline, did they? Fancy that.

Tempers in the hearing room became short. At a certain point the subcommittee's chairman, Senator Ferguson, wanted to go back to influence peddling and get away from the question of Brewster's relationship to Rockefeller and the Trippe plan. To do this, he wanted to bring Johnny Meyer back to the witness chair, but Meyer was not in the committee room when his name came up.

"Do you know where Meyer is?" Ferguson said to Hughes.

"No."

"Will you see that he is here at two P.M.?"

Pause. "I don't know that I will."

Newsreels show Hughes calm and self-possessed. Ferguson could not think what to say, so Hughes sat back and continued, "Just to put him up here on the stand beside me and make a publicity show? My company has been inconvenienced just about enough. I brought Meyer here twice. You had time for unlimited questioning."

"The chair feels that as president of the company, you should know where Meyer is. I must warn you of possible contempt. Give me your answer to the preceding question."

"I don't remember."

"I've just asked what your answer was."

"I don't remember—get it off the record."

Ferguson slammed his hand on the desk. "Will you bring

Mr. Meyer in here at two P.M.?"

"No. No, I don't think I will."

In a matter of moments, the hearing had turned into a shouting match. Brewster was desperate to regain the offense and chose to attack Hughes's pride by attacking the flying boat. He attacked its very concept, as though it were only the expression of the vanity of an individual and not of the hubris of an entire class. He called the plane "Hughes's flying lumberyard" and doubted that it would ever fly.

Hughes answered,

> I had to sweat five weeks in Washington to prevent cancellation of the contract from the start because a lot of people in government didn't like it. We got pushed around everywhere. I had to build up a staff of engineers from scratch. I designed every nut and bolt that went into this airplane. I designed this ship to a greater degree than any one man has ever designed any of the recent large airplanes. I worked for eighteen to twenty hours a day for six months on this plane. If the flying boat fails to fly, I will probably exile myself from this country. I have put the sweat of my life into this thing, and $7,200,000 of my own money. My reputation is wrapped up in it. I have stated that if it fails to fly, I will leave this country, and I mean it.

The hearings adjourned till November. Brewster retired to his home base. In spite of the "poisoned arrows" Hughes had hit him with, Brewster was confident enough to say, "My moral code will compare favorably with that of this young man [of 42] who found time while others were fighting the war to produce *The Outlaw*."

Early in November, before the hearings recommenced, Hughes moved the Hercules to a specially built hangar at Long Beach, where it was reassembled and prepared for flight (and where it sat until 1975, when it was broken up for museums[2]).

The Brewster side sneered at the Spruce Goose and predicted that the tables would be turned on Hughes when the hearings reopened. Hughes answered by inviting the whole of the Brewster committee to California for the Hercules's first flight. Brewster did not accept, but others on the committee had fallen under Hughes's charm or become intrigued with him and so came and saw and were conquered all over again, this time by his creation, this gigantic plywood flying boat with a tail ten stories tall and wings of 320 feet (60 percent larger than the 747's). But though its pieces were "as neatly fitted as a mandolin," it was still too early. It was wooden. Wood was wrong for such immense stresses and strains. It was powered by piston engines delivering too little thrust. It was a prefiguration of something still to come, not yet completely possible.

Yet on the last of several taxi runs at Long Beach that day, as Hughes explained, "it just felt so buoyant and light, I just pulled it up." He climbed to seventy feet and sailed along at that altitude for about a mile, then brought it down, satisfied evidently, because that was the single solitary flight of the Goose-Hercules. Brewster was destroyed.

The unmasking of Brewster as an agent of a deep-dyed conspiracy of Yankee bankers plotting to take TWA off Hughes's hands gives us a startlingly unobstructed glimpse into the workings of national power elites. It puts in sunlight the fact that a Yankee conspiracy against Hughes, aiming to take over TWA, existed as early as 1947. It shows us again how mainstream an instrument conspiracy is, how the best families do it, how it reaches the highest and squarest levels of business and government, how it is behind many events that seem disconnected, as with the Brewster hearings and the Trippe plan. It even shows how a rock-ribbed Republican stalwart from the superstraight state of Maine can thunder and roar and tear up about other people's moral deficiencies at the very moment and in the very act of conspiring with other, higher powers in a rip-off scheme of his own, still more perverse because it uses and humiliates the Congress as a whole. This is very deep corruption. It says something about where the moral gloom that overcame America in the fifties came from.

Hughes Grounded

The Soviet Union secretly exploded its first A-bomb late in August 1949.[3] A month later Truman gave the world the news that the American nuclear monopoly was broken.

Shortly thereafter Colorado Sen. Edwin Johnson accused Atomic Energy Commission Chairman David Lilienthal of conspiring to turn over U.S. atomic secrets to Britain. Lilienthal answered with an impassioned warning against the domination of the military in foreign affairs and resigned in the midst of a tense situation.

On February 1, 1950, against the advice of the AEC, Truman ordered the go-ahead on development of the H-bomb.

On February 9, in Wheeling, West Virginia, Sen. Joe McCarthy told an assembly, "I have in my hand 57 cases of individuals who would appear to be either card-carrying members or certainly loyal to the Communist Party, but who are nevertheless helping to shape our foreign policy."

Yankees countered. In February and March the chairman of the Armed Services Committee, Sen. Millard Tydings of Maryland, spoke out in a series of Senate speeches against the "defeatism" of the Truman line on Russia and communism, arguing that the presumption of inevitable conflict would lead to conflict inevitably. Tydings urged Truman to start moves toward a world disarmament conference. Connecticut's Sen. Brian McMahon, chairman of the Joint Committee on Atomic Energy, called also for conferences with the Soviet Union and argued that the best way to save the peace would be a program of massive aid to the poor countries. And Harrison Salisbury reported from

Moscow that the Russians wanted to meet with the Americans to discuss A-bombs and disarmament—Yankees for an early detente.

Then on April 28, in a big speech to the always right-wing American Newspaper Publishers Association, Herbert Hoover proposed expulsion of the Communists from the United Nations and the formation of "a new united front of those who disavow communism." The speech was met with a "thunderous, almost impassioned ovation."

Yankee publicist and secret Round Table member Walter Lippmann leapt into the breech. Was there not a fatal contradiction in the stance of these "old guard Republican forces?" he asked. How could they "reconcile their warlike and crusading fervor against communism and Soviet Russia with their growing opposition to the European Recovery Plan, military aid, Point 4, and all the other measures of that sort?"

At the same time, the view which Yankees denounced as isolationism was actually a rival internationalism—a rival strategy of expansion. Precisely in the manner of the Yankee Atlanticist looking to Europe, the Cowboy Frontierist looking to Asia was moved to view the problems of American life as originating in external pressures. As the Yankee was instinct with the need to reconstruct and consolidate in Europe, the Cowboy was instinct with the like need to maintain the Open Door in Asia.

And precisely as Hughes saw his wide open spaces being rationalized and regulated out from under him by the combined powers of the Established East, constantly encroaching, so he saw the traditional means of escape being sealed off by the rise of revolutionary communism in Asia. This is perhaps how he and so many other hard rightists could come to think of the New York bankers and the Reds as being in on the great rip-off together.

Hughes joined in the fight against bankers' communism so fiercely because it touched him so intimately, right in his airplane company. In the struggle that followed, like Joe McCarthy about the same time, Hughes found himself misallied against the Pentagon, the institution with which his political relations might have been more agreeable.

The issue was the old and recurrent one of corporate control and accountability. Hughes Aircraft Company had built up its position dramatically in the previous few years under the management of former Air Transport Command Chief General Harold George and the technical leadership of Simon Ramo from Cal Tech and Dean Wooldridge from Bell Labs. At the end of 1953, when the trouble long brewing between Hughes and his management team broke out, HAC sales stood at $200 million a year, almost every dollar of it a top military secret.

The trouble between Hughes and his Hughes Aircraft Company team began in the late 1940s when Ramo, Wooldridge, and George demanded a face-to-face meeting with Hughes to argue for a new lab, needed, they said, because of the expansion of the company's defense contracts. Hughes agreed to a new lab, but proposed to build it in Las Vegas. The HAC people were horrified. They wanted the research center and the production center together. They fought their boss's proposal. Hughes was angry and stubborn but at last gave way and let the lab be built in Culver City.

How can we characterize this rebellion? The *techno-structure*, as John Kenneth Galbraith and, after him, such other liberals as Andrew St. George would come to call it, wanted only to discharge its ultimate duties to its capitalist owner and master and therefore to its owner's customers. It wanted to make big money and to help secure the country against military threats. So from its own standpoint, it had not rebelled against its owner at all, it had only asserted the powers of rational action inherent in its contract, had only insisted upon its right to do what it was being paid to do.

But the more fundamental significance of this rebellion is that it showed that management and ownership, formerly indivisible politically, had diverged. Now they were not altogether as tight as before. It appeared now that management could actually sustain its bureaucratic interests over the objection of the owner, and especially could do this if the company was in effect a single-source supplier to the Pentagon of major weapon system components. And if to own a (defense) company was no longer to control it, then which end was up in the world of private capital and the American state?

In approximately June 1952, HAC management concluded that HAC's growth under their leadership had inspired jealousy in the parent organization, the Hughes Tool Company board of directors, to whom they were accountable, and that Noah Dietrich, the so-called financial wizard of the Hughes empire from the beginning and the main power on the Toolco board, was actually hatching a plot to snatch control of HAC away from themselves.

The occasion of the clash was an HAC revolving credit fund that General George wanted to establish at $35 million. Dietrich unilaterally and arbitrarily cut this back to $25 million. The HAC management team insisted that this posed a threat to national security. They threatened to complain to the Air Force. Hughes met with them a second time, but was unwilling to listen to their most important general complaint, that the company's once commanding position in the industry was being destroyed by Dietrich, who at best (they said) was misapplying the finance principles of boomtown oil to an altogether different business situation, and who at worst was maliciously engineering the troubles at HAC in order to fight off an imagined play for his own power.

Hughes reminded the rebels that Dietrich was a championship-class professional and that his sense of HAC's true needs could not be discounted. There was a perspective larger, after all, than that of a mere division like HAC, namely, that of the Hughes empire as a whole. And larger even than that was the perspective of Hughes the person, the rugged individual. What was good for HAC (or later, TWA) might not be good for Toolco, just as what was good for Toolco might not be good for Hughes the person. And Hughes the person, said Hughes, still happened to be in command.

Well, answered the technostructure, was *national security* not a perspective still larger than that of Hughes the person?

Which is when Hughes started thundering: *"Communism! Communism!*

Fortune somehow saved the following dialogue:

> HUGHES: You are proposing to take from me the right to manage my own property. I'll burn down the plant first.
>
> GEORGE: You are accomplishing the same effect without matches. I do not intend to preside over the liquidation of a great company.[4]

George thereupon quit, soon followed by Ramo and Wooldridge and virtually the whole of the top technical staff behind them. Secretary of the Air Force Harold Talbott flew to Culver City to meet with Hughes and find out what was happening. He found Hughes furious. They were all troublemakers, he said. The company would be better off without them.

> TALBOTT: You have made a hell of a mess of a great property, and by God, as long as I am Secretary of the Air Force, you are not going to get another dollar of new business.
>
> HUGHES: If you mean to tell me that the government is prepared to destroy a business merely on the unfounded charges of a few disgruntled employees, then you are introducing socialism, if not communism.
>
> TALBOTT: I intend to see that the Air Force contracts are protected.[5]

* * *

The overriding issue of modern capitalism, the issue of individual control versus social accountability, could hardly have been more frontally joined than between these two forces, free enterprise and the anti-Communist military, more usually imagined as locked in embrace eternal.

Hughes being Hughes, with his capacity for putting all his excesses in one basket, was fighting out that very same issue at that very same moment in a separate province of his empire. He had picked up the movie studio RKO in 1948, and it had promptly begun crumbling in his fingers. The explanation universally given for this business disaster was the same as the explanation given in the HAC case tumbling along at the side, the Spruce Goose case a little behind, and the TWA case developing underneath. The explanation was always that Hughes was a foolish, neurotic, procrastinating crank whose compulsive retention of control over the least rivet made him catastrophically unsuited for the management of large-scale corporate systems.

"It is impossible to estimate the damage done to RKO by Howard Hughes," said *Fortune* from the commanding financial heights of Yankeedom. "Where is the accountant who can set a figure on the hundreds of intangible losses that came from Hughes's inability to produce enough movies? With adequate production, RKO would have been able to develop stars of its own, rather than buying them from other studios at fancy prices . . . . The Hughes regime at RKO was about as dismal as it could be. . . ."[6] The assault on his ownership continued with $30 million in stockholder lawsuits that suddenly materialized out of nowhere.

In a double jam, crossed two ways for being a good capitalist in America, land of the free, etc., Hughes was at last forced to roll up RKO into a ball and sell out to Akron interests. His profit was more than $7½ million over his purchase price, but now he was shut out of the movie business and he had not wanted that.

* * *

It is not known for a fact that Hughes supported Nixon financially in the early part of Nixon's public career, from 1946 to 1952. Dietrich maintains that onward from the late forties, Hughes financed a great many politicians—"governors, congressmen, senators, judges, yes, and vice presidents too."[7] Still, this was written well after the fact and Dietrich may only have been recalling the famous "Hughes loan" of 1957.

This well-known but not so well understood episode is the first definitely recorded significant transaction between Hughes and Nixon. What Nixon got from Hughes was $205,000 for the benefit of brother Donald, whose Southern California fast-food chain was failing (it finally went broke anyway). What Hughes got from Nixon was approval of a previously denied St. Louis-Miami route for TWA, government reversal of a ten-year-old decision against letting Hughes lend TWA $5 million from HAC coffers, recomputation of mail transport credits to TWA generating a multimillion-dollar refund out of what had been a TWA debt, SEC approval of a TWA stock transfer that it had turned down four times previously, reversal of an unfavorable IRS judgment against Hughes's Medical Institute in Miami, and the dropping of a Justice Department antitrust action against Toolco.

The Hughes loan was expensive for Nixon. In fact, the Nixon-Hughes relationship throughout is charged with negativity and mutual destructiveness. In the current instance, word reached Nixon in the waning days of the 1960 presidential campaign that Kennedy scouts had discovered the Hughes loan and that Kennedy was waiting until just before the election to expose it, leaving Nixon no time to recover. Nixon decided therefore to break the story himself, hopefully thus to deflate it.

That proved a foolishly speculative decision. Nixon told the story and it erupted in his face. Possibly that was what kept Nixon out of the White House in 1960. Almost certainly it kept him out of Sacramento in 1962 when it boiled up again.[8] Then came the crescendo of 1972, Watergate, the reappearance of Hughes as a weight on Nixon. Hughes is Nixon's nemesis. It will appear in the following that Hughes may also be Nixon's victim.

The Flight of TWA

To understand Nixon at the time of Watergate, we must understand Hughes in 1970 and thus his situation in Las Vegas. To understand that, we must first know what made him go there. And that brings us to the battle for TWA, the exemplary illustration from the world of contemporary big business of the Yankee/Cowboy conflict in play, paradigmatic of the working contradictions of American capitalism, and along with the wreck of the Penn Central, the towering commercial conflict of the sixties.

Hughes acquired Transcontinental and Western Airlines and four smaller lines in 1939 and merged them into Trans World Airlines, pumping up the new corporation with an investment of $90 million of his own funds. He controlled 70 percent of its stock. It was his airline in a sense that no airline has ever belonged to any single person.

And this was indeed the crux of the struggle about to take place. Hughes wanted a banker who would lend him what he needed, then let him run his own business, but the bankers wanted to change the private Hughes empire into publicly traded properties.

David Tinnin makes this the central point of his detailed account of the Hughes-TWA affair, *Just About Everybody Vs. Howard Hughes* (Doubleday, 1973), upon which my summary is based. Hughes, he writes, "was fighting for a very personal cause—to retain sole possession of the country's last individually owned industrial empire. The Fricks, the Rockefellers and Fords had long since relinquished absolute ownership of their enterprises. This man alone held out." One doubts Tinnin's use of *relinquish* in this case, first because he is blurring the important distinction between "possession" or "ownership" and *control*, but more importantly, because the evolution of Rockefeller-Morgan magnitude power, displayed so awesomely in this fight, is in no respect a history of relinquishing; it is rather a history of how great financial power begets still greater financial power, and how financial power risen to new degrees necessarily begets new institutional requirements, and how these requirements ultimately come to transcend and dominate the personalities of specific princes. David Rockefeller does not share Hughes's autonomy as of 1960, but that is not because he has relinquished anything; it is because his empire weighs in the vicinity of $30 billion and is inextricably bound into a vast design of interlocking corporate powers reaching far beyond the Chase Manhattan Bank itself. As a consequence, it cannot be supported by the structures of individual personality. There was nothing smallish about Hughes's estimated worth of $3 billion, but that didn't even put him in Rockefeller's class. Hughes's control structures are therefore faster, but also lighter in weight.

This difference tends to be concealed in the Hughes-Rockefeller TWA fight as a difference of personal style. People on the Yankee side think themselves more cultivated. Those on the Cowboy side think themselves more virile. Tinnin might even be saying Rockefeller is more modest than Hughes, since he no longer struggles for so much personal control, and less eccentric, since his accomplished control seems so rationally bureaucratized. But the stylistic differences between them actually originate in the larger patterns of their unequal and differently structured empires. Tinnin's own rich narrative makes it plain that Hughes lost because he was the weaker of the two powers, not because he was eccentric or old-fashioned or on the wrong side of the law, and a thousand times not because he was more grasping than his adversaries or less willing than they to relinquish what he thought was his.

The Brewster prelude past, the great Hughes-vs-Rockefeller fight for TWA began to move toward its main battles slowly in the fifties with the coming of the age of jet transport aircraft. New engine technology developed under pressures of the Korean war made the Boeing KC-135 possible, and in 1955 the Air Force gave Boeing permission to produce it commercially as the 707. The airlines wanted and needed the new jets but were in no financial shape to buy them out of cash reserves, which were badly depleted in the Eisenhower recession.

Enter the big Eastern finance consortium formed up around Dillon, Read and Company and in one way or another involving the Metropolitan, the Equitable and the Prudential insurance companies plus Irving Trust, Chemical Bank, New York Trust Company, Manufacturers Hanover Trust Company, the Bank of America, and the Chase Manhattan. They had the money the transition to jets would need, saw the airlines' needs as opportunities, and were just willing to do whatever they could to establish control over this new high-growth sector of the national transportation system.

TWA was in worse shape to receive the jets than the other big airlines. This was partly because Hughes miscalculated the tempo at which the transition to jets would take place. He thought there was time for one more generation of propeller aircraft and so he bought for TWA a fleet of Lockheed Jetstream Super Constellations, possibly the most graceful planes of their kind, the China Clipper of flight. Too late. Other troubles arose from his persisting too long in the hope that a jetliner partly of his own conception and design, the design forerunner of the Convair 880, could be produced on a competitive schedule. It was finally not produced at all owing to a decision made by Convair's major creditors, Prudential and Chase Manhattan. Yankees everywhere.

So Hughes had been waiting for a jet that now was not coming. He had depleted his cash and credit in the top-dollar purchase of piston-engine airplanes that had become obsolete before they could be delivered. Antitrust regulations prevented his financing a TWA jet fleet from the immense profits of Hughes Tool or Hughes Aircraft, so he had to find external sources. And the Eastern banks were on the march to take the airline away, much more earnestly now than in 1947, their strategy the classic one: (1) make him a debtor, (2) foreclose.

First Hughes had to be convinced to take the Easterners' money. Once that happened, TWA's management could gradually be made accountable to the bankers' combine rather than to Toolco's board of directors. The plan drawn up by Dillon, Read & Company was many times revised, discarded, picked up and revised again, but its main elements stayed the same. The insurance companies would put up $90 million, the banks $70 million, and Toolco $100 million (through purchase of TWA subordinated debentures). With this loan of $260 million, TWA could pay off a sizable accumulation of debts and acquire its jet airplanes.

The terrible catch of it all from Hughes's standpoint was that in order to get this loan he would have to turn over the management of TWA to a three-person voting trust in which he would have one vote and the lenders two.

Hughes badly wanted this not to happen. Through his chief counsel in the TWA matter, Chester Davis, he argued that he was being raided by a financial conspiracy whose underlying purpose was to take away his airline. Said Davis, "There is a conspiracy, certainly concerted action, among these defendants [i.e., the banks in Hughes's countersuit]. These are not bare naked allegations."[9]

The larger world got a small taste of Davis's style in 1973 when he was called before an executive session of the Ervin committee to tell what he knew about the mysterious $100,000 Hughes gave Nixon in 1969 and '70, the money Rebozo said he kept for three years without touching and then gave back. Davis came to the hearing with a suitcase packed with that much cash and with the words, "You want the money, here's the goddamn money," dumped its contents on the table.[10] Tinnen calls him "forceful, blunt . . . irrepressibly obdurate." At the time Toolco retained him for this job, he was chief of the trial department of a powerful Wall Street firm. He soon set up his own office to deal exclusively with the Hughes case. (His partner in the new all-Hughes firm—one of the more engaging coincidences of Watergate—was Maxwell Cox, brother of the special Watergate prosecutor, Archibald Cox, who was fired by Nixon in the famous Saturday Night Massacre, according to some reports, for coming too close to the Hughes connection. Or was it because the Hughes connection was coming too close to him?)

Davis's rival attorney was John Sonnett, another all-star of another super-heavy Wall Street firm. Sonnett was more conventional than Davis in manner but equally suited to his task. On June 30, 1961, he launched the struggle by filing a complaint in the U.S. District Court for the Southern District of New York (in Wall Street's Foley Square), an antitrust action against Hughes on behalf of TWA.

An antitrust action by a company against its owner? Sonnett's argument was that TWA's chronic money problems and the constant and expensive turmoil of its upper management were all attributable (as usual) to the eccentricity of Hughes. If Hughes would leave TWA alone to behave in accordance with good business principles, TWA would make money, but he would not leave it alone, so it lost money. By rejecting the earlier versions of the Dillon, Read plan, Hughes had in effect kept TWA from getting jets at the same time as the other big lines, costing TWA money in lost profits.

How much? Scores of lawyers toiled for thousands of hours over TWA's complex financial records and arrived at a precise figure. Hughes's refusal to accept financing when financing was needed and available from the Yankee banks had cost his airline exactly $45,870,435.95. The rule of settlement in such cases is to multiply the damages by three, add fees, then start charging interest on the amount owed every day it remains unpaid. The bill to Hughes in this suit worked itself up to about $160 million.

To show the court the depth of Hughes's managerial irresponsibility to his own airline and his unfitness for motherhood of a public utility, Sonnett fastened onto the episode in 1957 when Hughes flew off to the Bahamas with one of the first of the new Jetstreams to be delivered to TWA, No. 313. TWA was short of airplanes and losing blood rapidly. If it could get its big new liners into service on the lucrative long-distance routes quickly enough, it might recover. Hughes knew this. Had he not gifted the Nixon brother to the tune of $205,000 that very summer to win Civil Aviation Board approval of the plush St. Louis-Miami route for TWA? Then what possessed him to take this badly needed equipment on a vacation?

He flew No. 313 every day for a month, landing and taking off over and over in the bright Atlantic sunshine, as though he were its only possible test pilot. It made no apparent difference to him that his executives at TWA were screaming. They were his executives, they worked for him, not he for them, just as No. 313 was *his airplane* to do with as he pleased, as indeed, what of TWA's was not his *personal* property? If what he pleased to do cost TWA money, that meant only that it cost *him* money, and his money was his business, was it not, and was it not the whole meaning of American capitalism that nothing was allowed to interfere with that privileged intimacy between a businessman, his property, and his money? He flew No. 313 back alone one night across the country to Los Angeles. He told the mechanics to change the engines and said no more about it.

Well, what was the use of being a rich man if you couldn't take off in your airplane for the Bahamas when you wanted to? One might ask why he didn't fly his own plane instead of TWA's, like other rich men. But this distinction between "his" and "TWA's" was precisely the distinction he was fighting not to accept. The idea that TWA might have an identity, never mind a will, that was in any way separate and alienable from his own proper person was, for Hughes, simply wrong, was a bad idea, a mistake in thinking.

Remember too that Hughes's tenacity in the cause of big airplanes was rooted less in proved successes than in a faith that solutions to the many technical problems must exist. The solutions would come with new metallurgy, new electronics, new magnitudes of concentration of technology and capital, mountain ranges of technical and administrative bureaucracy beyond anything Hughes's generation had yet seen. These were still to come. In his time, the task was still to determine whether the vision of "the airways" was illusion or reality. In retrospect, the airways may seem to have been realized quickly and logically. Hughes's life bears out the old truth that for those involved in the actual making, the individual concrete steps are often uncertain and accidental and dangerous. Hughes had personally experienced nothing but trouble in getting big airplanes to fly. In 1946 he had nearly been killed test piloting the XF-11 when a bug in the electronic control system suddenly, in midflight, reversed the thrust of the propeller on the righthand engine.

Then a scant year and a half later had come the failure of the Goose-Hercules. True, it had flown, had proved itself an actual airplane, had saved Hughes's reputation and extended his legend and given him a dramatic final triumph over Senator Brewster. But for all its eight engines, it did not begin to have the power Hughes knew he needed for safe flight, and it took him just a few taxi runs up and down Long Beach and one mile-long flight at seventy feet to understand and accept that.

Ten years later, down in the Bahamas in 1957, Hughes at last found himself at the controls of an airplane that solved the former problems (in piston-engine terms) and with considerable engineering and design elegance. But the Jetstream was obsolete even as he proved it out. The problems it solved so well were being put behind. The jets were coming on and everything was being changed by this faster than Hughes thought it would be.

As Sonnett told the story of No. 313 before the New York court five years later, it was only more proof of Hughes's madness, a madness, Sonnett argued, that disgraced TWA, spoiled its profitabilities, and made its sharpest executives want to resign. TWA could not be allowed to remain the plaything of a crank. The airlines were public utilities. TWA had a schedule to keep, like the rest of them. Its managers were morally bound to pursue maximum profit lines to the enrichment of the owners. Hughes's eccentricity, in other words, had made it impossible for others to fulfill their bounden contract duties toward him. And in this, said Sonnett, was Hughes himself not culpable on his own terms, a criminal under his own law?

Chester Davis answered that TWA had indeed been hurt, but not by Hughes. It was the Eastern banking cabal, he charged, that had nearly wrecked the company, and it had done this through conspiratorial efforts to force its financing plan upon Hughes, when Hughes had known perfectly well that this plan was only the opening wedge of a takeover campaign, a raid. Hughes did not need New York bankers to tell him that he needed money in the amount of $100 million a year for two or three years. That was plain on the situation's face. If the Dillon, Read group actually cared that much about the health of TWA as an airline rather than as a future Rockefeller property, they would prove their concern better by staying out of Hughes's efforts to secure more favorable financing terms elsewhere.

One of Hughes's alternative plans, for example, involving nine banks plus Convair and Lockheed, fell through at the last minute because Convair's main creditors vetoed its participation. The creditors were Prudential and Chase Manhattan, leading members of the Dillon, Read consort. At about the same time, top officers of Equitable and Metropolitan, major TWA creditors, advised TWA President Charles Thomas to resign, which he did in a rancorous public episode that cost Hughes dearly in prestige.

Then the lenders drew on their power as TWA creditors in

a handful of smaller loans to force TWA not to accept any aircraft from Hughes. This crippled other financial schemes Hughes was working on which entailed the purchase of the new jets by Toolco. Toolco, which easily could afford them, would have leased them to TWA on easy terms. The lenders also unilaterally advanced the due dates for two of these loans.

Only after these moves had put him up against the wall did Hughes capitulate to the Yankee plan. He asked only that he be allowed to repay the loan at any time without penalty. But not even that was acceptable to the Yankee bankers. "We have made up our minds," said Ben Sessel of the Irving Trust. "The banks do not want to do business with Howard Hughes."[11] Either Hughes would accept the Dillon, Read plan with its penalty clause, its high interest rate, and its voting trust, or the lenders would foreclose, throw him into bankruptcy and TWA into receivership, seize Toolco and open its files, and sell off enough of its assets to meet Hughes's obligations to themselves, his creditors.

Hughes's cash and credit position was badly deteriorated by this time. He was forced to send a squad of his security men to the Convair plant in San Diego to seize some dozen 880s being readied for delivery to TWA and hold them at an isolated corner of the airfield. He could not allow them to be delivered because he could not pay for them. The angry Sessel said, "It is time for Howard Hughes to realize that he is in the hands of the banks and will do what we say."[12]

But how had this happened? It had happened, said Davis, because the banking conspiracy wanted to get TWA. The banks cared little how badly their manipulations might damage the airline before they got it. "During the years from 1947 through 1960," said Davis, "TWA realized earnings before taxes of $95,600,000. Upon information and belief, TWA in 1961 [when the banks were in control] lost in excess of $30 million."[13]

So Davis attacked with a countersuit by Toolco against the banks. The major claim was that the Easterners had conspired, first, to keep TWA from getting capital from anybody else but them, and second, to impose the voting-trust stipulation that completed Hughes's loss of control. That is what disrupted TWA's jet procurement program, forced Hughes to accept financing at loan-shark rates, and created TWA's bad situation. Hughes's putative eccentricities had nothing to do with it. Because of this conspiracy, said Hughes, TWA had suffered damages in the amount of $45 million and Toolco in the amount of $77 million. Times three equals $366 million. That was Hughes's answer to the bankers' $160 million suit against him.

Sonnett's original antitrust action against Hughes was based simply on the idea that Hughes owned Hughes Aircraft Company, presumably a manufacturer of aircraft, and so was disallowed under the antitrust laws from owning an airline too. To this, Davis answered, first, that as Sonnett ought to know, the Federal Aviation Act exempted the airlines from antitrust regulation; second, that issues such as those raised by Sonnett's action ought to be raised before the Civil Aviation Board, not in the courts; and finally, that the CAB had in fact spoken on precisely these questions when it first approved Hughes's original acquisitions. Davis asked the court to throw the case out.

We jump ahead ten years to January 1973 when the Supreme Court at last spoke on *TWA* v. *Hughes* to note that this is exactly and completely the position finally upheld. Justice Douglas, writing for the majority, adopted the line of reasoning Davis had taken from his first day on the job, namely, that the case ought never to have gone to court. Jurisdiction belonged with the CAB; the antitrust law did not apply. So much for a few hundred thousand hours of the highest-price lawyering downtown Manhattan has for sale, with combined fees running close to $10 million.

But that was 1973. Until then, Hughes lost every battle. In 1960 he was forced to accept financing he did not want under provisions that left him powerless over his own company. In 1965, on the strength of Sonnett's ultimately flawed antitrust argument, he was forced to divest himself of his 78 percent holding and get out of TWA and the airlines altogether. And in 1970, he was told by the court that he owed $160 million in damages to the very people who had robbed him of his airline.

How could there have been so wide a difference between the final judgment of the Supreme Court and the earlier judgment of the district and appellate courts? The lower court judges involved and the special masters they appointed to hear the depositions were angered by Hughes's refusal to appear in person and be deposed like everyone else. The 1970 judgment against him was partly motivated by their irritation over this. Yet to award, on grounds of mere default, the largest amount of money in damages ever awarded by any court seemed a large, wild thing to do. This is why Special Master Herbert Brownell, who heard the depositions for Federal District Judge Charles Metzner, took almost a year to study the arguments and make his report. Then Judge Metzner took nineteen months more to study Master Brownell's report and affirm its recommendations.

Moreover, at every step of the way, Davis appeared to have the better of the debate with Sonnett, so clearly as to color the speculation that Hughes lost in some part because the game was being played in the other side's arena with hometown referees. Once, in 1964, Davis almost won the Supreme Court review that might have given him his win ten years before it finally came. The Supreme Court had just made a ruling in a strikingly similar case, the *U.S.* v. *Pan American World Airways, W.R. Grace & Co., and Pan American-Grace Airways* (shortened to *Panegra).* The ruling in that case seemed exactly to support Davis's central argument, i.e., that jurisdiction lay with the CAB, not the courts. But the very next moment, with no explanation, the Supreme Court accepted Sonnett's contention that the decision to review the *TWA* v. *Hughes* case had been "improvidently granted." Apparently the justices thought either that there was no need for a review or that a review was not yet possible, but the practical effect was the irrevocable dismissal of Hughes's countersuit. The default judgment against him was allowed to stand and the presumption of his guilt was supported.

So the wheel would remain in spin for another eight years, first causing Hughes to divest his TWA stock, then requiring the painful hearings to determine the precise amount he would have to pay the new owners of his old airline for the damage he had done in trying to keep it from them.

The divestment occurred on May 3, 1965. Ordinarily the sudden sale of so much stock would depress the price, but the community had followed *TWA* v. *Hughes* closely and understood why Hughes was selling, so the price was firm at $86 a share. Merrill Lynch handled the transaction with the help of 410 other domestic and foreign underwriters. Public sale of the six-and-a-half million shares took half an hour. The underwriters deducted their fee of $4 per share, then wrote Hughes a check for the remainder: $546,549,771. Taxes reduced this to about $486 million free and clear. Only the Ford stock sale of 1956 was bigger.

So Hughes was out one airline and his overall empire had been brutally shaken by those five years, and more was coming, and worse. But at that moment, as of the sale of TWA, he had ready cash again and could start looking for another game.

Hughes in Vegas

Hughes responded to divestiture aggressively by using his $486 million cash in hand (he was lugging it around the country in suitcases) to go after the Lansky Syndicate's monopoly of big-time gambling.[14] He hovered for a moment in Boston undecided whether to attack in Montreal, the Bahamas, or Las Vegas, but shortly determined upon Las Vegas. By Thanksgiving 1966 Hughes was sliding quietly into his new headquarters at the Desert Inn penthouse which his advance man—reenter Robert Maheu—had prepared for him. He would remain there, for four years to the day, then disappear under circumstances much more mysterious than those of his coming.

There can be no serious doubt of Hughes's intentions of establishing a Nevada empire and of competing head-to-head with Lansky. Editor Greenspun of the *Sun* pushed for such an establishment from Hughes's first day in town on the shortsighted argument that Las Vegas's best weapon against the Syndicate was just such a capitalist as Hughes—strong and independent.

And of course, ambitious. We have already cited Dietrich to the effect that in the West Coast phase, Hughes tried to buy up the entire local governing infrastructure from tax assessors to senators. In 1974, the then-deposed Maheu testified to the same ambition in Hughes: "I clearly recall explaining to [Hughes's Nevada lawyer] Tom Bell the desire of Howard Hughes to own the state of Nevada, to own the judges in Nevada, to own all the officials of Nevada. I was concerned about the desire of Mr. Hughes to want to own the President of the United States."[15]

By 1968, Hughes's Nevada operations had grown under Maheu's management to a worth estimated at well above a half billion dollars. Hughes was the state's biggest employer with a staff of over eight thousand and a $50 million payroll and a private security force (under another ex-FBI man, Jack Hooper) easily a rival of the official and criminal agencies with which it might have to contend. He had put some $400 million into hotels and casinos. He owned the Desert Inn, the Sands, the Castaways, the Frontier, the Landmark, and the Silver Slipper. He was angling for the Silver Nugget, the Stardust, and the Dunes. He also owned Alamo Airways and McCarran Field and was on his way to getting Air West. He owned KLAS-TV. He owned the Krupp Ranch and thousands of square miles of other Nevada real estate and some $30 million in mining claims.

Governor Paul Laxalt said flatly, "Howard Hughes's operations are as important to Nevada as U.S. Steel is to the nation or General Motors to Michigan."[16]

Reflecting and furthering that eminence, Hughes in 1968 gave $150,000 to Nixon (two-thirds of it covertly), $100,000 to his presidential opponent Humphrey (half of it covertly), $70,000 to Senator Cannon, $50,000 to Senator Bible, and— strangely—$25,000 to the estate of the recently assassinated Senator Robert Kennedy.[17]

Let us take a moment with this Kennedy contribution, superficially so out of character for Hughes. It has been explained as a Hughes sympathy gift to help with the costs of the funeral. But Hughes? The Kennedys? We might find a more plausible explanation if we set this $25,000 in the context of another gesture Hughes was making at the very same moment in the direction of the again-bereaved Kennedy camp.

On June 28, 1968, two weeks after Robert Kennedy's death in Los Angeles, Maheu concluded a lengthy handwritten memo to Hughes with the following item:

Larry O'Brien—He is coming here on Wednesday next for a conference as per our request after the assassination of Senator Kennedy. He is prepared to talk employment and has received a commitment (without any obligation whatsoever) from the four or five top men in the Kennedy camp that they will not become obligated until they hear from him.[18]

O'Brien Associates of New York and Washington did indeed subsequently sign a consulting contract with Hughes-Maheu, but my efforts to find out from O'Brien's office and home what he was doing for Hughes were unproductive. No one better equipped to get an answer seems interested, even though as I write one of the prevailing theories of the Watergate DNC break-in is, in substance, that the Nixon people were afraid that O'Brien's stint with Hughes-Nevada had taught him, and thus the Democrats, something useful about the Nixon-Hughes relationship, and that they sent the Plumbers into the DNC to try to find out what that could be.[19]

But what was Hughes's original interest in Larry O'Brien and the other superliberals of the RFK staff? What could have been O'Brien's interest in a figure of Hughes's far-right ideology? And was it not a little early after the prince's murder for his ministers to be sifting job offers from a kingdom of the ideological opposition?

Investigator-journalist Jim Hougan, who has made a special study of Intertel[20] (see below), guesses that by the phrase "the four or five top men in the Kennedy camp," Hughes actually meant the attorneys, notably Robert Peloquin and William Hundley, who played roles in Robert Kennedy's early 1960s campaign against organized crime. By 1968 Hughes was moving irreversibly toward his confrontation with the Syndicate over control of Las Vegas gambling. Hougan thinks that in reaching out to the RFK anticrime staff, Hughes may have been simply seeking to strengthen his front.

We do not know whether this was the basis of Hughes's interest in the Kennedy staff people or of theirs in him or how far any such common interests might have been realized in joint projects. We do not know how to evaluate the importance of Hughes's now-exposed special relationship to the CIA (Glomar, the Maheu-Roselli link, etc.) in terms of the antagonism between elements of the CIA and the Kennedy group. But we do know for a fact that the Hughes contact with the RFK staff was made, that it came about at Hughes's initiation through Maheu, that Hughes did contribute the $25,000, that the job offers were made and at least in O'Brien's case accepted, and that all this coincided (a) with Hughes's efforts to reverse several antitrust decisions limiting his further expansion on the Lansky Strip and (b) with his tortuous payment via Richard Danner to Nixon of $100,000 in cash for which Nixon would be accountable to no one—*not even Lansky*.

The following passage from Maheu's June 1968 memo to Hughes shows how conscious Maheu and Hughes were of the anti-Syndicate aspect of their expansion. Maheu wrote:

> Howard Cannon called me this afternoon to inform that he and Senator Bible have been told all day long—by fellow Senators—that they can depend on full support and assistance in sustaining their position that we obtain the Stardust. Cannon stated that Justice was severely ridiculed for having taken action which precluded the accomplishment of what the criminal division has tried to do for fifteen years—when particularly the result was only 52 hours away.

And Hughes answered:

> Now also, re the club being a gathering place for North Las Vegas's less respectable citizens, all the more reason for us to control this very dangerous gathering place for less desirables to the result that it no longer continues to be a gathering place for the less desirable element. For this reason, Bob, I am determined we under no circumstances bring Moe [Dalitz of Cleveland's infamous Mayfield Road Mob] or any of his group in to run it under our control. This is the very very last thing I feel we should do. So please don't discuss the Nugget with Moe or any of his group at this time.

Hughes goes on in the same memo to approve a Maheu offer to approach the chief of the Nevada FBI. "At the same meeting, please try to arrange that Mr. FBI of Nevada will convince Dickerson [of the Nevada Gaming Commission] also of the likewise importance of our buying out the Silver Nugget of NLV because of the criminal element now gathering there and the hope that under our management this would be discontinued."

Whether this was indeed Hughes's purpose or just convenient rhetoric, certainly Maheu's buying spree was having the advertised effect. As crime-writer Richard Hammer wrote a few years later, "though the Organization never completely abandoned the Las Vegas gold fields, its influence and control began to wane with the increasing dominance of Hughes. Before, there had been a widespread feeling that only the mobsters could run casinos profitably; the Hughes operations proved that this was only a Mob-perpetuated myth. And the arrival of Hughes also pushed some Nevada officials out of their easy chairs to take a closer look at the casinos that they had long claimed could not be controlled."[21]

How and why did the Syndicate let this happen? It cannot be simply that Hughes was too strong to be kept out and that Lansky had no choice but to bow before his billions. The fact is that Hughes could never have come to Las Vegas to begin with if Lansky had not decided to permit and support it. Maheu cultivated a close relationship in particular with Moe Dalitz (see Hughes's memo to Maheu, above). Maheu actually purchased from Dalitz the hotel-casino the Desert Inn, where Hughes made his headquarters. "Not only did I depend very much upon the advice of Mr. Dalitz," said Maheu, "but so did Mr. Hughes. Repeatedly he would ask me to get Mr. Dalitz's advice. Mr. Hughes recognized, as I did, that we had no expertise in the gambling business and that there was no one in the Hughes world at that time who did."[22]

Fortune speculated that the Syndicate's earlier friendliness to Hughes was predicated on Lansky's sense that Hughes's "entry into gambling lent respectability to a sleazy business; stock in gaming companies enjoyed a considerable vogue at the time."[23] There may be something to that. It conforms with Lansky's usual style of legitimizing previously criminal business operations. But it would not tell us why

Lansky let Hughes drive him out of one of his major bases without an apparent fight.

Could Lansky in fact have been playing on a bigger field than Hughes knew? I think there is a case that he was, and that Hughes was ultimately no more the victor in the struggle for Las Vegas than in the struggle for TWA. The reason I say this involves the case of John Meier.[24]

John Meier—do not confuse with Johnny Meyer, Hughes's aid in the Brewster episode (above)—was in his early thirties when he joined Hughes's Nevada operations in 1968. He was diagrammatically at Maheu's level in the organization in that he reported to Hughes through the throneroom guard, though he had none of Maheu's power in the larger works. He had a background in ecology, systems analysis, and the Rand Corporation and had been a member of Nixon's Resources Aid Environmental Task Force. In 1970, he ran unsuccessfully for the Senate from Nevada. With Hughes, his special province was silver mining claims and other real estate. His job was to find claims worth buying and to recommend purchases to Hughes. The altitude this had him flying at is roughly indicated by current estimates valuing Hughes's Nevada land and mining holdings in the $20 million range.

Two grand juries in Las Vegas later decided that what was actually happening was that Meier was in cahoots with Syndicate fronts in a massive land fraud in which Hughes was the victim. One of Meier's confederate groups was Georgetown Research and Development, which materialized in a Watergate address one day, sold off its worthless holdings to Hughes the next, and dematerialized that night. A more constant companion was the Toledo Mining Company of Salt Lake City, whose president, Anthony Hatsis, is identified by Senate Select Committee investigators as an executive-level officer of the Lansky Syndicate.[25] Hughes's losses to such Syndicate fronts on land and mining deals may have totaled as much as $10 million in the brief period, less than two years, during which Meier occupied his advantageous position.

What happened to all this money? Part of it went into a trust in the name of Meier-Callandria at Overseas, Ltd., a Swiss bank with a Robert Vesco connection. A larger part was routed out of the country through banks in the Bahamas and Montreal holding companies into a Dutch firm called Maatschappil Intermovie.

The money, thus laundered in Europe, was then funneled back to the States, where Meier and Hatsis may have used it to finance business ventures involving Nixon's brother, Donald. The three men visited the Dominican Republic in September 1969. Dominican President Juan Belaguer staged a classy public reception and sold what the *Wall Street Journal* termed "valuable" concessions to Hatsis's Toledo Mining, whose stock rose to $30 per share. In a splashy public ceremony, Donald Nixon conspicuous at the side, Belaguer decorated Meier for "Hughes's charities" in the Dominican Republic, and Meier and Hatsis scratched back by giving blocks of Toledo stock to various Dominican officials "for services rendered in regard to securing a mining concession."

The relationship developing between John Meier and Donald Nixon was observed from the White House with some anxiety. The president's personal tax accountant, Arthur Blech, was told to review all of Donald's proposed projects, including the Dominican ones. Blech is said to have turned them all down. Then White House pressure against Meier's relationship to Donald intensified. Rebozo called Maheu in Las Vegas and told him to keep Meier away from Donald. Nixon's famous brother-bugs were put in. Donald was put under twenty-four-hour White House surveillance. The FBI hassled Meier, Donald, and Hatsis together at a Florida airport in September on one of their trips to the Dominican Republic.

Maheu answered Rebozo that he too wanted to get rid of Meier, but that Meier worked for Hughes, not for him. Maheu said that Hughes liked Meier, and that all Maheu could do was to ask him to keep away.

Maheu also put a tail on Meier and thus found him and

Donald Nixon trysting in October in the Orange County Airport. As a result of the intense reaction this provoked, Hughes at last cut Meier loose. Maheu said he was fired, Meier called it resigning. Meier was taken on at once by Hatsis at Toledo Mining as a $6,000-a-month consultant. In the summer of 1975, he was avoiding indictments in British Columbia.

The Thanksgiving Coup

The conflict developing here between Hughes and Lansky, with the Meier branch of it curving through the foreground, forms the strategic context of the events of November and December 1970, the Thanksgiving coup of Hughes's Nevada Operations and the overthrow of Maheu.[26]

We are concerned in this coup with a power struggle between two parts of the Hughes empire in which various outside parties participated, not always openly. On one side, the main force was the Toolco board of directors and the main actor was Chester Davis. On the other side, the main force was Hughes's $400-million Nevada Operations and the main actor was Maheu.

Davis and Maheu were not new men to the Hughes empire. Davis had come on to fight the TWA case in 1960 and was still astride it. Maheu had come in through the FBI and a private career in the security business. The hotel-dicks-at-heart who make up this insulfurated subculture must see their highest dreams realized in Maheu's life. Before his fall, this entailed a $600,000 mansion to live in rent free and an annual salary of $520,000 to play around with, never mind the fishing and hunting lodges, the private airplanes always ready to go anywhere, the constant company of millionaires and their kind of people. He had come to Hughes in the late fifties as a security and intelligence expert with a background of FBI work in Chicago. As noted, he took charge of such seamier chores of Hughes-tending as matchmaking the CIA with the Roselli-Giancana crowd in the plots against Castro's life and against the life of who knows who else besides. He got it on with Syndicate heavies like Dalitz in order to operate casinos successfully in Las Vegas. After the Castro work, he turned up next in the Boston interlude after the divestment of TWA when Hughes first decided to take on the Syndicate for control of Las Vegas. Maheu put together the whole secret move to Las Vegas, including the impenetrable security precautions, and allowed Hughes to arrive while Lansky slept or pretended to. He quickly became the chief officer in charge of Hughes's boisterous Nevada expansion.

Maheu was fearful as early as March 1968 that the old Hughes guard of Houston and Los Angeles, the Toolco board, would grow jealous of his unique closeness to Hughes. The Toolco board's authorization was still required for most of Maheu's deals in Vegas. Although the board would never refuse a specific order from Hughes, it could be dilatory in the absence of such an order. It could cut Maheu off. Maheu sought reassurance from Hughes in 1968 against any problems the intrinsically touchy situation could lead to. Hughes answered him as follow:

> Bob, I have your message. I do not feel your apprehension in the least unjustified. If I give you my word to find a solution promptly, such as a voting trust for my Hughes Tool Company stock [which of course would have made Maheu the legal master of the whole Hughes empire], and if I put the formalities into a state of effectiveness for your scrutiny without any unreasonable delay, will you consider it done as of now, so your mind will not be filled with these thoughts in the near future? I will assume an affirmative answer and proceed accordingly.[27]

Hughes never got around to doing that, but at the same time he stayed available to Maheu by memo and phone, sometimes (so 'tis said) spending twenty hours a day on the phone with him.

In January 1970 Hughes put Maheu in charge of the TWA case, an act which set in train the events leading to the major climax of his career, the Thanksgiving coup, and possibly thence to Watergate. Hughes's tone as he undertook this move was definite:

> "Bob, please understand one thing which I do not think you have understood heretofore: you have the ball on the TWA situation. You do not need further approval from me to a specific settlement of a specific sum of money....If I am to hold you responsible for the overall outcome of this litigation, I must give you the complete authority to decide which law firm you want to handle each phase of it. I repeat, Bob, you have *full* authority."[28]

Maheu convinced Hughes to say this to the Toolco directors. He did, they accepted the news with whatever inner murmurings but no recorded protest, and indeed issued Maheu "the necessary authorizations to handle all the phases and aspects of the TWA suit, including a settlement."[29]

This gave Maheu strength but left him exposed. There were first of all the troubles normal and natural to the TWA case itself. On April 14, 1970, Judge Metzner handed down a final judgment in favor of TWA against Hughes of $145,448,141.07. By the time the Supreme Court threw the whole thing out of court three years later, chargeable expenses had worked that amount up to about $160 million. That was what Maheu was looking at, and his job was to succeed where Davis had failed in finding a way not to have to pay it. On top of this, he had the additional problem of having to work without the sympathy of the powerful Toolco directors.

No sooner does Hughes turn the TWA problem over to

Maheu than Maheu learns—this is in February 1970—of a large-scale land fraud operating somewhere inside Nevada Operations. Now we can sense the Lansky pressure, but all Maheu had to go on then was a rumor. Taking up the TWA task with one hand, with the other hand he began to track down the silver mining swindle.

Maheu seems to have done everything you and I would have done to avoid getting shredded to pieces by the corporate violence implicit in his situation. Especially on the TWA matter, it is hard to see how he could have covered himself any better than he did, first in getting Hughes actually to tell the Toolco board that he was putting Maheu in charge, then in getting everything confirmed in explicit Toolco authorizations.

Maheu's first step with TWA was to hear everyone out on the question of what to do. First he heard Chester Davis, whom he thought too defensive of his own role in the preceding legal defeats. Davis might well have been very defensive. These defeats amounted to the loss of a very large airline and the threatened loss of a very large amount of cash. The Supreme Court would finally agree in January 1973 that Davis was right and had been from the first day. But early in 1970, facing a damages bill for $160 million and a lost airline, Maheu thought Davis's efforts to defend himself and his strategy too self-serving to be true.

So Maheu went to four blue-chip law firms with the question: Given everything that has happened and the situation as it is, what should Hughes do to save whatever can be saved out of the TWA mess? Maheu went to Washington to Clark Clifford's firm of Clifford, Warnke, Glass, McIlwain & Finney. He went to New York to Welch & Morgan, the Morgan being Edward P., a close friend of Maheu's and the Hughes lawyer whose advice originally decided Hughes on going to Las Vegas. He went to New York's Donovan, Leisure, which represented Toolco throughout the damages hearings. And he went to the Beverly Hills firm of Wyman, Bautzer, Finell, Rothman &

Kuchel, whose Gregory Bautzer was a long-time associate and Hollywood friend of Hughes.

Each one of these firms told Maheu to do the same thing; namely, get Davis off the case. This was not necessarily because they found Davis a bad lawyer. It was because rightly or not the arguments he stood for had been rejected by the bar, and what was necessary for Hughes now above all was to get the case back in court. That required new arguments and new arguments necessarily required a new chief counsel. So Davis had to leave the case. One could think up the new arguments later. Perhaps there were even some good ones. It did seem strange, after all, that the largest damages claim ever yet awarded in the history of civil law should have been awarded in behalf of a company against the man who built, made, and owned that company. And it was also strange that the claim was not awarded on the merits of the case at all but because some inexplicable inner compulsion kept Hughes from appearing personally to testify in his own behalf.

What about Hughes's solitude? Why could he not show his face to save $160 million? Does this not go beyond eccentricity? Sometimes it seems Hughes must have died, as so many insist, long before April 1976. The only people who claim definitely to have seen and had daily transactions with Hughes are the so-called Mormon Mafia, or the Big Five, the mostly Mormon superstraights who were said to tend him as nurses and secretaries. They were all recruited by Bill Gay of the Toolco board, and they are of course loyal to Gay. Parties to the events they served, partisans, these five men alone assured us of Hughes's existence. That he did as they say he did, willed as they say he willed, we have no word but theirs.

But this is getting us too much ahead. We are thinking here of the standing mystery of Hughes's reclusiveness, and we note that, come to think of it, with a tiny number of doubtful exceptions, the only people who actually *saw* Hughes since 1970 were Gay's men.[30] Maheu later took his place in the ranks of ministers who must observe ruefully, as he did, "All you have to do is control the palace guard, because that is who really controls the empire."[31]

But Maheu's rue came a year later. In early 1970, armed with the best legal opinion Hughes's money could buy, he opened his reign as strawboss of the TWA project by informing Toolco and Davis that Davis was off the TWA case. Not that he was no longer Toolco's chief counsel; Maheu never claimed the power to fire Davis from his corporate bastion. Only that the universally recommended legal strategy in the TWA case required the use of new attorneys.

At that moment, Hughes suddenly moved Maheu in two new directions simultaneously.

First, he launched him in an effort to penetrate gambling in the Bahamas. Hughes's consciousness of what this entailed is indicated in a fragment from an early 1970 phone conversation (taped) with Maheu: "If I were to make this move I would expect you to wrap up that government down there to a point where it will be—well, a captive entity in every way."[32]

Hughes's interest in the Bahamas was not new. His choice came down to the Bahamas or Las Vegas in Boston in 1966. But actually activating Maheu to start thinking of ways to take on and beat the Lansky apparatus in the Bahamas— that would look new and different from a Lansky perspective, all the more so because of Hughes's concurrent gyrations with Nixon in Washington.

And, second, Hughes got Maheu going on a secret campaign to find out what Meier was up to in his theretofore secluded little silver-mining corner. In other words, Hughes was now opening two new fronts against the Syndicate on top of his already achieved preeminence on the Las Vegas Strip. He was expanding to the Syndicate's other capital, and he was about to discover someone who may well have been the Syndicate's man in his machine.

As Maheu was thus preoccupied, Davis mobilized his

response to the TWA dismissal notice. Davis informed
Maheu that his notice naturally meant nothing to him or to
Toolco, and would Maheu please stay out of matters lying
far outside the scope of his contract as a consultant on
gambling and hotel security.

Maheu answered:

> To date you have lost this case at every level with
> catastrophically adverse financial and other injury to
> the defendant.... You were previously before the
> Second Circuit on this case and sustained a crushing
> defeat. This must not be repeated. You have repeatedly
> assured me that no antitrust violations were involved
> and that in consequence TWA could prove no damages.
> I must conclude that you were either wrong or wholly
> ineffectual, for the judgment now stands at a staggering
> figure. The time is at hand for other counsel to endeavor
> to achieve a favorable result.... I deeply resent your
> presumptuous request that I "cease interference with
> counsel in charge and responsible for the case." There
> has been no interference on my part other than taking
> steps to accord other counsel an opportunity to salvage
> a case which you have tragically lost.[33]

The Toolco directors behind Davis were meanwhile
taking four concrete steps.

1. They voted the dismissal of Maheu.
2. They mandated Director Bill Gay to have the
Mormon Mafia cut off Maheu's communications. Maheu
was from now on losing this particular game.
3. They ordered the two chiefs of the throneroom guard,
Howard Eckersley and Levar B. Myler, to enter in unto
Hughes with a one-sentence proxy conferring full powers of
attorney on the Davis group. This proxy was signed by
Hughes, according to Eckersley who notarized it and Myler,
who witnessed it. Hughes had now assigned to the Toolco
board the right to run a large section of his empire.

This was November 14. Myler took the signed proxy to the Nevada State Bank in Las Vegas and put it in a strongbox.

4. Toolco promoted a whisper-in-Hughes's-ear campaign against Maheu. "No outsider so far is privy to the exact details," writes Tinnin, "but in essence, the reports informed Hughes that Maheu had developed into a disloyal and avaricious employee, who was taking his trusted employer for all he was worth." The story on Maheu was that he was pocketing part or all of the finder's fees for everything Hughes was buying in Nevada. These charges were never proved. It now is clearer that what was happening was that Toolco was accusing Maheu of the crimes that the Syndicate was committing and that Maheu had begun to stumble onto.

Hughes's Nevada security chief, Jack Hooper, left unguarded the back stairway leading down from Hughes's Desert Inn penthouse to a backdoor opening onto a parking lot. Hooper had taken off the door handle and assumed the doorway was now permanently closed. On November 26, 1970, the palace guards, the Eckersley-Myler group, took Hughes down nine flights of back stairs, out that door, and into one of several waiting station wagons. In a variation on the Boston departure of 1966, a decoy caravan of black sedans with California plates was dispatched to Hughes's McCarran Field, while the actual Hughes party drove to Nellis Air Force Base. There they were met by a Lockheed JetStar, leased from the Lockheed Aircraft Corporation, come to carry Hughes away to the Bahamas.

Hughes was met in the Bahamas on Thanksgiving Day by an Intertel official named James Golden, whose presence in the melodramatic episode is interesting because of his reputation as "Nixon's man."[34] Secret Serviceman Golden was assigned to Vice-President Nixon in 1957. He accompanied Nixon to Russia and Central America. They got stoned together in Venezuela. They grew close. When Nixon left the White House in 1960, Golden left the Secret Service to take a job as security chief for Lockheed. In 1968

Lockheed gave him a leave of absence to join Nixon's campaign as director of security. After Nixon's election he became Resorts International's deputy director of security on Paradise Island. He was a founding officer of Intertel and one of its vice-presidents at the time of the events of November. He later joined the Hughes Las Vegas staff. As of summer 1975, he was at the Justice Department as chief of the Organized Crime Strike Force of the Law Enforcement Assistance Agency.

Golden's presence in the coup raises the question of a Nixon influence, since "Nixon's man" either means nothing or something. Could Nixon have been involved in the plot of Thanksgiving 1970 to overthrow Maheu, abduct and confuse Hughes, and radically change the nature of the crime-connected, FBI-connected, and CIA-connected Hughes empire? Was the motive to protect the Meier-Donald Nixon racket against exposure? Was it to resolve the tensions of a Hughes-Lansky conflict within the Nixon coalition? Golden's possible role constitutes a workpoint for future investigations.

For the next four days, Hooper's guard kept routine vigil at their closed-circuit TV displays which showed every means of access to Hughes except the one actually used by the intruders. Then Greenspun got a tip from a Syndicate friend at the Desert Inn to the effect that Hughes's suite had been strangely quiet lately. Greenspun got this intelligence to Maheu. Maheu tried to put through a call to Hughes. A second-level aide finally answered and told him Hughes was no longer there.

The next day, December 3, the *Sun* headlined, "Howard Hughes Missing." A Toolco director later said that Hughes saw this headline on December 4 on Paradise Island and was infuriated. Throneroom guardsman Levar Myler claims to have heard Hughes say that Greenspun by himself would never have dared print such a headline and that Maheu therefore had to be behind it, and thus that Maheu should be fired at once. Myler said Hughes then told him to release the November 14 proxy.

On that same day, December 4, Toolco battle commander Davis summoned his adversary's friend and lawyer, Ed Morgan, to a meeting in Beverly Hills. Morgan had been active that summer in the transfer of the Danner-Rebozo money (and would be again active in its return three years later). On this trip to face Davis, in fact, Morgan brought Danner along. Danner's reputation is that of an intimate of Nixon's. He was also at this time a manager of one of Hughes's hotels in Las Vegas.

Morgan and Danner found Davis awaiting them in Beverly Hills with Toolco directors Bill Gay, Calvin Collier, and Raymond Holliday. Davis told Morgan that Morgan's client, Maheu, was thereby formally and officially fired by Davis's client, Toolco, which was sole representative of Hughes. Davis flashed the November 14 proxy to prove it. Hughes had lost confidence in Maheu, said Davis. Nevada operations were not doing well. Earnings were less than 5 percent on a turnover of about $5 million. Only the Sands was showing a good profit. (And Danner was also fired, screamed Holliday, "number five on a list of 155." This was a mistake soon corrected. Holliday had perhaps not appreciated the importance of Danner's relationship with Nixon. Danner is last seen, post-Watergate, running the Sands.) Both groups flew back to Las Vegas that same day.

December 4, 1970, transfigured Vegas night. In swooped the Davis command—secretaries, files and telephones going full speed from first landing. Davis commandeered the penthouse at the Sands. The Sands was at that time managed by Maheu, but like the rest of Hughes's Nevada holdings, it was actually owned in the name of Toolco. The Sands and the rest fell within the legal authority of the Toolco board and Davis.

Davis liberated and occupied his chosen headquarters swiftly. He installed a tough-looking security guard and announced that he alone spoke for Hughes, that Maheu was now out, and that a whole new order reigned.

Simultaneously, Davis commanded his "small army of special agents from Intertel,"35 flashing their mysterious credentials, to move with no more than necessary force into the sacrosanct cashiers' cages in all the Hughes casinos. The Intertel men stuffed the cash into paper bags and boxes with no explanation other than their story about "a new management" and no credentials other than their advantage in surprise and force. They could as easily have been robbers as cops. They completely succeeded in putting the law's first nine parts to work for Toolco. Subsequent discussion about who actually should boss the casinos was much influenced by the fact that Davis did.

We noted above that Maheu had feared something like this all along and had repeatedly sought Hughes's reassurances that he was doing just what Hughes wanted him to do. Now he had no access to Hughes and therefore no reassurances and therefore nothing. The lawyers Morgan and Bell were loyal to Maheu, as were Greenspun with his paper and Hooper with his shamefaced security force. These people gave Maheu some capability for tactical defense but not enough. Without Hughes's voice to animate it, Maheu's world turned back into a pumpkin.

But Maheu did make a good argument of it. He gave four solid reasons in support of his outrageous theory that Hughes had actually been abducted by his enemies.

1. Hughes's health was too poor for so sudden and hurried a trip. *Newsweek* reported on these events in its issue of December 21, 1970. This story scornfully informed its readers that "Maheu's group spread another story that Hughes had been visited by a heart specialist (or in one version, three heart specialists) in November, that he was too ill to be moved anywhere but to a hospital, and that he had been kidnapped." But actually, one of the few hard facts in this case accepted by all sides is that in the early part of that month, Hughes's health had so sharply declined that Hooper's security agents and Gay's throneroom guards were

compelled to open the airlock and let a doctor-human from the normal world, Dr. Harold Feikes, come into the innermost bubble to examine Hughes in the flesh, forbidding task. Davis quickly got a court order shutting Feikes up on what he had observed behind the screen at Oz, but in the split second before the order fell, Feikes said enough to confirm the general lines of Maheu's claim.

According to Feikes, Hughes stood six feet four inches and normally weighed about 150 pounds. Now, said Feikes, he weighed 97 pounds and was suffering from an active heart condition, pneumonia, and anemia stemming from chronic malnutrition. (Malnutrition in one of the world's richest men? His routine lifelong diet was cookies and milk.)

Feikes gave him immediate blood transfusions and said later that he was still on transfusions at the time of his sudden departure for the Bahamas, a departure carried out so hastily, however long it may have been considered, that he actually left behind his till-then precious or even indispensable life-support equipment. Maheu may well have found this sufficiently improbable to raise doubts about Davis's claims.

2.   Maheu thought it was strange that Hughes should choose Davis and Gay as his personal trustees in a matter as sensitive as this. Maheu said he once suggested to Hughes that Davis be brought to Las Vegas for a certain legal task, and that Hughes answered, "God damn it, Bob, you must be losing your mind. If we allow this man to come to Las Vegas, in 24 hours the whole city will be devastated, and in 48 hours the entire state of Nevada will be in chaos."[36] This is of course self-serving on Maheu's part, but it was apparently true that Davis had been in bad standing with Hughes. Hughes had tried to take Davis off the TWA case and may easily have sensed and resented his resistance. The Toolco directors of course knew all about this, having gone through the ritual transfer of authority from Davis to Maheu earlier in the year.

Gay was also on the outs with Hughes. In 1965, Hughes

backed a new major corporate undertaking on Gay's recommendation. This was a computer company, Hughes Dynamics, aimed at capturing a piece of IBM's action. Hughes Dynamics collapsed within a year with a loss of about $9 million. When Hughes was preparing his clandestine entry into Las Vegas, he turned to Maheu for security, Gay's former preserve. According to Maheu, Hughes also gave instructions that Maheu was "not to invite Bill . . . and not to permit him to be privy to our affairs . . . . I no longer trust him. My bill of complaints against Bill's conduct goes very deep."[37]

Said Maheu,

> I explained this to Bill Gay in great detail. But he resented it to the extent that he began to move into areas of my domain . . . . Shortly after we had arrived here [in Las Vegas], I asked [Hughes] if, on land problems, I was to take instructions from Bill Gay. Whereupon he literally went into a tirade and explained . . . that Bill Gay was less important in his world than his aides [i.e., than the throneroom guard]. He said that Bill Gay's only assignment in life was to keep his relationship with Mrs. Hughes intact . . . and to keep Mrs. Hughes's name out of the newspapers. He said Bill was just a baby-sitter for Jean.[38]

Maheu then cited a passage from a later Hughes memo on Gay: "Bill's total indifference and laxity to my plea for help in my domestic area, voiced urgently to him week by week, throughout the past seven or eight years, have resulted in a complete, I am afraid irrevocable loss of my wife. I blame Bill completely for this unnecessary debacle. I feel he let me down—utterly, totally, completely."[39] (Hughes and Jean Peters were formally divorced in 1970.)

3. Maheu argued that it was certainly peculiar for a man like Hughes, engaged as he was at that exact moment in a battle for control of the Las Vegas-Bahamas gambling axis,

suddenly to abandon old friends and helpers in the game, people like Maheu himself and Hooper, and to leap headlong down the spiderhole of an organization like Resorts International, "a company which operates a casino in the Bahamas...in direct competition with those in Nevada."[40] This in spite of bad health and only on the counsel of formerly distrusted executives. On top of all, what would possibly lead him to employ as over-all manager of this trip a security organization, Intertel, 94 percent of which was owned by Resorts International?

So even if Intertel was not the CIA of the Lansky Syndicate,[41] it was still at least the CIA of Resorts International, and Resorts International, whether it was a Syndicate front or not, was still Hughes's chief competition.

4. Lastly, Maheu raised the question: If Hughes was so down on him, why not simply terminate his contract? Why so much fuss? Why the seemingly deliberate attempt to provoke a public controversy? And was it not another stupendous coincidence that Hughes should have closed himself off to Maheu at the very moment the Toolco board felt most threatened by him? One moment Maheu is a good guy with Hughes doing a hard job honestly and well. His communication lines are open to the top. He bends over backward to keep his face and hands clean. He is studiedly correct in all things. Then, pop! The mandate he won by that very competence, the TWA mandate, brings him up against the power of Davis and Toolco. So Gay tells the throneroom guard not to carry Maheu's memos to Hughes anymore, not to put his phone calls through, to tear up his Valentines and badmouth him to Hughes—and thus lead Hughes to the belief that Maheu was responsible for the Syndicate's silver-mining swindle.

The force of Maheu's self-defense grew with developments, the following two in particular.

First, after years of digging in the records of Maheu's Nevada administration, Toolco attorneys were unable to find a single fault to stick him with. Then in July 1974, in Los Angeles, Maheu won a jury verdict in his multimillion-dollar libel suit entered against Hughes in 1972 after Hughes told reporters (in a telephone interview growing out of the Clifford Irving "hoax" biography affair) that Maheu was "a no-good, dishonest son of a bitch and he stole me blind,"[42] a view Hughes held on the strength of information he got from the Toolco throneroom guard service, the Mormon Mafia.

The Las Vegas battle was finally resolved not by the force of anyone's arguments or by the integrity of either side, but by the Eckersley-Myler proxy of November 14. Myler got it from the strongbox and presented it to the court on December 10. Eckersley arrived the same day from Paradise Island with a long letter purportedly from Hughes in support of Davis. Two days before, phoning from the Britannia Beach Hotel, Hughes spoke to Governor Laxalt and District Attorney George Franklin. Both of them said they were positive the person they heard calling himself Hughes over the phone was the same person they had heard every other time they believed themselves to be talking to Hughes. Hughes told them he was alive and reasonably well, that Maheu was a disloyal employee and had been fired, and that Davis spoke for him in all matters.

Maheu produced a handwriting expert who swore that the Hughes signature on the proxy was a fake. Davis produced another handwriting expert who swore it was genuine. The court found Davis's expert the more convincing one. Maheu lost his job.

In the aftermath came a complete reconfiguration of the over-all Hughes empire. In place of the old Toolco, a new creature materialized, the Summa Corporation. And stock in the drillbit company from which it all had started was publicly traded on the New York Stock Exchange. The CIA relationship was continued within the structure of Summa and the Hughes Medical Institute of Miami.

Something had come full circle. Hughes the individualist tycoon had now disappeared altogether behind exactly the kind of closed corporation that had been hounding him all his life—perhaps the master, but perhaps, after Thanksgiving 1970, the slave and victim of an ambitious and resourceful staff in revolt.

The Greenspun Caper

Maheu could not prevail against Davis, but he protected himself against annihilation by stashing away, in the safe of his ally Greenspun, his large private collection of Hughes documents and tapes.[43] It contained memorable items not only from the teeming four years of happiness in Las Vegas, but also from all Maheu's adventures with Hughes before that, such as the time Maheu got the CIA and the Syndicate together. Since Maheu was at one time or another immersed in these activities, his documents presumably painted an insider's picture of the larger relationship emerging between Hughes, Toolco, the CIA, and the Syndicate.

Rumor of the scope of Maheu's document trove finally prompted Robert Bennett, president of the CIA-linked public relations firm of Robert Mullen and Company, to convene a meeting in Washington between himself, Howard Hunt and Ralph Winte. Winte was the new Hughes-Nevada security chief after the coming of Toolco. He has an Intertel background. Bennett assembled this group in order to discuss "the communality of interests" among them in the contents of Greenspun's safe. Bennett is the son of Utah Senator Wallace Bennett, a high official of the Mormon Church. He joined Mullen and Company as its president early in 1971, bringing the Toolco-Davis account with him.

Mullen and Company was incorpated in 1959. According to Senator Baker's special report on the CIA and Watergate (July 2, 1974), Mullen "maintained a relationship with the CIA" from then on and was providing cover for agents in

Amsterdam and Singapore at the hour of the Watergate breakin. Besides Hughes, Mullen was also close to ITT and CREEP. It helped raise some $10 million for the 1972 Nixon campaign. Douglas Caddy worked out of Mullen offices during the halcyon days of the Huston Plan.

Hunt told the Ervin Committee what he had told McCord, that there was some scandal *on Muskie* in Greenspun's safe. Hunt's tenacity in struggle is better than this story. Greenspun's denial, the partial revelation of the Maheu papers, and the whole subsequent flow of the situation persuade us that McCord's estimate the following December was better: that Nixon and Mitchell thought "Greenspun had other material which would personally incriminate the President and his friends." We need only wipe away the dust to see that this material was the Maheu collection.

The February 1972 meeting at Mullen's Washington office determined upon a straight-ahead, Liddy-style approach to the problem, i.e., burglary, a Plumber favorite.[44] McCord's testimony is that Liddy told him that he, Liddy, shortly thereafter handled a first-installment Hughes contribution of $50,000 to CREEP, the money flowing from Hughes through Bennett. In November, also flowing between Bennett and Liddy at the Mullen/CIA office, another Hughes cash dose for CREEP came through, this one for $100,000. Was Toolco hiring the services of the White House Plumbers?

In April, Liddy went to Las Vegas (again according to McCord) to case the layout of the *Sun* a second time. McCord does not say the break-in was actually attempted, but his account indicates that plans and preparations were carried to extensive detail. The Maheu documents and their White House thieves were to have been flown out of the country to a Central American haven in an airplane provided for that purpose by Toolco.

An unsuccessful attempt to open the *Sun's* safe was reported that month. It has never been conclusively linked to the Plumbers. But whether the Greenspun document heist was abandoned in the planning stage or muffed in the attempted execution, it remains an abiding fact of American history that it did not end the interest of the Nixon people in the contents of Greenspun's safe or the Hughes problem. The best current explanation of the actual Watergate break-ins of June 1972 is that they were motivated by fear that something on Hughes and Nixon—possibly also on the whole question of Cuba, the CIA, and the attempted Castro assassination—had fallen into the hands of the McGovernites of the Democratic party. Even in the glaring publicity of the Senate Watergate hearings, the Nixon people still could not resist a last little try to get these papers back for Toolco. On May 23, 1973, the day after McCord told the Ervin Committee and the world of the Greenspun break-in plot, two IRS agents showed up at Greenspun's office with a pretext for demanding the Maheu material. Greenspun went to court and got that stopped. The safe remained inviolate, and Maheu's treasure helped serve him a victory in his Los Angeles libel suit against Hughes.

The Hughes-Nixon Connection

We opened this exploration of the political-economic Hughes with the words that first brought his name into Watergate, those of McCord to Ervin on May 20, 1973. In view of the specific light cast by the story just reconstructed, I think we now know how to decode the McCord statement. He is telling us the technical truth, but he is also telling us that a significant detail is wrong, that something else was afoot, that we should look for a twist. He is saying through clenched teeth that Nixon was the presidential figure whom the Maheu-Greenspun documents posed a threat to, not Muskie. Decoded, his original statement would then read:

Liddy said that Mitchell told him that Greenspun had in his possession blackmail type information involving

NIXON [*not Muskie*] *and Mitchell wanted that material, and Liddy said that this information was in some way racketeer-related, indicating that if this candidate, NIXON* [*not Muskie*] *became president, the racketeers or national crime syndicate could have a control or influence over him as president.*

I submit that this is the "other motive" McCord hinted of, the unnamed motive he thought might actually have prompted the Greenspun caper. The link between the "presidential candidate" and organized crime existed, but if I am ever to be too obvious, the motive of the attempt on Greenspun's safe was to *protect* that secret, not to *acquire* it, because the link did not run between Lansky and Muskie, it ran between Lansky and Nixon and Hughes.

Theory: Hughes and Lansky both had a piece of Nixon. When Hughes and Lansky got along, as they did so well on the Cuban question, things went well. They went badly after about 1968, when Meier appeared. The Hughes-Lansky conflict over Nevada was a conflict internal to the Nixon coalition, essentially a conflict for control of the presidency and the president. The Cowboy's need to protect that secret and the Yankee's ability to penetrate and manipulate it constitute the inner drive of Watergate.

7

The Watergate Plane Crash

Context

One workday morning in the capital, early in October 1972, McCord got a call from Gerald Alch, his CREEP-appointed attorney of that moment. Alch said he had important news to convey, could they meet for lunch. When they met, says McCord, Alch's opening words were, "I have just come from Bittman's office [White House attorney William Bittman]. Nobody gets up on that (witness) stand during trial. In return, they will get executive clemency, money while in prison and rehabilitation afterwards." Alch assured McCord that this was a good deal under the circumstances. "Nobody," he repeated, "gets up on that stand."

Alch then asked McCord, "Why aren't you taking the

money from Mrs. Hunt?" In McCord's account of Watergate, *A Piece of Tape*,[1] from which I borrow this dialogue, he writes, "I went over my concerns that the whole business had the appearance of a control mechanism to keep the men quiet prior to the Nixon election by the use of money as a weapon and tool. Between that concern and the surveillance I had experienced on the 19th of September, I had decided to take no further money in order to be completely free to pursue whatever course of action my conscience dictated without being obliged."

McCord says Alch "berated" him for taking this stand, then popped a question which McCord found "rather unusual in the wording and context." Said Alch, "Just what would it take for you to turn state's evidence?" McCord says Alch's tone and manner made it clear that he was not sponsoring this alternative. It was "as though he were feeling me out for someone else." McCord told Alch that he would follow his own course of action. Alch, he notes, "fell silent at that statement."

MACHO BARKER: The next day I got a call. "Do you recognize my voice?" And I said yes. It was Dorothy Hunt. She told me to go to Miami and stay in the airport and meet the next flight of the same line. I made sure that Dorothy was not being followed, and then we went to my home. She said, "From now on I will be your contact," and it was quite evident that the Dorothy that I had known had a split personality, because for the first time she used operational terms that Howard and I had always used. She said not to trust Rothblatt too much, that she didn't like him. She said to start figuring out how much assistance we would need. Up to this time, we had not had any at all. She said remember the spirit of the old organization—that if you are caught by the enemy, two things will be done: (1) every effort will be made to rescue you, and (2) all expenses and your family will be taken care of. Even today, the families of those who were lost at the Bay of Pigs are being aided, and it is something you expect on a mission.[2]

Late October 1972. Dorothy Hunt called Colson's office in an agitated voice demanding to speak to Colson, who declined. By Colson's later account, she was "upset at the interruption of payments from Nixon associates to Watergate defendants."[3]

November 15. Colson met with Nixon, Haldeman, and Ehrlichman in the Laurel Lodge presidential office at Camp David to play a tape of Hunt expounding his blackmail threat. That same afternoon, Dean flew to New York with this tape to play it for Mitchell, meeting in safe rooms at the Metropolitan Club. A week later, Hunt called Colson in order to have it recorded that ". . . we are protecting the guys who are actually responsible . . . and of course that is a continuing requirement, but at the same time, it is a two-way street. . . ."[4]

Late November. McCord: "In addition, Mrs. E. Howard Hunt, on or about November 30, 1972, in a personal conversation with me, stated that E. Howard Hunt had just dictated a three-page letter which Hunt's attorney, William O. Bittman, had read to Kenneth Parkinson, the attorney for the Committee to Re-elect the President, in which letter Hunt purportedly threatened to 'blow the White House out of the water.' Mrs. Hunt at this point in her conversation with me also repeated the statement which she too had made before, which was that E. Howard Hunt had information which would impeach the President."[5]

December 2 (Saturday). The president met at Key Biscayne with Colson and Rebozo to discuss the growing blackmail threat. Dorothy Hunt in Washington meanwhile was hounding Colson's secretary, Joan Hall, with phone calls about "the problem." She demanded that Hall get the word to Colson <u>to get the word to Nixon</u> "to get something done about it."

Mitchell was ultimately reached, and he reached for Dean. Mitchell told Dean to use some White House cash to get the Hunt situation settled down. Haldeman came into the picture and told his staff assistant Gordon Strachan to deliver a certain amount, either $40,000 or $70,000. LaRue cranked up his mill and soon got the money on its way through Kalmbach to Ulasewicz to Bittman. There may have been a relaxed moment before information came rippling back from Hunt to Bittman to Ulasewicz to Kalmbach to Mitchell to LaRue to Dean to Haldeman and to Nixon that, even so, the blackmailers were still not satisfied.

Haldeman finally told Strachan to deliver all of $350,000 to CREEP but to get a receipt for it from LaRue. LaRue accepted the money but refused to write a receipt. LaRue testified to the Watergate committee the following May that he paid out a total of about $250,000 to buy Hunt's silence.[6]

December 4 (Monday). Judge Sirica told defense and prosecution attorneys that the jury would want to find out who ordered, who funded, and who organized the Watergate operation.

Early December. Dorothy Hunt complained to McCord that she was tiring of her role in the Watergate blackmail.

December 8 (Friday). United Airlines flight 553 inbound from Washington crashed a mile and a half short of Chicago's Midway Airport, where it was trying to land, killing two people on the ground and forty-three of the sixty-one people on the plane. Dorothy Hunt was one of the victims.

President to Dean, morning of February 28, 1973: "Well you can follow these characters to their Gethsemane, I feel for these poor guys in jail, particularly for Hunt with his wife dead." The blackmail threat, of course, was still on as of that moment.

The President and Dean, in their novella-like meeting on the morning of March 21, 1973, the "cancer on the presidency" meeting, feel each other out simultaneously, while simultaneously pretending not to, on the grave question of how much they know about each other, particularly with respect to Nixon's ties to organized crime and Dean's formal ignorance of such ties:

DEAN: ... Kalmbach raised some cash.

NIXON: They put that under the cover of a Cuban committee, I suppose?

DEAN: Well, they had a Cuban committee and they had—some of it was given to Hunt's lawyer, who in turn passed it out. You know, when Hunt's wife was flying to Chicago with $10,000 she was actually, I understand after the fact now, was going to pass that money to one of the Cubans—to meet him in Chicago and pass it to somebody there.

Later, same scene:

DEAN: ... You've got then, an awful lot of the principals involved who know. Some people's wives know. Mrs. Hunt was the savviest woman in the world. She had the whole picture together.

NIXON: Did she?

DEAN: Yes. Apparently, she was the pillar of strength in that family before the death.

NIXON: Great sadness. As a matter of fact there was discussion with somebody about Hunt's problem on account of his wife and I said, of course commutation could be considered on the basis of his wife's death, and that is the only conversation I ever had in that light.

DEAN: Right. So that is it. That is the extent of the knowledge....

This dialogue about "the knowledge," weaving its way throughout the transcripts, is fundamental to the Nixon tragedy of power, just as it is fundamental that most of the actors knew they were talking into hidden microphones every second of their lives. Thus, Dean is here simultaneously in touch with the double personage of *Nixon* and *the president* as well as their implicit electronic audience. His function indeed forces him in his ceremonial innocence (pretend ignorance) to teach the Nixon-person how to be the Nixon-president before an unseen listening audience which they both must pretend not to notice.

Dean continues with a precise summary and an understated suggestion which manages to say to Nixon the man that he certainly must employ his own special resources in this fight to prop up the presidency. Though Dean always talks to the mask of Nixon-president, he still has his sense of limits, as though carelessly, laid across Nixon's private parts. Thus the poignancy of Dean's next speech:

DEAN: ... So what are the soft spots on this? Well, first of all, there is the problem of the continued blackmail which will not only go on now, but it will go on while these people are in prison, and it will compound the obstruction of justice situation. It will cost money. It is dangerous. People around here are not pros at this sort of thing. This is the sort of thing Mafia people can do...

Now the dialogue unwinds, constantly returning to the question of Hunt.

NIXON: Your major guy to keep under control is Hunt?

DEAN: That is right....

NIXON: ... the vulnerable points being, the first vulnerable points would be obvious. That would be one of the defendants, either Hunt, because he is most vulnerable in my opinion, might blow the whistle and his price is pretty high....

... You can't keep it out if Hunt talks....

... I think Hunt knows a hell of a lot more....

... You have no choice on Hunt....

And finally, breaking at last into a whole utterance:

... But my point is, do you ever have any choice on Hunt? That is the point. No matter what we do here now, John, whatever he wants if he doesn't get it— immunity, etc., he is going to blow the whistle.

Then this cabalistic exchange at a later meeting the same day in which Haldeman and Ehrlichman sail in over Dean's head:

DEAN: ... Hunt has now sent a blackmail request directly to the White House.

NIXON: Who did he send it to? You?

DEAN: Yes.

NIXON: Or to me?

DEAN: Your counsel.

HALDEMAN: That is the interesting kind of thing, there is something there that may blow it all up that way and everything starts going in a whole new direction.

EHRLICHMAN: That he would hurt the Eastern Asian Defense. [?] Right there. That is blackmail.[7]

The FBI and the Crash

The criticism of the official pilot-error theory of the Hunt crash has been overwhelmingly identified with Sherman Skolnick, a Chicago-based private investigator, and his

colleague, companion, and bodyguard, Alex Bottos, who
has a murky background and claims former FBI, CIA, and
narcotics connections. Skolnick and Bottos are a pungent
Dickensian pair. Skolnick has been confined from birth to a
wheelchair. He is intense, loud, overbearing, quick,
suspicious, sometimes merry, all upper torso and arms,
boisterous, gnomic-faced. Bottos is more somber and
sepulchral. He says he was at Opalaka in 1960-61 with Hunt
on the Bay of Pigs campaign. He carries a pistol and is fond
of flashing it. He dresses with old-fashioned nattiness and
polishes to a high gloss both his black hair and his black
patent leather loafers. Skolnick and Bottos have seen each
other through great controversies. They project an ominous,
swirling, shadowy atmosphere, Skolnick wheeling and
challenging, Bottos in a tailored flak jacket brooding on
collapse.

The instrument of their collaboration is Skolnick's
Citizens Committee to Clean Up the Courts. Their most
spectacular hit so far—until United flight 553—was
Chicago's once-immaculate liberal, Governor Otto Kerner,
whom they discovered and exposed in a race-track payoff
scheme. Skolnick and Bottos have also helped put away
several Illinois Supreme Court judges on corruption counts.

Skolnick was instantaneous in charging that the crash of
United flight 553 was the result of sabotage and that there
was a big Watergate connection. In the weeks immediately
following the crash, he claims to have received a flood of
information from protected inside sources supporting him in
this belief. He also tried to make that information public,
thus to generate a controversy and a demand for a new
investigation of the crash.

In the furor of claim and counterclaim that followed,
Skolnick's voice often reached an intensity that many found
hysterical. Anyone who disagreed with him about anything
(your author much included) he denounced as a secret agent
of the CIA. The controversy over his personality came to
interfuse with the controversy over the crash. He made it

easy for his detractors to ridicule him for rampant paranoia and to ignore his specific claims as wild raving.

Yet in the instances in which the dispute has been resolved by a subsequent factual disclosure, Skolnick's contentions have been substantially borne out. The question of FBI involvement in the crash investigation is the perfect case in point.

The Boeing 737 had barely hit, said Skolnick, before the crash site was aswarm with large numbers (he sometimes said "carloads," sometimes "200," sometimes "dozens") of "federal people" who shouldered Chicago police and firemen aside and kept to themselves why and on what authority they were doing so. When I first encountered the array of Skolnick's arguments about the crash, I dismissed this particular item—the 200 FBI agents prowling the wreckage within moments of the crash—as an improbable piece of melodramatic adornment. In my original summary of Skolnick's case in the *Boston Phoenix* (May 15, 1973), I left the point out altogether, concentrating on what I regarded as his more impressive arguments.

But then came the disclosure, as a result of Skolnick's agitation in Washington, of the two letters which I reprint in their entirety below. The first is from the chairman of the National Transportation Safety Board, John Reed, to acting FBI Director William Ruckelshaus. The second is Ruckelshaus's reply. The NTSB is a putatively independent branch of the Department of Transportation with responsibility for investigating all accidents involving commercial airliners. It investigated the crash of United 553. The NTSB chairman's letter is dated June 5, 1973.

Dear Mr. Ruckelshaus:

As you may know, the National Transportation Safety Board is currently investigating the aircraft accident of the United Air Lines Boeing 737, at Midway Airport, Chicago, on December 8, 1972. Our investigative team assigned to this accident discovered on the day following the accident that several FBI agents had taken a number of non-typical actions relating to this accident within the first few hours following the accident.

Included were: for the first time in the memory of our staff, an FBI agent went to the control tower and listened to the tower tapes before our investigators had done so; and for the first time to our knowledge, in connection with an aircraft accident, an FBI agent interviewed witnesses to the crash, including flight attendants on the aircraft prior to the NTSB interviews. As I am sure you can understand, these actions, particularly with respect to this flight on which Mrs. E. Howard Hunt was killed, have raised innumerable questions in the minds of those with legitimate interests in ascertaining the cause of this accident. Included among those who have asked questions, for example, is the Government Activities Subcommittee of the House Government Operations Committee. On the basis of informal discussions with the staff of the Committee, it is likely that questions as to what specific actions were taken by the FBI in connection with this aircraft accident, and why such actions were taken, will come up in a public oversight hearing at which the NTSB will appear and which is now scheduled for June 13, 1973.

In order to be fully responsive to the Committee, as well as to be fully informed ourselves about all aspects of this accident so as to assure the complete accuracy of our determination of the probable cause, we would appreciate being advised of all details with respect to the FBI activities in connection with this accident. We would like to have, for example, the following information: the purpose of the FBI investigation, the reasons for the early response and unusual FBI actions in this case, the number of FBI personnel involved, all investigative actions taken by the agents and the times they took such actions (including the time the first FBI agents arrived on the scene), and copies of all reports and records made by the agents in connection with their investigations (we already have copies of 26 FBI interview reports; any other documents should be provided, therefore).

While we have initiated action at the staff level between our agency and yours to effect better liaison and avoid engaging in efforts which may be in conflict in the future, we have determined that some more formal arrangement—in the nature of an interagency memorandum of agreement of understanding, for instance—would seem appropriate. It would clearly delineate our respective statutory responsibilities and set forth procedures to eliminate any future conflicts. We would therefore appreciate it if you would designate, at your earliest convenience, an official with whom we may discuss this matter and with the authority to negotiate such a formal agreement with the Safety Board.

In the interim, however, we would like to receive, in advance of the scheduled June 13, 1973, public oversight hearing, the specific information concerning the actions of the FBI in connection with the Midway accident and the reasons therefore, in order to enable us to be as fully responsive as possible to the House Subcommittee.

Sincerely,
(Original signed by
John H. Reed, Chairman)

FBI Director Ruckelshaus answered on June 11, 1973.

Dear Mr. Reed:

Your letter dated June 5, 1973, concerning the FBI's investigation into the crash of a United Air Lines Boeing 737 at Midway Airport, Chicago, Illinois, on December 8, 1972, has been received.

The FBI has primary investigative jurisdiction in connection with the Destruction of Aircraft or Motor Vehicles (DAMV) Statute, Title 18, Section 32, U.S. Code, which pertains to the willful damaging, destroying or disabling of any civil aircraft in interstate, overseas or foreign air commerce. In addition, Congress specifically designated the FBI to handle investigations under the Crime Aboard Aircraft (CAA) Statute, Title 49, Section 1472, U.S. Code, pertaining, among other things, to aircraft piracy, interference with flight crew members and certain specified crimes aboard aircraft in flight, including assault, murder, manslaughter and attempts to commit murder or manslaughter.

FBI investigation of the December 8, 1972 United Air Lines crash was instituted to determine if a violation of the DAMV or CAA Statutes had occurred and for no other reason. The fact that Mrs. E. Howard Hunt was aboard the plane was unknown to the FBI at the time our investigation was instituted.

It has been longstanding FBI policy to immediately proceed to the scene of an airplane crash for the purpose of developing any information indicating a possible Federal violation within the investigative jurisdiction of the FBI. In all such instances liaison is immediately established with the National Transportation Safety Board (NTSB) personnel upon their arrival at the scene.

Approximately 50 FBI Agents responded to the crash scene, the first ones arriving within 45 minutes of the crash. FBI Agents did interview witnesses to the crash, including flight attendants. Special Agent (SA) Robert E. Hartz proceeded to the Midway Airport tower shortly after the crash to determine if tower personnel could shed any light as to the reason for the crash. On arriving at the tower, SA Hartz identified himself as an FBI Agent and explained the reason for his presence. He was invited by Federal Aviation Administration (FAA) personnel at the tower to listen to the recording made at the tower of the conversation between the tower and United Air Lines Flight 553. At no time did SA Hartz request to be allowed to listen to the tapes. After listening to the tapes, SA Hartz identified a sound as being that of the stall indicator on the aircraft. The FAA agreed that SA Hartz was right and immediately notified FAA Headquarters at Washington, D.C.

The FBI's investigation in this matter was terminated within 20 hours of the accident and on December 11, 1972, Mr. William L. Lamb, NTSB, was furnished with copies of the complete FBI investigation pertaining to this crash after it was determined there was apparently no violation of the DAM or CAA Statutes.

In order to avoid the possibility of any misunderstanding concerning our respective agencies' responsibilities and to insure continued effective liaison between the NTSB and the FBI, I have designated SA Richard F. Bates, Section Chief, Criminal Section, General Investigative Division, FBI Headquarters, Washington, D.C., telephone number 324-2281, to represent the FBI concerning any matters of mutual interest.

Sincerely yours,
William D. Ruckelshaus
Acting Director

Based on the facts agreed upon by both sides, it is at least apparent from these letters that the FBI was all over Dorothy Hunt at the time of the crash, despite Ruckelshaus's protest that Dorothy Hunt's presence on 553 was "unknown to the FBI at that time." There is no obvious way such a large response as fifty agents within the hour could have been generated from a standing start as of the moment of the crash itself. The closest FBI office is forty minutes from the crash site and there are never fifty agents available at once without warning. It is tradition that FBI agents do not gather in offices waiting for calls but stay in the field. When a really obvious intelligence agent, Hungarian Freedom Fighter Lazlo Hadek, died in a crash the next summer at Boston's Logan Airport, leaving a trail of secret NATO nuclear documents strewn down the center of the runway, the FBI was barely able to get a solitary agent to the scene on the same day as the wreck. That this same FBI could get fifty agents to the scene of the Chicago crash within an hour is to my mind an arresting piece of information. How could the FBI have done this if it had not had Dorothy Hunt's airplane, for whatever reason, under full company-scale surveillance before the crash ever happened? And why might the FBI have been doing that?

Note in this connection that it was specifically the airplane itself that was being followed, and not the person of Dorothy Hunt. That is, no FBI agent was aboard the plane.[8] *If the FBI was tailing Dorothy Hunt, why was she not being followed on the plane?* Was it that her flight was too sudden? But it was delayed on the ground for fifteen minutes. Michelle Clark of CBS, who was on the same flight, knew she was going to be on it and may have been her companion in the first-class cabin. The Hunts took enough time at the airport to buy $250,000 worth of flight insurance.[9]

Ruckelshaus does not meet Reed's main questions. He reads the book with a straight face as though Reed had asked him what were the statutory grounds of the FBI intervention instead of why, suddenly, this time and no other time, and so massively, and hence with such a semblance of advance contrivance, were these grounds taken up and acted upon. One understands that the FBI will always be able to demonstrate a rudimentary legal basis for whatever it takes it in its head to do. What we want to know is where these whims and fancies bubble up from.

We wonder finally what in the world made the FBI think 553's crash might have been a case of "willful disabling of a civil aircraft," or of "crimes aboard aircraft in flight, including assault, murder, and manslaughter"? Not that any of this necessarily happened or did not, but the FBI does not usually behave as if it might have. Does it? How does Ruckelshaus account for this, especially in view of his assertion that the FBI acted with no knowledge of Dorothy Hunt's presence? What was the chain-of-command activity and what were the reasons that had so many FBI agents waiting to move when that plane came down?

The Plumbers and the Crash

The White House also responded immediately to the crash. Nixon moved Egil Krogh, Alex Butterfield, and Dwight Chapin, three of his remaining special agents, to positions of vantage around the crash investigation.

Krogh was the organizer of the Nixon White House's Special Investigative Unit, the "Room 16" group. Chapin was a key Haldeman aide who recruited and directed Segretti in his sabotage and espionage tasks.[10] Butterfield, who so airily exposed the White House secret taping system on Friday, July 13, was a Haldeman man from UCLA, where their wives were sorority roommates. He has an Air Force background and some of his biographies say he flew with the Blue Angels. He served Nixon as White House liaison with the CIA.

Here is how these agents were deployed in the days following the December 8 crash.

Krogh

On Saturday, December 9, 1972, Krogh was suddenly made an undersecretary of the Department of Transportation, the DOT being the seat of larger bureaucratic responsibility for the crash investigation. There was no prior announcement of this appointment. There was no explanation of why it had to be implemented the same day it was announced, a Saturday, not normally a business day in

Washington. Once installed in the DOT, Krogh proceeded to pressure the NTSB to speed up its reports and restrain its criticism of DOT or face "discipline."[11]

Butterfield

Ten days later, on December 19, Butterfield was appointed administrator of the Federal Aviation Administration, the parent body of the actual technical-investigation arm, the Bureau of Aviation Safety. Butterfield's appointment was delayed to March because of a provision prohibiting any military or retired military officer from holding the position Nixon wanted to move him into. As when General Alexander Haig joined Kissinger's National Security Council later, Butterfield had to resign his commission temporarily.

Chapin

Early in January, Chapin left the White House behind a story that he was being drummed out because of his role in the activities of CREEP. He soon joined the staff of United Air Lines Chicago office as a "director of market planning." He was present every day at the NTSB public hearings into the 553 crash that opened on February 28, 1973, in Chicago. He spent some of his time fending off Skolnick and Bottos and some of it intimidating the media with licensing threats.[12]

Then there is the matter of *Richard Spears*.

In May 1973 stories reached the Senate Commerce Committee, overseer of the NTSB, that "officials of the White House or the Department of Transportation were trying to improperly influence members of the [Safety] Board in the pursuit of their lawful duties."[13] On May 3,

Chairman Warren Magnusen (D.-Wash.) asked Chairman Reed to respond to these stories.

On May 9, exposed as a Plumber in the Fielding burglary, Krogh resigned his post as number two man in the DOT.

Magnusen's inquiry motivated Reed and the Senate Commerce Committee to convene the sessions of May 21 and 23. These sessions were attended only by Senator Howard Cannon (D.-Nev.), although Senator Frank Moss (D.-Utah) submitted two questions to each witness remotely suggesting a suspicion of sabotage. But the most important development at these hearings was the clash between a Nixon appointee to the NTSB, General Manager Richard Spears, and the director of the Bureau of Aviation Safety, C.O. Miller.

Spears became a "consultant" to the NTSB in January 1971 shortly after the end of the term of Senator George Murphy (R.-Cal.), whom he formerly served as administrative assistant. Spears moved in as head of the NTSB after a Nixon-inspired change in the regulations created the position of "NTSB general manager" and defined it as a political-patronage job. Spears had no former experience in the field of aviation safety, a specialized technical field.[14]

According to Miller, Spears immediately began trying to run the NTSB. A quarrel developed between them. It boiled up in February 1973 just as the NTSB hearings into the Hunt crash were opening in Chicago. As BAS director, Miller was the boss of the technician, William Lamb, who would oversee the entire program of investigation, analysis, and report on the crash of 553.

Late in February, Miller took off from his normal duties to attend a sixty-day Federal Executives Institute. When he was safely out of the building, Spears replaced him in the BAS directorship and let it out that his duties would be different upon return. Before Miller could return to challenge this personally, Spears himself rewrote the NTSB's definition of "probable cause" of a crash, directed NTSB investigators to make fewer safety recommendations, and called for quicker completion of investigations and reports on all projects, including the 553 crash.

Miller returned for confrontation in April. He testified that Spears told him, "I have got orders from the only people that hire and fire me to become chief operating officer of the NTSB."[15] Asked by Senator Cannon how he interpreted this, Miller said he thought it meant that Spears "had some knowledge of some power base in the executive branch. One of the very serious impacts on the effectiveness of our Bureau, in my opinion, has been the use of this reference to outside power to, in a sense, intimidate the people who perhaps are a little more concerned about their jobs than I am, to get things done without question."[16]

Miller's appeal to the full NTSB was successful. He was restored to his former position as BAS director. Somewhat later, however, he began complaining of heart trouble and was obliged to retire.[17]

What are we to make of Nixon's evidently intense interest in the crash of the Hunt plane? FBI men intervening so quickly at company-level force; the three secret Nixon agents fanning out to positions of control around the crash investigation; Spears going to the report-writing center, cutting directly into the 553 investigation: What might all this mean?

This brings us to the detailed technical analysis of the NTSB report on the crash. It is a boggy and noxious area to explore because it entails necessarily technical exposition. At the same time, it is in the technical areas that our intuitions have found strength before, so let us plunge ahead.

The Analysis of the Crash

We briefly and tersely dismissed Sherman Skolnick's claims. We investigated thoroughly and found not a shred of evidence indicating the Dorothy Hunt plane was sabotaged.

—Brad Dunbar,
NTSB spokesman
September 23, 1974[18]

The technical questions of fact and interpretation in the crash of United 553, for better or worse, have taken form in the course of a polemic set in train by Skolnick's early accusations of sabotage and cover-up. In this section, we will take up several particular questions emerging from this polemic.

We begin with the question of cyanide poisoning not because it is the strongest of Skolnick's claims—indeed it is much the weakest—or because it is the most important, which it is not, but because it is the question on which Skolnick's critics have concentrated most of their fire.

Then we will move to consider the more substantial technical doubts about the precise mechanisms of the crash, most of which involve questions also first articulated in some form by Skolnick.

Finally we will take up the theory of the crash developed by the NTSB and advanced in their final report, "Aircraft Accident Report 73-16, United Airlines, Inc., Boeing 737, N9031U, Chicago-Midway Airport, Chicago, Illinois, December 8, 1972," dated August 29, 1973.[19]

The Question of Cyanide

James Walsh, administrative assistant to the Cook County coroner, told James Brady of *New York* magazine, "We found seven bodies which contained enough cyanide to kill them. We are not *saying* cyanide killed them, but that there was enough of it to have done so."[20]

Brady notes that Walsh refused to say whether or not the

pilot's body contained cyanide. But Skolnick had already unearthed FAA technical exhibit No. 6A, docket No. SA-435, entitled "Human Factors Group Chairman's Factual Report," by C. Hayden LeRoy. Page 8 of this exhibit contains in its entirety a typewritten table introduced by the words, "Federal Aviation Administration, Civil Aeromedical Institute, Aviation Toxicology Laboratory, Oklahoma City, Oklahoma, examined specimens from three aircraft occupants. Results were as follows." Among other things, the table shows that the three whose bodies were examined by the Civil Aeromedical Institute were Captain Whitehouse, Flight Officer W. O. Coble, and a first-class passenger otherwise unidentified. (According to NTSB spokesman Slattery, Dorothy Hunt was flying in the first-class cabin forward, just behind the cockpit.) By the item, "Cyanide (Conway Diffusion, NaOH)," the value entered for Captain Whitehouse is 3.9 micrograms per milliliter. In the columns for Coble and the first-class passenger there are hyphens indicating that the test for cyanide was not carried out on them.

What does it mean that Whitehouse had 3.9 micrograms per milliliter of cyanide in him? For the record, let us first note that the NTSB had some trouble in establishing this figure. The Chicago coroner's office reported to begin with that Whitehouse's blood showed cyanide in the amount of 0.211 *milligrams* per milliliter, an extremely high amount which by itself would establish a prima facie case of foul play.

A defender of the no-sabotage theory, Ronald Dorfman, editor of the *Chicago Journalism Review* (true to character, Skolnick denounces it as a CIA front), wrote[21] that he checked this figure out with Dr. Paul W. Smith, chief of the Aviation Toxicology Laboratory of the Civil Aeromedical Institute and that Dr. Smith told him, "We were very unhappy, and frankly don't know how they did their measurements." He is talking about the Chicago coroners, a handful of whom were fired for "incompetence" on account of this controversy. Smith continued, "They picked up cyanide in ten or twelve victims and they were all very high. Then they realized they probably made an error, which they interpreted to be a decimal error, and they altered their report. In moving the decimal their figures became innocuous—all less than one microgram."

There are a few problems with this simplification, however. Dr. Smith proceeded to analyze a blood specimen from the pilot (but not the others) to see how much cyanide actually was present, and the value he came up with was not "an innocuous" 0.211 *micrograms* per milliliter, which is the value arrived at by assuming that there was an error in the placing of the decimal point. Rather, it is the 3.9 micrograms per milliliter value we found in Exhibit 6A. That value, in the first place, does not bear out the Chicago coroner's guess that their assumed error was in the decimal; there is still a difference of a whole magnitude between their adjusted value of 0.2 micrograms per milliliter and Dr. Smith's new value of 3.9 micrograms per milliliter is not an innocuous level, a fact which even Dorfman concedes indirectly when he notes that this "is the highest blood cyanide reading [Dr. Smith] has ever recorded in a crash victim." Dorfman continues: "A research toxicologist I consulted confirmed that while a concentration of 3.9 micrograms is more than enough to kill, it is quite possible—depending on the concentration of cyanide gas in the air and the physical condition of the victim—to inhale that much before death occurs."

Very well, but observe how far this shifts the grounds of the argument. A moment before, we were being told that the pilot died a normal cyanide death, period. Now we are only being told that it is not absurd on the facts to *speculate* that he did.

The NTSB report states (p. 13) that "elevated hydrogen cyanide levels were found in the captain and in six fatalities in the crash," but it says nothing of the new record poor

Whitehouse set and does not pause to tell us what these "elevated levels" were, even though it notes (p. 14) that "smoke inhalation with carbon monoxide asphyxia and blood cyanide accumulation" was finally determined to have been the cause of the captain's death.[22] It merely explains that plastics used extensively in the cabins of commercial airliners give off hydrogen cyanide as a gas when burned.

The crash was indeed followed by an intense fire in the center section, mainly in the first-class cabin where Dorothy Hunt and Michelle Clark were traveling. But there was little fire in the captain's half of the cockpit, possibly because the nose and cockpit section broke off from the cabin and split in half. The NTSB report states (p. 12): "The left side of the cockpit and the left forward entry door were relatively intact. The captain's seat was intact and sustained only minor fire damage." And in any case, not to be too elementary, the *possibility* of a crash-normal cyanide gas poisoning would hardly cancel out the *possibility* of a *non*-crash-normal cyanide gas poisoning (as with a canister delivery mechanism). The existence of a convenient explanation (as in the use of potassium and cortisone as poisons) is actually the leading advantage of such a method.

It is certainly true, as Dorfman says, that Skolnick goes beyond the evidence in a self-discrediting way in claiming that shadows like the above demonstrate intentional poisoning in the 553 crash. Here Skolnick seems at his most lurid, turning, in Dorfman's words, every "assumption" into a "conclusion," every "hunch" into a "fact."

Still, Skolnick's informed misses teach us more of the truth of Watergate power politics than the baseless reassurances Dorfman prefers. That is because, first, Skolnick's overall conception of what goes into politics, what constitutes it, what comes out, is currently rooted in real experience. So even wandering at his most hysterical through dismal swamp, as perhaps with the cyanide question (and perhaps not), Skolnick still makes more sense and does more good teaching than those who use modest rhetoric to tell us there is nothing wrong. Something in fact may be quite wrong, the wrong may be of Satanic magnitude, and there is no way the standard statistic-ridden, political-sociology models employed in conventional federal-academic discourse can even focus the structured character of what is wrong. These models, these assumptions, give us a lone madman here and a lone madman there, as though our time's violent assault on presidential figures were the purest contingency, purest acts of God, unstructured, random events lying outside the events constitutive of "politics" proper and of no greater interest to the "political scientist" than the normal airplane accident or the normal heart attack.

Finally, as inadequately supported as it no doubt is, Skolnick's assertion about 553 and cyanide poisoning still ought not to be dismissed altogether. A palpable residue of doubt remains, partly because the authorities have seemed so anxious to shut the question up, but also partly because these are not bare, naked allegations. In view of the extreme political sensitivity of Dorothy Hunt's death, it might appear to the trusting among us that the public officials responsible would bend over backwards to follow every shadow of doubt all the way through to the end. What had they to fear? As it was, the very day after the crash, even as Plumber Krogh was being scrambled to the number two spot at the Department of Transportation over the FAA and NTSB, the official voices began their choral chant that there was no possibility of sabotage, "not a shred of evidence," and let slip no chance to heap more vituperation on Skolnick. The FBI was saying *no sabotage* within twenty hours of the crash, before it was even announced to the public that Dorothy Hunt was among the victims, and NTSB spokesmen were saying it early in May at a moment when the analysis of the data had barely begun. There is too much intensity in this, too much head-shaking. Too much protest betokens fear of some discovery. It reeks of cover-up whether it is one or not.

In view of the report of the Cook County coroners and

Dr. Smith's own results in the retest of the captain's blood, for example, why did Dr. Smith and the NTSB not press to examine the other seven or ten or twelve bodies said to contain "elevated levels" of cyanide? In view of the queer behavior of the FBI, why was not every angle looked into, every doubt openly faced, before the curtains started being closed on the play?

I have been nagging some version of this question, or it me, through many passages of this book: why the cover-up? A paragraph from the short-lived polemic that flared up between Dorfman and me in the *Nation* contains what may be a hint of an answer. Dorfman wrote:

> I do not disbelieve in conspiracies. I have helped uncover a few myself. My quarrel is not even with Oglesby's own treatment of the December crash, which as he suggests has been carefully hedged about with distinctions between what is known and what needs to be known. Rather, I take issue with, and he defends, a style of political thinking [i.e., Skolnick's] which turns assumptions into conclusions and hunches into facts, which are in turn [note:] broadcast to an increasingly receptive public content that, since the forces at work are not only beyond their reach but omnipotent, there is nothing they can or need do about public problems.[23]

In other words, gentle reader, it is your despair that Dorfman fears. If you come to think that such theories as the sabotage theory of the Hunt crash are not crazy on face, and that such things can actually happen and the offenders not be caught, then your faith in politics will wither and die, and where shall we all be then.

To this I answer, first, that there is no point in trying to set preconditions on the truth. Either the airplane was sabotaged or it was not, just as John Kennedy, Martin Luther King, Robert Kennedy, and George Wallace either were or were not attacked by conspiracies acting behind cover stories of lone, mad, diary-writing gunmen. And either we can do something about this or we cannot. Nothing whatever is served by hiding from the question. If we cannot, then, indeed the age of politics is behind us and we are the creatures of a new millenium.

Second, Skolnick's track record does not entitle his detractor to such airy contempt. Dorfman may be unable to muffle a boast about helping to "uncover a few" conspiracies himself (he is too modest to remind us what they were), but Skolnick is something else. We have already noted his major works: the bust of some half-dozen federal and other judges in Illinois and Indiana, including three members of the Illinois Supreme Court, and the exposure of Kerner in 1969.

Finally, something in the turn of Dorfman's last phrase in the above passage reminds me again that what academic liberals are typically so worried about is not the lapse of people's faith in politics so much as the lapse of their faith in the politics *of the current system.* But it is the power and invisibility of that system's demonstrated current corruption that threaten political demoralization, not the fact that a handful of people with virtually no resources are trying to expose it, analyze it, name it, and raise in public forums the question of direct political action to do something about it. To Dorfman I say, if that is what we are really talking about, preserving the people's faith in a corrupt political system, I know I am not the only democratic-minded patriot who will say, let it bleed.

Technical Doubts

Skolnick and others have raised much more substantial questions about the actual mechanisms of the crash of United 553: that the in-flight recorders were sabotaged and stolen from the wreckage, that the altimeter was sabotaged, that the runway system at Midway was used irregularly on this landing, that an electronic landing aid was unaccounta-

bly switched off at a crucial moment, and that the crew failed
even to take note of, much less to act on, the actuation of a
cockpit stall-warning signal designed expressly to be
imperative.

The Flight Recorders. The Boeing 737 carries two data-
recording systems, both designed to survive crashes of much
greater violence than that of 553. In the shock test, each
package must withstand the blow of a five-hundred-pound
steel bar dropped from ten feet. This is because their only
purpose is to help crash investigators determine as
absolutely as possible the cause or causes of a crash.

One is the Cockpit Voice Recorder (CVR), a super-
quality but otherwise ordinary tape recorder system wired
through a network of microphones to tape a whole range of
cockpit sounds—the distinctly different clicks, chimes,
rattles, horns, and whirrs of the controls—besides every
word of cabin conversation and any signals incoming from
outside the aircraft, as from a tower, another airplane, or an
electronic beacon on the ground. In other words, it is
designed to record the total acoustical signal environment of
the crew. This record of the cockpit acoustical environment
is so sensitive that General Electric engineers, working with a
tape that had been badly damaged (see below), were
nevertheless able to reconstruct from its acoustical data
precise thrust settings, left and right, for each of the 737's two
tail-mounted jet engines, right up to the moment of impact.

The other is the Flight Data Recorder (FDR). It is by far
the more important of the two from the standpoint of
technical crash analysis. The FDR keeps a continuous
graph-paper trace on the state of the aircraft's nerve center,
the Central Air Data Computer, mounted with the FDR in
the tail because that is the safest part of the aircraft. The
FDR records such parameters as air speed, barometric
(coarse) altitude, transponder (fine) altitude, and aircraft
roll and pitch angles, and it also records instrument
presentations to the crew, in order that errors in instrumentation can be discriminated from errors in sensing or

servomechanization or the like.

The critical points in connection with the CVR and the FDR are threefold:

First, the NTSB did not recover these instruments from the crash, even though its technical team was already in the field early Saturday morning. News accounts at the time said that *both* recorders were turned over to the NTSB team by James McConaugh, commissioner of the Chicago Department of Streets and Sanitation, who actually held a little ceremony of handover to which he invited a handful of newspeople.[24] No one asked, however, what the Department of Streets and Sanitation was doing with these instruments. They could not have simply tumbled into the street. The NTSB report tells us in fact that the nose and the tail sections of the aircraft suffered relatively little damage. News accounts incuriously note that the two recorders "had been recovered from the wreckage." They do not pry into such questions as: By whom were they recovered, and in what way, and under what power and authority, whether by Streets and Sanitation people or others? What would Streets and Sanitation people know about extracting these recorders from a still-burning wreckage? Not that they *could* know nothing, but what *did* they know? In the immediate aftermath of a horrifying mid-afternoon plane crash in the heart of a residential neighborhood, when there were survivors still screaming in the wreckage, why would Streets and Sanitation people be in such a hurry to save the flight-data recorders? Not that there *could* be no innocuous explanation for this, but what *is* it? And if Streets and Sanitation got the recorders from the FBI agents also present, as seems likely, then the question is: Why was Pat Gray's FBI so hot to get its hands on the technical instruments needed for a precise reconstruction of the crash?

The second critical point bears on the state of the Cockpit Voice Recorder. A Dwight Chapin-inspired Chicago news story from the March NTSB hearings in Chicago ran as follows:

"United Air Line investigative committee members are

suggesting that hydraulic pump failures may have contributed to the crash. They point out that the Cockpit Voice Recorder was filled with hydraulic oil when recovered from the wreckage, and some four days were required in the laboratory to clean the tape sufficiently for it to be played back to Safety Board listeners."[25]

There is no mention of this oil, however, in the NTSB's final report, or of any need to treat the CVR tape in any way whatsoever, never mind for four days, before unnamed minds accounted it fit to be heard by the NTSB investigators.

The report reads, "Although the CVR showed evidence of extreme fire and heat damage, the entire tape was recovered with only moderate damage to a nonpertinent area" (p. 8); although another passage tells us that the normally high-fidelity "CVR tape contained a high-level background noise which tended to mask meaningful frequency data" (p. 16); and in another context (p. 8) notes without explanation that there were "variances" of up to six seconds in the "times of identical events recorded by Air Traffic Control sources [ground-based] and the CVR." The transcript of the last eight minutes of the CVR tape, printed in the NTSB report as Appendix F, shows fourteen "unidentified voice" entries and ten "unintelligibles," ever so reminiscent of those other tape transcripts boiled in oil. Or was Haig's Sinister Force at Chicago, too?

The third critical point involves the all-important Flight Data Recorder, the one mounted in the tail near the Air Data Computer. The FDR on 553 was found to have broken down one quarter of an hour before the crash.[26] Yet cockpit discussion of the malfunctioning FDR shows that the crew did not get a suggestion of any FDR failure until about eight minutes later than that, and that up until about five minutes before the crash, the circuit and tape functions were still indicating positive.[27]

Without exploring this side canyon, the NTSB report nevertheless acknowledges the importance of the simultaneous loss of capability in both recording systems at once: "The absence of FDR information, the [inherent] imprecision of the [ground-based Automated Radar Terminal Service] ARTS-III data, and the high ambient noise level of the CVR recording preclude a precise determination of the nature and tempo of events during the 60 seconds from the call for the final descent check until impact" (p. 26).

The Altimeters. Skolnick claimed shortly after the crash that the flight instrument actually sabotaged on 553 was the altimeter. He said his information from an FAA source inside the investigation was that the diaphragm of a barometric-pressure-sensing device had a pinprick in it. The NTSB established that the pilot's altimeter had no such pinprick and showed that the copilot's instrument was smashed too badly in the crash for a positive determination to be made.

There the NTSB laid the matter to rest and proceeded with its own reconstruction. In the course of this reconstruction, however, it appeared that there were indeed serious technical peculiarities in the performance of the altimeter system as a whole.

There are actually two independent altitude measuring and display systems on the Boeing 737, one for the pilot and one for the copilot. Each system begins with a barometric-pressure-sensing device mounted outside the aircraft on "independent Pitot/static probes which have no common connections." The signals from each sensor go to one of two Central Air Data Computers (CADC) which continue the parallel redundancy of the system. Each CADC then supplies inputs to identical and independent altitude indicators, one at the pilot's instrument console and the other at the copilot's.

Indeed, the altitude-measuring system's only catastrophic failure is the situation in which both the pilot's altimeter *and* the copilot's altimeter fail or malfunction in precisely the same way, in precisely the same magnitude, at precisely the same time. I am not a mathematician and will not try to compute the probability that these three conditions will ever be met in actual performance, but one's inner ear says that the chance would be low, all the more so because of the unsurpassed reliability performance record of the Boeing 737. The only wreck this model ever had was the wreck it got into a mile and half short of Midway.

What do you know, these three conditions appear nevertheless to have been met in the case of the crash of 553. "Both CADC units were capable of normal operation," reads the NTSB report (p. 24), "but their altitude synchros, as recovered, showed an altitude higher than that of the crash site. The altitude differences, which could have been transmitted from the [independent] CADC units to the captain's and first officer's servo altimeters, were 157 feet and 103 feet, respectively."

These are not trivial errors in either altimeter by itself, and it is putting it mildly to say they are not trivial when they occur in the two independent systems at once.[28]

Runway Utilization. Midway is an old airport with few of the modern electronic instrumentation systems which jet flight has come to depend on. One of its runways, however, runway 13R, is longer than the others and better equipped for jets. It has an electronic glideslope, a system that automatically tells the captain whether he is descending at the right altitude and rate throughout the whole length of the final approach. Wind not being a factor (a light 4-6 knots at the time of the crash), it is the runway normally assigned to the few airline jets that still land at Midway instead of O'Hare. Use of this runway is all the more appropriate under conditions of low overcast, as on December 8, when the ceiling was about five-hundred feet.

The question of when and why flight 553 was reassigned to runway 31L, which is shorter and lacks a glideslope, is lost in the confusion of the lost "approach clearance," that is, the word given, or in this case *not* given, by O'Hare tower (which handles all traffic circulating around Chicago) that 553 could come out of its holding pattern and start in for a landing. O'Hare claims it "forgot" to give this clearance (Appendix E of the NTSB report) and Midway's story was never told. The whole question of O'Hare's hand-off of 553 to the Midway tower is muddy with irregularities.[29]

Related to the evident uncertainty in the cockpit of 553 about the landing procedure is the question of the light private plane, a two-prop Aero-Commander, that landed just ahead of 553 on Runway 31L. The more appropriate runway for such a small plane was 31R, which parallels 31L. Indeed, at one point the CVR transcript shows that Midway considered having the Aero-Commander go to that runway, but then changed its mind.[30]

Less than twelve seconds later, with no communications intervening, the Midway tower sent its next and last message to 553: "United five fifty-three, execute a missed approach, make a left turn to a heading of—one eight zero, climb to two thousand."

Nineteen-and-a-half seconds later came the crash. There were no further communications between the tower and 553 either way. The reason Midway gave for the wave-off was that 553 was going too fast and the distance between it and the Aero-Commander had closed to an unsafe margin. On its first approach to the runway, 9VS had been well ahead of 553, some three miles. Unaccountably, its pilot requested a missed-approach clearance from Midway tower and was given permission to pull up, circle, and come back for another try, all without giving place to 553 coming in behind it out of its holding pattern. The reason for the Aero-Commander's missed-approach request is not given in the NTSB report.

The Kedzie Outer Marker. Skolnick's original claim was that the Kedzie Localizer/Outer Marker was turned off as 553 passed over it. This is a vertical electronic beam emitted by a transmitter located on Kedzie Avenue, 3.3 miles from the runway, on direct line with runway 31L. Especially in overcast conditions, it is needed to ensure that landing aircraft are headed in properly toward the runway.

The NTSB report ignores Skolnick's assertions and puts a good face on the performance of the Outer Marker. The CVR transcript shows the Kedzie beacon tones sounding just after 553's approach is handed over from O'Hare to Midway tower, a little less than two minutes before the crash. No irregularities are noted, and in its only remote approach to the point, the report says only (p. 7) that "all navigational facilities associated with this approach procedure were flight-tested by the FAA immediately after the accident and were found to be operating within prescribed tolerances. None of the flights using the localizer before or after the accident reported any problems."

One must have access to the part of the CVR transcript not published with the NTSB final report to know of the following snatch of dialogue from the cockpit:

"Is Kedzie Localizer off—off the air, is that it?"

"I beg your pardon?"

"Is Kedzie Localizer off the air? There's an inbound, ah, there's an in-bound on 31."[31]

As to the significance of the shut-off of the Kedzie Outer Marker, the NTSB report scatters fragments of the answer throughout its pages and never brings them together so that the meaning can come out clearly. On page 9 it tells us that 553 crashed "¼ mile to the right of the localizer approach course." From the report in Appendix D, we learn that the magnetic heading of the path of the wreckage across three city blocks, hence the heading of the aircraft at impact, was 340 degrees. From Appendix E we learn that the magnetic heading of runway 31L was 312 degrees. Thus, a little more than a mile-and-a-half after it had crossed the suddenly turned-off Kedzie beacon, in spite of the fact that its crew was turning 553 left for the missed-approach exercise in the moments just before impact, it was still a quarter-mile off course to the right on a magnetic heading in error by 28 degrees. This is precisely the kind of error that the electronic marker system is installed to prevent.

* * *

The Stickshaker. The eeriest technical oddity about this crash is the behavior of the flight crew when the stickshaker went off.

The stickshaker is a no-uncertain-terms warning device installed in the cockpit expressly to warn the flight crew if the airplane is ever in danger of going into a stall. It is operated by the Air Data Computer, which constantly monitors and reflects upon the airplane's total flight state, including airspeed, engine thrust, and aerodynamic configuration. By aerodynamic configuration is meant the positions of the variety of movable surfaces on the wings and tail—tabs, flaps, spoilers, landing gear, etc.—that affect the drag and lift of the airplane while moving through the airstream. Under some combinations of airspeed, thrust, and aerodynamic configuration, drag exceeds lift, the nose spools up, and the airplane stalls. If a stall happens at a high altitude, the plane will go into a spin; if at a very low altitude, as with 553, it will crash tail first.

The stall is thus an eventuality not to be trifled with, and the designers of the super-safe Boeing 737 make it as unlikely an event as they can, partly by building into the crew's control system a stall-warning device designed for absolute infallibility.

The warning system has two parts. One is a noisemaker in the roof of the cockpit. Its alarm is described as sounding something like a rattlesnake but louder. It is made to sound as alarming as possible, since its purpose is to get the crew to do something. The other part of the stall-warning system, from which the over-all system gets its name of "stickshaker," is a mechanism for actually shaking the flight controls in the pilot's and copilot's hands. It produces something like the jerking felt in the steering wheel of a car when load exceeds power and the engine begins to lug, except that the stickshaker action is purposely more intense.

Commercial airline pilots say the stickshaker warning system should be heard and felt only during training flights. "The sound of the shaker," says the NTSB's chief investigator, William Lamb, "should trigger an immediate alarm" in the crew.[32]

The fact is that in the case of 553 it produced no apparent reaction whatsoever, though it came on twenty seconds before the crash and stayed on all the way to the end. The transcript of the well-oiled, well-cleaned CVR tape has it that two seconds after the stickshaker alarm went off, an unidentified voice in the cockpit spoke "two to three hurried words at very low amplitude and masked by noise of stickshaker" (p. 52): the stickshaker went off simultaneously with the word "execute" in Midway tower's abrupt command, "United five fifty-three, execute a missed approach." Six seconds later, Flight Officer Coble "was almost languid"[33] (NTSB report, Appendix F) in response to the tower's command to "make a left turn to a heading of— one eight zero, climb to two thousand." "Okay," Coble radios the tower, "left turn to one eight zero—left turn, okay?" A preliminary NTSB statement said, "The inquiry, which is far from concluded, has found that the final words of the plane crew showed no concern or alarm about the planned landing" and that "no vocal or other indication was received from United's three-man flight crew that an emergency had developed aboard. Instead, the voice of Second Officer E.J. Elder [the final NTSB report assigns this speech to Coble] was almost languid as he responded to Midway tower's instruction to 'take it around again, you are too close to the Aero-Commander ahead.'" (This last language, incidentally—about being too close to the Aero-Commander—is quoted here in the NTSB statement as though it were the actual language of the tower, but no such words can be found in the CVR transcript of Appendix F.)

The stickshaker warning signal that was not evidently noted by the crew of 553 was not noted by tower personnel either until (in the story Ruckelshaus told Reed) FBI Special Agent Robert E. Hartz "proceeded to the Midway Airport tower shortly after the crash to determine if tower personnel could shed any light as to the reason for the crash.... After listening to the [tower's] tapes, SA Hartz identified a sound as being that of the 'stall indicator on the aircraft. The FAA agreed that SA Hartz was right and immediately notified FAA headquarters at Washington, D.C."

How is this to be explained? What chance is there that the sound of the stickshaker was electronically imposed on the tapes by some such Startrekish infernal device as the "degaussing gun" with which Charles Colson once considered erasing the White House tapes from a position beyond the White House grounds? I do not know if an instrument that can do that exists, but we know for a fact that the CVR tape transcript published in the NTSB report gives not the slightest indication of any vocal or operational reaction by any of the three flight crew members to the activation of a warning system designed to be irresistible. That intrigues me. If I had been the NTSB and known that the tapes had been in the possession of the Nixon-Gray FBI and Chicago Streets and Sanitation and/or others for twenty hours, I should have inquired further into it. The NTSB did not. But then, Krogh and Spears and Butterfield were telling them to hurry.

To sum up this much, I am saying that we face serious technical doubts in six areas connected with the crash of this airplane:

1. The elevated levels of cyanide shown in the pilot's body and at least six others aboard the flight.
2. The fate of the flight recorders, including:
   a) the missing fourteen minutes of the FDR record;
   b) the oil-pollution and "special treatment" to which the CVR tape was subjected for four days and the garbled nature of its final input to the investigation;
   c) the irregular way these vital instruments came into the hands of the NTSB through Streets and Sanitation.
3. The parallel and common errors occurring simultaneously in the captain's altimeter system and the

> copilot's altimeter system, physically independent of
> each other.
> 4. The irregular utilization of the runways.
> 5. The malfunction of the Kedzie Outer Marker on an
>   apparently exclusive-to-553 basis, leading 553 a
>   quarter-mile astray inside a mile and a half.
> 6. The apparent failure of the crew to respond in any way
>   to the activation of the stickshaker stall-warning
>   system.

I am not saying that these technical doubts cannot
possibly be resolved in innocuous ways or that they
constitute by themselves a proof of the sabotage theory of
the plane crash. I am saying only that they have not yet been
resolved, innocuously or not. In the Appendix to this book, I
argue further that the NTSB's technical explanation of the
crash, a "pilot-error" theory, is based on assumptions
contradicted by the NTSB's own technical findings. What
remains to be seen is whether a more likely reconstruction of
the event can be put together.

The Sabotage Theory

I have mentioned Skolnick's bodyguard and companion
Alex Bottos. Following is an outline of the story he tells of
the Hunt crash.

In September 1971, Bottos and other Skolnick associates
quietly began investigating records of the Lake County
Coroner's Office in connection with a number of mysterious
deaths of people figuring in one way or another in court
actions pending in Hammond, Chicago, and Omaha against
former executives of Northern Natural Gas Company and
an assortment of public officials in Hammond and East
Chicago. This is the same Northern Natural whose lawyers
Blodgett and Krueger will bring the so-called Mitchell
documents aboard United 553 a year and a half later.

Northern Natural had been accused of a basic big-utilities bribery scheme involving the regional price structure and the seduction of pliant officials in a variety of levers-of-power positions. The indictment was originally to have been drawn in June of 1972. It was delayed by the stir created by new Skolnick-Bottos disclosures to the effect that the case had precipitated a string of cover-up crimes including murder and the falsification of death records. By September, when the indictment was finally brought, several more new victims of calculatedly accidental death had piled up, all key figures in the case, including an East Chicago councilman, a city clerk, a city controller, and the chiefs of the Lake County Mechanical and Incineration departments. Then a Lake County ambulance driver who had given critical testimony to the grand jury reversed himself and claimed that he actually had seen no evidence of wrongdoing. He later said members of the Gary Police Department had terrorized him into this reversal, but the case was never reopened.

During this same period, Bottos either came upon or was delivered to an opportunity to penetrate one of the functioning layers of a Lansky Syndicate-linked operation based in Chicago's North Side, the Joseph Sarelli mob, specialists in high-technology in-flight airplane robberies.

On August 17, 1972, the North Central Airlines' afternoon flight from Chicago to Milwaukee was carrying a bundle of Brinks securities valued between $25 and $50 million. At the beginning of the twenty-minute flight, one of the twenty-four passengers, a Sarelli technician, complained of airsickness and locked himself into one of the washrooms. Inside, he removed a certain hidden panel and thus gained access to the compartment where the valuables were carried. The thief was cool and ripped off only a tenth or a twentieth of what he had reached. The haul was $2.5 million in securities easily negotiable at almost any bank (said FBI Area 6 Burglary Commander Patrick Heraty) for up to 70 percent of their face value.[34]

Later in August, through a contact with a bar owner in an

industrial suburb of Chicago, Bottos stumbled on—or was
delivered to—the opportunity to fence some of these stolen
securities. Because Skolnick and his associates are on
constant guard against being set up, Bottos immediately
took this information to the FBI. The FBI brought him to
the Justice Department's Organized Crime Strike Force in
Chicago in the persons of federal prosecutor Sheldon
Davidson and Douglas Roller. They were impressed with his
story and quickly began building a Sarelli prosecution
around it.

Their strategy was for Bottos to stay inside the mob and
not surface until the actual moment of the trial itself. He was
holding in that pattern, the Sarelli indictment was being
drawn, and the case was poised to go into the arrest and
courtroom phase on December 8 when 553 crashed.

The crash had no immediately visible effect on the Sarelli
case. In January the arrests were made. The Strike Force
began to prepare Bottos for his courtroom role of key
witness.

But during the time of that preparation, Bottos's cover
still being on, he was approached again by the same contact
as before. In spite of the arrest of its boss and a key operative,
the Sarelli people were continuing their operations. They
had new booty to put on the market. Could Bottos help
again? This was how Bottos came to discover that the Sarelli
mob was connected somehow to the crash of 553. In
particular, Bottos told Davidson and Roller that the Sarelli
mob was talking about:

1. A large amount of cash it took from the belongings of
Dorothy Hunt. This was not merely the ten thousand dollars
the Chicago police said they found in her handbag, the
"Good luck F.S." roll of one-hundred dollar bills, but as
much as $2 million in securities, presumably White House
blackmail money. It was in her luggage.

2. In the possession of the Northern Natural Gas
Company lawyers Blodgett and Kreuger were the so-called
Mitchell documents. These documents related to another

case of big-time utilities bribery in 1969 involving Northern Natural's biggest competitor, El Paso Natural. El Paso was supposed to have turned over a large sum to the Nixon group in exchange for favorable antitrust treatment by the attorney general in their acquisition of Pacific Northwest Gas. Whoever possessed these papers could prove it, and in those days so long before the full flowering of Watergate, that made them valuable. Bottos's information was that the documents finally brought $5 million on the underworld market.[35]

As Bottos saw it, this meant that the Sarelli mob had something to do with the 553 crash. The way he pieced the story together, a group which Bottos occasionally follows General Haig in calling "the Sinister White House Force" was strongly desirous that several passengers aboard 553 not reach Chicago alive: Dorothy Hunt, because of her involvement in the blackmail operation; Michelle Clark of CBS, because she could put Dorothy Hunt on the big stage; Kreuger and Blodgett, because they had the Mitchell documents, part of the Huntmail. Because of the short time in which the technically difficult job had to be contracted for and carried out, the Sinister Force betook itself to the Syndicate group with the greatest technological capability of carrying it out, the Sarelli group. The hit group then employed a technique classically indicated for do-or-die situations, the use of double cutouts, i.e., of a number of independent hit-men each acting in ignorance of the others to get rid of the same people. The kill mechanisms employed overlapped and produced the overkill of 553. Bottos claimed also that elements of the FBI and other federal agencies were involved.

The 553 investigation was meantime heating up on its own burner and Skolnick and Bottos, pressing their views where they could, were demanding, but not winning, a chance to present evidence and arguments at the NTSB public hearings.

On March 1 Skolnick presented the NTSB Board of

Inquiry chairperson, Isobel Burgess, with a letter outlining his claims and requesting an opportunity to present them in a regular public session. Burgess rejected this petition on the spot without comment or explanation.

On March 2 Skolnick denounced the hearings as "a sham and a pretense" and filed suit against Burgess in the Cook County District Court.[36]

On March 5, Bottos was suddenly taken prisoner by federal marshalls acting on the order of another Chicago federal judge. Without formal charges, hearing, or trial, Bottos was spirited away for sixty days of "mental observation" at the Federal Medical Facility in Springfield, Missouri, a prison-hospital long reckoned by cognoscenti to be the main high-technology dungeon of the high-technology state, a "Clockwork Orange" subcellar. Bottos was released without harm after about forty days owing to the intervention of the Northwest Indiana Crime Commission, a citizens' watch agency connected with Skolnick. By this time, however, the Sarelli case had gone by and he had not given his testimony.

Bottos is convinced that it was to keep him from testifying in the Sarelli trial that he was taken off to Springfield. A point cited against him in the "mental observation" period, in fact, was that he had been pushing so irrationally hard to be heard as a witness in that case. Davidson and Roller wanted him out of the picture, he came to believe, because they were protecting the Sarelli-White House link in the 553 crash.

This was only obliquely denied by Peter Vaira, Davidson's successor as head of the Justice Department's Organized Crime Strike Force in Chicago. Vaira told me in a telephone interview in late September 1974 (before all the CIA stories broke), "We did not put Alex on the stand because once he gets started, God almighty, he'd be all over the place. He talks about the CIA, the Bay of Pigs, all kind of weird stuff. Says he knew Howard Hunt at the Bay of Pigs. We figured the Jury's got enough problems. So we used the agent who listened into Alex's conversations."

The result even so was convictions for Sarelli and Chiodo. But as Vaira added sadly, "Unfortunately for us, they both got quick probation. I'd have thought they'd have done time. They got a lot of money."

One of course lacks the means to evaluate the Skolnick-Bottos version of events from a distance; no doubt it is lurid and frightening. It goes beyond the image-frame of normal politics and so gives us an unwelcome, vertiginous sense of suddenly not understanding politics any more. The act imputed is indeed so monstrous that the imputation itself seems a monstrous act. Would this *Sinister Force* of ours really kill so many innocent people to protect itself? Would it actually do that? In the time of My Lai? Secret wars? Allende? Dallas? Memphis? Los Angeles? Laurel? Fred Hampton's bedroom in Chicago? The Audubon Ballroom in Harlem? The road to Selma? Jackson State? Kent State? Watergate?

8

McCord, Double Agent

McCord explicitly rejected the theory that he was a double
agent for the CIA or anyone else, or that anyone else at
Watergate was a double agent, in a face-to-face interview I
had with him on June 20, 1974, in a Boston hotelroom. The
following exchange took place:

QUESTION: May I ask you your reaction to Petersen's
remark about you yesterday?

MCCORD: What was his remark?

QUESTION: "The phoniest of the lot was McCord," he
said. "The phoniest! I wouldn't trust him from here to
there."

MCCORD: I want to respond to that. I have attacked
Mr. Petersen in Senate Watergate testimony before the
same committee he's testifying to, and I've said I believe
he's part of the cover-up, and I still believe it.... So I
think it's natural for Petersen and I to have some very
great differences. They're never going to be resolved,
because I think he's part of the conspiracy.

QUESTION: Was there another conspiracy that you
were part of?

MCCORD: What?

QUESTION: A conspiracy to expose the Plumbers at work?

MCCORD: The answer is flatly no. But the answer is also that, knowing what was going on, I had the greatest responsibility of my life to speak out about it. If I hadn't spoken out when I did, it may not have come out. It's my children's future.

McCord had actually taken up this question of CIA involvement in his Washington *Newsletter* of May-June 1974, which I had not seen at the time of our interview. In this he says that Colson "has recently been throwing up a smokescreen for Nixon trying to accuse the CIA of involvement in the Watergate operation. This ploy was long ago discredited—there is nothing to the story. Nixon has continuously tried to use it as a diversion—to confuse the public and to try to get the spotlight off him. It will not work.... Colson... is still covering for Nixon."

As McCord says, Nixon people had at that late moment still not abandoned the theory that Watergate happened because the CIA was out to get Nixon. In January 1974 Vice-President Ford told the agricats of the American Farm Bureau convened at Atlantic City that "a coalition of AFL-CIO, ADA and other powerful pressure groups is waging an all-out attack on Nixon," aiming "to crush Nixon and the policies for which he stands."[1] He might have been talking, of course, only about the attack everyone could see in the Eastern media and the Congress. But next month, in conservative Queens, Nixon aide Bruce Herschenson went further in implying that the plot must also have included the ambush of the Plumbers at Watergate by some conscious contrivance: "We witness an attempted coup d'etat of the U. S. Government through well-measured steps... by a non-elected coalition of power groups."[2]

But McCord was always prompt and unflinching in his denial of personal and CIA involvement in such doings. In his most considered language, the famous letter to Judge John Sirica of March 19, 1973, which set the final-stage collapse of Nixon in motion, McCord wrote: "The Watergate operation was not a CIA operation. The Cubans may have been misled by others into believing that it was a CIA operation. I know for a fact that it was not."

This passage actually is what startled me into wondering about McCord and led me to publish in the April 3, 1973, *Boston Phoenix* the first of a three-part essay roughly sketching out in early form the ideas advanced below about McCord's role in Watergate. In brief, as I put it then, "McCord . . . is a double agent from the Yankee kingdom of the Northeast who infiltrated the Nixon Cowboy group at its highest level and arranged for it to undergo the disaster of Watergate. . . ."

Turning McCord's denial upside down and taking it as a virtual confession may seem cranky, but look more closely at his language, especially in the passage we have quoted from the Sirica letter, in which he was writing as cogently as he could. How could McCord "know for a fact" that "the Watergate operation was not a CIA operation" unless he was at that time sufficiently privy to the doings of the CIA, notoriously multitudinous, to "know for a fact" that the Watergate job was not one of them, *in spite of* the presence of Howard Hunt, whom McCord knew as a lifelong CIA officer with a stylistic penchant for covert operations, *in spite of* the presence of the Cuban Bay of Pigs vets, all visibly connected to the CIA Operations wing, and *in spite of* the speedy and unquestioning service with which McCord saw the CIA greet Plumber Hunt's every request for technical support? In McCord's shoes, knowing only these things, how could you or I have known "for a fact" that the Watergate operation was *not* a CIA operation? Did it not have a palpably CIA-like motive to it, this alleged pursuit of the putative Castro connection to the McGovern Democrats? Who should be investigating such a connection if not the CIA? How could this "former CIA officer," supposedly two years retired at the time, know with such blunt certainty what no one at all but an active member of the CIA elite could possibly know under any conditions? And if McCord was at Watergate as an active officer of the CIA, then by all the definitions, the CIA was monumentally present in the Watergate operation, involved in it, even if in spite of itself, through the power of its officers to involve it, secretly entangled with the Plumbers even if only through a struggle against them.

There is a simple ambiguity to this term, "Watergate operation," which I sense the honest McCord plays on to keep from lying as he misleads us about this. If by *Watergate operation* we mean the break-in at the DNC, then we can completely agree with McCord. It was not the Helms CIA that conceived this and carried it out. It was the Nixon White House. It is only *incidental* in this respect that except for Liddy, formerly of the FBI, all the bagmen had Agency backgrounds and active Agency contacts. *Incidental.* These people will have been merely moonlighting.

But the *Watergate operation* can also mean the *arrest*, the capture of the Nixon men at their work in the DNC redhanded. It is in this sense that I say the Nixon people were right, Watergate was a plot and Nixon was undone by a component of the CIA he had not been able to bring under White House control. *Just as with Kennedy a decade before, only in political reverse.*

Thus, the theory we are about to pursue: that McCord was the pointman of an anti-Nixon plot formed within the CIA whose purpose was to disrupt a larger White House plot having police-state ramifications. This theory is based on analysis of five factors: (1) an indication that whispers of an impending anti-Nixon plot were circulating before Watergate; (2) the denunciation of McCord by his confederate Plumbers; (3) direct evidence of a still-concealed CIA involvement in Watergate; (4) intimations of Yankeehood in McCord's career; and (5) McCord's overall role in the development of Watergate as a public issue.

Preknowledge

The charge that Nixon's private Plumbers were set up for the bust at Watergate was made most explicitly by Robert Vesco. Vesco was interviewed late in March 1974 by CBS's Walter Cronkite in a remote video hookup, Cronkite in New York, Vesco in Costa Rica, where he sat in defiance of U.S. courts. The interview ran in part:

CRONKITE: Mr. Vesco, you said last January that six months before the Watergate break-in, the Democrats had come to you with a plan for impeachment of the President. Can you tell us what that plan was?

VESCO: Well, let me just correct you for a moment. I don't think I said that the Democrats came to me. I said a group did. I don't believe I identified who. The plan was essentially as I have stated previously, where they were going to attempt to get initial indictments of some high officials, using this as a launching board to get public opinion and—in their favor and using the press media to a great degree. The objective was to reverse the outcome of the public election.

CRONKITE: Why would they have come to you with this plan?

VESCO: Way before the Watergate affair got to the current stage that it's at, there were—there was a—an article that appeared in the *Washington Post* alluding to the fact that there may have been a secret cash contribution made to the Republican party. And it was that article that triggered their interest.

CRONKITE: And was the suggestion that you would help them finance their plans?

VESCO: No, it did not come to a suggestion to help finance their plan. They were more interested in gaining the information from the details that I may have, with respect to the contribution and certain other things, and to exploit those.

CRONKITE: Now are they getting to the President, Nixon, through Mitchell and Stans and you? Is that the point?

VESCO: That—that was the essential ingredients. And with the full knowledge that the grand jury process being what—that it—or being what it is, that with a limited amount of selected testimony and withholding, in effect, what might be countertestimony or cross-examination, they could achieve the indictments. Whether they actually got a conviction is somewhat irrelevant, just as it is in the case of Mitchell and Stans. If they can draw public opinion to a degree that they have, a conviction is almost irrelevant.

CRONKITE: Was the idea of the plot to neutralize the Administration in its—in its policies, or to secure Mr. Nixon's resignation, or to actually force the matter to impeachment?

VESCO: I do not believe that that was their intention, at that time, to impeach the President but—or to force him to resign. I would think that today, if they had any sense at all or any respect for the future of the United States, they would not pursue impeachment because that would solve nothing.

CRONKITE: How many people involved in this plot?

VESCO: I don't know how many were involved. I only dealt with three people.

CRONKITE: Were these people of importance?

VESCO: They were names that everyone would recognize.

CRONKITE: Were they officials? They hold elective office?

VESCO: No, but they had held extremely high posts in past administrations.[3]

In an interview with *New Times* writer Neil Cullinan about the same time,[4] Vesco did not mention this group of three (Ball? Harriman? Clifford?) but made other observations again indicative of his belief that the Watergate bust arose from a power struggle, was an intentionally created event, and that the motive of the plotters was to stop Nixon. Vesco paints his legal problems and explicitly those of other major (Cowboy) powers "Howard Hughes, H. Ross Perot, Armand Hammer and C. Arnhold Smith," as arising from "an attempt to shatter the mandate received by Richard Nixon in 1972 and to destroy in the process any large economic interests who support the President publicly."

Vesco continued in this faith, though we may think he garbled it ideologically when he said in December 1974, fighting expulsion from Costa Rica, "The forces that threatened me are the same politically that eliminated President Kennedy [?] and then President Nixon and want to eliminate all of Nixon's associates."[5]

Then there is the fact that Detective Lt. Carl Shoffler and his crew double-shifted for the first time ever the night of Watergate. Shoffler was the chief of the special district police team that arrested the Plumbers. He and McCord were prior acquaintances. Normally off duty at midnight, Shoffler departed from otherwise unbroken routine the night of Watergate and with his entire crew signed on for a second shift. He and the three other arresting officers were sitting parked a minute from the Watergate building when Watergate Security Guard Frank Wills found the second tape and called for police help. Did Shoffler know he had someone to arrest that night?

Denunciation

McCord's cohorts denounce him as follows:

Martinez, writing in the October 1974 *Harper's*, describes the first unsuccessful attempted break-in:

All seven of us in McCord's army walked up to the Watergate complex at midnight. McCord rang the bell, and a policeman came and let us in. We all signed the book, and McCord told the man we were going to the Federal Reserve office on the eighth floor. It all seemed funny to me. Eight men going to work at midnight. Imagine, we sat there talking to the police. Then we went up to the eighth floor, walked down to the sixth— and do you believe it, we couldn't open that door, and we had to cancel the operation.

I don't believe it has ever been told before, but all the time while we were working on the door, McCord would be going to the eighth floor. It is still a mystery to me what he was doing there. At 2:00 AM. I went up to tell him about our problems, and there I saw him talking to two guards. What happened? I thought. Have we been caught? No, he knew the guards. So I did not ask questions, but I thought maybe McCord was working there. It was the only thing that made sense. He was the one who led us to the place and it would not have made sense for us to have rooms at the Watergate and go on this operation if there was not someone there on the inside.

Barker, writing in the same magazine: "McCord had the highest rank of our group in jail then, and so we looked to him for leadership. But we didn't trust him totally, because McCord was very friendly with Alfred Baldwin, and to us Baldwin was the first informer. To me, Baldwin represented the very lowest form of a human being. McCord was also different from the Cuban group because he did not know about the Ellsberg mission." And later:

After the trial, we were waiting for the sentence in jail, and we were all under tremendous strain. And McCord told me one day: "Bernie, I am not going to jail for these people. If they think they are going to make a patsy out of me, they better think again."

So I said, "Jimmy, you are probably a lot more

intelligent than I am and you know a lot of things, but let's face it. In my way of thinking, you don't do this because of these people. You are going to have to live with McCord, and I am going to have to live with Barker. I don't do this because they are deserving or underserving, but because I have my own code."

Howard was very proud that we had stood up. We had played by the code and not broken. We took everything they had, and it was plenty. The judge sentenced me to forty-five years and the others to long terms, and he told us that our final sentence would be affected by what we told the grand jury and the Watergate Committee, by our cooperation. We were very worried, but we did not let out the Ellsberg thing. We were exposed by the very people who ordered us to do it—without their even being in jail.

Hunt, interviewed by *Time* correspondent David Beckwith: "There were just too many fishy things that occurred. What was the Mod Squad [Shoffler's group] doing out on the street some two or three hours after they were supposed to be off duty?" Again: "Baldwin was a very convenient fellow. He had a girlfriend at the Democratic National Committee, and he somehow came up with the floor plan of the DNC headquarters. He was never checked out at all—McCord got him off a job-wanted list of former FBI agents. He didn't do his job; he didn't alert anybody about the police until they were running around the DNC with their guns drawn." McCord was an "electronic hitchhiker who shouldn't have been allowed on our operation.... There were just too many things that went wrong for them all to be coincidence."[6]

Martha Mitchell, the true sibyl of Watergate, another kind of victim, for whose personal security McCord had been made responsible, told UPI's Helen Thomas immediately upon the publication of McCord's March 19 letter to Sirica: "My first thought was that McCord had been a double agent. In all faith, I never trusted McCord." Asked whom she thought he was working for, Mrs. Mitchell answered, "That is your problem. I don't know. It's a $64,000 question."[7]

The CIA Presence

The CIA was obviously involved much more deeply than it has so far admitted, whatever the *mode* and the *motive* of involvement turn out to be.

1. The CIA always knew what was happening with Hunt and followed the formation of the Plumbers from the beginning. Martinez says Hunt summoned him to the Bay of Pigs Monument in Miami, under the old Cuban invasion code name of *Eduardo*, on April 16, 1971, the tenth anniversary of the invasion. Martinez writes, "We talked about the liberation of Cuba, and he assured us that 'the whole thing is not over.' Then he started inquiring: 'What is Manolo doing?' Manolo was the leader of the Bay of Pigs operation. 'What is Roman doing?' Roman was the other leader. He said he wanted to meet with the old people. It was a good sign. We did not think he had come to Miami for nothing." Now a key revelation: "Generally I talk to my CIA case officer at least twice a week and maybe on the phone another two times. I told him right away that Eduardo was back in town, and that I had had lunch with him. Any time anyone from the CIA was in town my CO always asked me what he was doing. But he didn't ask me anything about Eduardo, which was strange." And later:

I made a point of telling my CO at our next meeting that Hunt was involved in some operations and that he was in the White House, even if they said he wasn't. After that the CIA chief of the Western Hemisphere asked me for breakfast at Howard Johnson's on Biscayne Boulevard, and he said he was interested in finding out about Howard Hunt's activities. He wanted me to write a report. He said I should write it in my own hand, in Spanish, and give it to my CO in a sealed envelope. Right away I went to see my CO. We are very close, my CO and I, and he told me that his father had once given him the advice that he should never put anything in writing that might do him any harm in the future. So I just wrote a cover story for the whole thing. I said that Hunt was in the Mullen Company and the White House and things like that that weren't important. What I really thought was that Hunt was checking to see if I could be trusted.[8]

2.   Helms was notified immediately of the arrest of McCord, actually within minutes. Equally interesting, at a concert intermission the very next night, he bragged about that to a gaggle of capital gossips, including *Washington Star* columnist Carl Rowan, who reported the story. Helms volunteered that the duty officer had awakened him at 4:00 A.M. with a full report.

Andrew St. George's description of this, also based on privileged information, runs as follows:

Both the CIA and the FBI had long known, of course, about the existence of the Hunt-Liddy team. The CIA had infiltrated it with a confidential informant just as if Hunt and Liddy had been foreign diplomats, and the informant, an old Company operative named Eugenio Martinez [in my view, of course, St. George is wrong about Martinez but right about the infiltrator], code-named "Rolando," who had reported in advance on the Watergate project, was in fact at that moment himself under arrest for his part in the break-in. "Ah, well," Helms said. "They finally did it." He chatted for a few moments with the young watch officer, who said it was "a pity about McCord and some of those guys." "Well, yes," Helms said. "A pity about the President too, you know. They really blew it. The sad thing is, we all think 'That's the end of it,' and it may be just the beginning of something worse. If the White House tries to ring me through central, don't switch it out here, just tell them you reported McCord's arrest already, and I was *very* surprised."[9]

3. The CIA destroyed documents and tapes bearing on McCord and the Plumbers in defiance of Senator Mansfield's written appeal that it retain all Watergate "evidentiary materials." One week after the Mansfield letter, sometime in the week of January 22, 1973, just before Nixon pushed Helms out of the CIA and exiled him to Iran, Helms ordered the destruction of all tapes in the CIA's central taping facility. The CIA said there was nothing irregular in this, but this was nevertheless the first time the CIA had destroyed all its tapes at once. Its former practice was to destroy tapes only as they become ten years old.[10]

Senator Baker's investigation also discovered in the files of the CIA's Office of Security a reference to a five-inch reel of tape labeled, "McCord Incident/18-19 June 1972." The Baker report notes, "It is not known what is contained in this tape, but its importance is obvious." The CIA has refused to make this tape available.[11]

Finally, as the eleventh and last item in its list of "miscellaneous recommendations," the Baker report reads, "Michael Mastrovito of the Secret Service should be interviewed concerning his Agency communications of June 17, 1972. Agency documents indicate that Mastrovito agreed to downplay McCord's Agency employment; that Mastrovito was being pressured for information by a Democratic state chairman; and that Mastrovito was advised by the CIA that the Agency was concerned with McCord's emotional stability prior to his retirement."[12]

4. The CIA sent an agent to McCord's house, one Lee Pennington, to destroy something immediately after the arrest, then clumsily tried to cover up the fact that it had

done so. For all his public volubility, McCord has never accounted for this, the so-called "Pennington Matter." Senator Baker's investigation (reads the report)

> clearly shows that the CIA had in its possession, as early as June of 1972, information that one of their paid operatives, Lee R. Pennington, Jr., had entered the James McCord residence shortly after the Watergate break-in and destroyed documents which might show a link between McCord and the CIA. This information was not made available to this committee or anyone else outside the CIA until February 22, 1974, when a memorandum by [Howard Osborn] the then Director of Security [McCord's old job] was furnished to this committee.
>
> The evidence further shows that in August of 1972, when the FBI made inquiry about a "Pennington" the Agency response was to furnish information about a former employee with a similar name.

Baker details his discovery that CIA Director of Security Osborn ordered Pennington material removed from CIA Watergate files before the files were handed over to Congressional investigating committees, and points out that the information on Pennington came to light in the first place "only as a result of the position taken by a staff employee of the Personnel Security Division." This staff employee "was so concerned that the documentary evidence of the Pennington information would be destroyed by others in the CIA that he and a co-employee copied the relevant memoranda and placed them in their respective personal safes." An unsung Ellsberg, this staff employee. The "relevant memoranda" referred to appear to be a single internal CIA report by Paul Gaynor on the results of agent Pennington's trip to the McCord house several hours after the Watergate arrest. As we shall see, Gaynor remained in close contact with the McCord operation from then on, at least up to the March 19 letter and the opening of the Sirica phase.

One or both of these anonymous CIA "staff employees" (intelligence analysts?) balked at going along with a CIA letter notifying the Ervin Committee that it had seen everything the CIA had to show on the question. According to a Jim Squires story appearing in the *Boston Globe*, March 26, 1974, Gaynor's report had been kept secret over a year by Security Director Osborn, who "took an early retirement last month." Paul Gaynor also "retired from the Agency last year." Heads falling in the forest—do they make any sound. "Our investigation in this area," continues the Baker report,

> also produced the fact that, contrary to previous CIA assertions, the CIA conducted a vigorous in-house investigation of the Watergate matter, starting almost immediately after the break-in. As one member of the Security Research Staff stated, they were in a state of "panic." In November and December of 1972 [blackmail-Hunt crash period] the Executive Officer to Director of Security was specially assigned to then Executive Director/Comptroller Colby to conduct a very secretive investigation of several Watergate-related matters.

This executive officer "was instructed to keep no copies of his findings and to make no records."

There is still no telling what the Pennington-Gaynor operation was really about. Says the Baker report:

> Less clear than the aforementioned efforts to suppress the Pennington information is an understanding of Pennington's actual role or non-role in the destruction of documents at the McCord home shortly after the Watergate break-in. Pennington has testified that he did not go to the McCord home for the purpose of searching for or destroying CIA-related documents,

but does acknowledge witnessing the destruction of documents by Mrs. McCord and others. [Others?] It is clear from the testimony of others [the same others?] that the CIA received more information, evidently from Pennington, indicating more active participation by operative Pennington.

Pennington, a CIA "old boy" died of reportedly natural causes at age seventy-two in 1974.

5. Immediately after the arrests, the CIA closed the Singapore and Amsterdam offices of one of its cover organizations, the Washington "PR firm" of Robert Mullen and Company. We run across this outfit everywhere. It takes over the Toolco account in the collapse of Maheu, sets up Hunt the day after he "retires" from the CIA, has ties to ITT, the GOP, CREEP, and the Democratic party, and gets up to its neck in Watergate. The Baker report reads:

On July 10, 1972 [Mullen President Robert] Bennett reported detailed knowledge of the Watergate incident to his CIA case officer [Martin Lukasky]. The case officer's report of this meeting was hand-written and carried to Director Helms on or before July 14, 1972, in this form because of the sensitivity of the information. It revealed that Bennett had established a "back door entry" to E.B. [Edward Bennett] Williams in order to "kill off" revelations of the Agency's relationship with the Mullen and Company in the course of the DNC lawsuit. He agreed to check with the CIA prior to contacting Williams. Our staff has confirmed that Bennett did funnel information to Williams via attorney Hobart Taylor and that this information was more extensive than the information Bennett had previously given the Grand Jury. The CIA has acknowledged paying one half of Bennett's attorney's fee for his Grand Jury appearance.

Baker discovered "no indication that these facts were

disclosed to the FBI."[13]

The report goes on to suggest still deeper intrigues:

A memorandum drafted by the Chief of the Central Cover Staff, CIA, on March 1, 1973, notes that Bennett felt he could handle the Ervin committee if the Agency could handle Hunt. Bennett even stated that he had a friend who had intervened with Ervin on the matter. The same memorandum suggests that Bennett took relish in implicating Colson in Hunt's activities in the press while protecting the Agency at the same time. It is further noted that Bennett was feeding stories to Bob Woodward who was "suitably grateful"; that he [Woodward] was making no attribution to Bennett; and that he was protecting Bennett and Mullen and Company.[14]

Was Sam Ervin himself compromised? Was Bob Bennett Deep Throat? Moral: The sense of politics implied by the double agent theory of McCord *understates* the degree of clandestine involution actually present in American politics.

In sum, the Baker report tells us that CIA knowledge of the White House Plumbers' operations long preceded the Plumbers' arrest at Watergate on June 17. The CIA was actually aware of the Plumbers from early on and well informed on White House strategy for putting them to use. The CIA's postarrest responses were prompt and strong. These responses centered immediately on protecting some then-current relationship between itself and McCord.

Certainly there are other departments of the CIA-Watergate connection not directly involving McCord (e.g., Hunt, Martinez). I am not trying to inflate the role of McCord out of proportion. Yet the shadows around McCord's role are centrally and decisively what Baker set forth to dispel, and his investigation only left them all the deeper.

McCord's true purpose was to my knowledge challenged first by myself in the April 1973 *Phoenix* articles already alluded to (see also *Esquire*, November 1973), then by Martha Mitchell, then in June 1973 by three British journalists in the (London) *Sunday Times* (see below), and then in Fall 1973, and in a most complete fashion, by the conservative and liberal CIA experts to whom we have already adverted, Copeland and St. George (chapter 2).

Reads the Baker report, "In the September 14, 1973 issue of the *National Review*, Miles Copeland wrote an article entitled 'The Unmentionable Uses of a CIA,' suggesting that McCord led the Watergate burglars into a trap. In the November 1973 issue of *Harper's* magazine, an article entitled 'The Cold War Comes Home,' by Andrew St. George, indicated strongly that former CIA Director Helms had prior knowledge of the Watergate break-in."

The report goes on to say that the two writers were questioned, at Senator Baker's insistence, by Senator Symington and the Senate Armed Services Committee, and that this committee "heard testimony from CIA officials that the Agency was not knowledgeable of the Watergate break-in before it occurred; had not led the burglars into a trap; and that the magazine allegations had no basis in fact."

The Baker report points out that on the St. George charges, Symington did not even bother to collect ritual disclaimers. It then plunges into an account of the findings of its understaffed, underfinanced, hurried investigation of this most difficult and demanding substream of Watergate—the CIA connection. The report ends with its original questions not having been answered and with a substantial claim of having established, in spite of all its technical difficulties, positive evidence of some still hidden Watergate-CIA link around McCord.

McCord's Past

McCord's biography sets him apart and indicates a general Yankee orientation, just as his high rank in the CIA, the special and critical nature of his capabilities, his career trajectory and position at the time of "retirement" in 1970, and other considerations as will emerge, all weigh against the "retired CIA technician," bungling-Nixon-agent version of his person and his big adventure.

This already comes through in the schematic resume supplied by the CIA:

JAMES McCORD
BORN: January 26, 1924, Waurika, Oklahoma.
HIGH SCHOOL: McLean and Electra, Texas.
EDUCATION: Master of Science, George Washington University, 1965. Bachelor of Business Administration, University of Texas, 1949. Graduate class of 1965 [sic] Air War College.
1942-43: FBI, Washington and New York. Radio intelligence duties.
1943-45: US Army Air Corps officer.
1948-51: FBI special agent, San Diego and San Francisco, California.
1951-70: CIA, chief Physical Security Division, Office of Security. From 1962-64, CIA senior security officer in Europe.
MILITARY: Lieutenant Colonel, USAF Reserve. Former commander National Wartime Information and Security Programme and detachment, Washington USAFR.
CIVIC AND OTHER: Member National Legislative Affairs Board, National Association for Retarded Children and member board of directors, Cerebral Palsy Association and Montgomery County Workshops for the Handicapped, Montgomery County, Maryland.
AWARDS: Distinguished Service Award for outstanding performance of duty from director of CIA. Retired August 1970 after 25 years Federal service.

This skeleton begins to take on flesh in the following recapitulation, the curriculum vitae McCord prepared for promotional purposes at a moment in mid-1973 when the book he subsequently published privately as *A Piece of Tape* was still to be called *View From the Watergate* and to be published by Exposition Press, a vanity publishing house in New Jersey. Exposition's president, Edward Uhlan, courteously supplied my request for a copy of this McCord document. Uhlan had made a few slight editorial improvements in McCord's single-spaced typescript, which for purposes of record I remove in the following text. The most important of these was his deletion of McCord's opening sentence:

The work of James W. McCord, Jr., has always been in the national interest.

Born in 1924, he has spent a lifetime in intelligence and security. In 1942-43 he worked in a highly-secret wartime FBI intelligence operation in which he and FBI Agent Jos Parsons set up and operated next door to the Russian Spy Chief in the United States, whose network included figures later named as spies by Whitaker Chambers and Elizabeth Bentley. The story of this and a related program against Russian spies in which McCord later worked while with CIA has never been told. In the early 1940's McCord was also a member of a special wartime FBI intelligence operation against German Spies in the US and South America. In 1943-45 McCord was a flying officer with the Army Air Corps and trained for B-29 duties in the Far East.

Following assignments as a Special Agent with the FBI on the West Coast in 1948-51, McCord joined CIA and for the next 19 years was an officer there where his duties included liaison with certain Senior European Security officials on Soviet and Intelligence and Security matters in the 1950s and 1960s. After a tour in the early 1960s as the Senior CIA Security Official in Europe he returned to the United States where [he] directed the Technical Security and later the Physical

Security activities for CIA. In the late 1960s he cooperated overseas with British Intelligence officials on a highly secret operation involving the security of the British government.

McCord retired in 1970 after 25 years Federal service. In August 1970 he received the Distinguished Service Award from CIA for outstanding performance of duties while with CIA.

McCord has a Masters of Science degree in International Affairs and has done further advanced work in Red Chinese military and government affairs. A graduate of the Air War College, as a Reserve Lt. Colonel, he commanded a Special Air Force Reserve Detachment in a Joint AF-Army-Navy unit set up to plan and implement a National Wartime Information and Security Program, with McCord's assignment that of developing highly sensitive technical operations to detect wartime spies operating in microdot, secret inks and other esoteric spy communications fields.

Regarded as a leading U.S. authority on security and investigative work, he has his own company, Security International, organized to provide security systems and services in the U.S. and abroad. These services cover the complete range of security from the design of a system for a large corporation or a small business, including guard services, alarms, CTV, audiocountermeasures, identification and badging systems for foreign dignitaries and VIPs overseas and the training of personnel to operate such systems. The address of his company is Security International, Maryland National Center, Rockville Md. 00850 Telephone 301/340-8110.

McCord brings a unique insight into U.S. and international government and politics. Working inside the FBI for 4 years and the CIA for 19, he also worked inside the Republican National Committee and the Committee to ReElect the President as their Chiefs of Security in 1971 and 1972. Presumably he also has some unique insight into the operations of the Democratic National Committee, and the Democratic Party, based on the story he has to tell in his book, *View From the Watergate*, as a member of the 5-man team arrested in the Democratic National Headquarters in Washington D.C. on June 17, 1972.

His family includes a wife Sarah Ruth, a son Michael who is a Junior at the Air Force Academy, a daughter Anne at the University of Maryland and a second daughter at Kennedy Institute. His hobbies include genealogy and he has a second company, Bicentennial Research International, which traces genealogical lines in the U.S. and overseas.

His interest in this field grew over the years in tracing his own ancestors who came over from Northern Ireland in 1719 and were frontiersmen before statehood in each of the states of Pennsylvania, North Carolina, Tennessee, Alabama and Oklahoma and Arkansas. Over 50 of the McCords fought with the American Revolution. Several were at Valley Forge with Washington. The family line in Scotland goes back to a Clan Chieftain under one of the three Stuart Clans of the Royal Family of Scotland. Family histories describe the McCords as "men of daring, cool under fire, with a love of country and of religion, quiet of demeanor, who throughout history have taken on any odds in defense of principle." McCord has taken on the highest odds of all, the Presidency, in his almost single-handed battle to establish the truth behind the Watergate operation of June 17, 1972.

Contrast this picture with the early impression that McCord was a low-level spook with some technical competence in bugging. As the British authors Lewis Chester, Cal McCrystal, and Stephen Aris observed in their *Sunday Times* (London) piece of June 3, 1973,

* * *

...under the Senate's diligent scrutiny, McCord has shown an intellectual capacity that belies this image. A memorandum which McCord wrote for his lawyer was described by one Senator with legal training as "a remarkable legal argument." Questioned at an ideological level, McCord said that the consequences of White House pressure on the CIA "smacked of the situation which Hitler's intelligence chiefs found themselves in in the 1930s." One witness, an ex-policeman, Anthony Ulasewicz, thought McCord must be "one of the best wiremen in the business."... A former number two man in the CIA described McCord's job as "highly responsible, requiring great accuracy with details." Allen Dulles, a former CIA chief, is said to have described him as "my top man." McCord knew and liked Dick Helms, another professional who rose to the top of the CIA until Nixon effectively banished him to the ambassadorship of Iran earlier this year.

The fact that McCord was indeed a superspy of extensive operational and technical competence is already established by the detail of McCord's assignment in Europe (NATO senior security official) and his later responsibility for security at Langley CIA headquarters. The existential quality of this fact is suggested by a story recounted by McCord's professional friend, retired Air Force Lt. Col. Fletcher Prouty. About a year before the U-2 of Gary Powers came down in Russia, wrecking the Paris Summit of Eisenhower and Khrushchev, a C-118 fitted out as the airborne command station of CIA Director Allen Dulles, freighted with footlockers filled with sensitive national security documents, missed a turn at some Turkish mountain and drifted by error into Russian airspace, where it was forced to land by MIG interceptors. The crew and plane were of course detained in Russia while the Russians conducted negotiations with the United States. During this period, the pilot was allowed a fishing excursion to a mountain lake of a remote province, where the Russians found a high-school English teacher to serve as the pilot's host and guide. When the crew was returned to the United States, a team of top intelligence specialists was assembled for the debriefing. McCord was among these specialists. On the basis of the pilot's descriptions, McCord identified the high-school English teacher as one of the KGB's top intelligence specialists and was able to show the pilot a photo. That was not the work of a mere bagman. He is said to have "retired" from the CIA in August 1970 when he was only 46.

He spent a year traveling the world, according to the *Sunday Times* investigators, trying "to establish a desperately unprofitable security business." Then suddenly he emerged as security chief to CREEP. With that, the Watergate egg is inseminated. The *Times* team report that he was at once a big hit at CREEP—for his electronics skill, his management ability, his intelligence, and his bearing. Mitchell entrusted his and his family's personal security to him. "He was drawn into the highest counsels of the organization. He could advise on the costings of the bugging equipment before Liddy's presentations to Mitchell. He became the CRP's top intelligence (as well as security) expert and personal liaison between CRP and the Justice Department's Internal Security Division. He was inside Nixon's machine."

Note the absence in McCord's visible record of a Cuba period. There is no apparent McCord link to the Bay of Pigs group until the Plumbers period. He is the only "former" CIA man at Watergate of whom this is true.

Note second that McCord's rise and standing in the CIA, his place in career, his relatively youthful age, and his otherwise solid claim to be living a dedicated life of service are inconsonant with his apparent retirement in 1970. Imagine. He stood at the highest levels of CIA command.

The conflict between the Agency and the White House was going into a new intense phase. The White House, as McCord has himself testified, was trying to extend its control over the previously autonomous Agency "intelligence assessments and estimates" function—over the reputedly more liberal Intelligence Division. He was in the prime of his life and at the peak of his career at a moment just before his beloved Agency was to be plunged into its long-building confrontation with Nixon. What a moment for a Clan Chieftain to quit the field! What a time for so doughty a partisan to show up gainfully employed by the very menace his Agency comrades most feared, the secret Nixon political police!

Note third that the strength of character and intelligence McCord made evident in his performances before Ervin, Sirica, and the media are inconsistent with his outwardly weak-willed inability to accept, as could all his confederates, the dictates of an undercover agent's code in protecting the secret client. Remember that at first the reason given for his decision to tell Sirica all he knew was that he was frightened by the prospect of a long prison term and felt abandoned by the White House and the other Plumbers. Only later and bit by bit did it materialize that, no, McCord told on the Plumbers and Nixon because he was angry at them for trying to blame the CIA.

The Break-in

Without McCord's direct advice against the instincts of all the other Plumbers, the second Watergate-DNC break-in, the fatal one, would not have taken place. Without his naive-seeming technical blunder of the taped door, the arrest would not have been made. Without his relentless agitations in the aftermath and refusal to accept CREEP discipline, the "scandal" would not have become the crisis that brought Nixon down.

These claims bear on two sets of events. Here we consider the mechanics of the actual arrest. In the following item, we will take up the second, McCord's activities after the arrest. Collecting testimony:

HUNT: The decision to re-tape and go back in was McCord's.[15]

BARKER: So we said, well, the tape has been discovered. We'll have to abort the operation. But McCord thought we should go anyway. He went upstairs and tried to convince Liddy and Eduardo [Hunt] that we should go ahead. Before making a decision, they went to the other room; I believe they made a phone call, and Eduardo told us to go ahead.

McCord did not come in with us. He said he had to go someplace. We never knew where he was going. Anyway, he was not with us, so when Virgilio picked the locks to let us in, we put tape on the doors for him and went upstairs. Five minutes later McCord came in, and I asked him right away: "Did you remove the tapes?" He said, "Yes, I did."

But he did not, because the tape was later found by the police. Once inside, McCord told Barker to turn off his walkie-talkie. He said there was too much static. So we were there without communications. Soon we started hearing noises. People going up and down. McCord said it was only the people checking, like before, but then there was running and men shouting, "Come out with your hands up or we will shoot!" and things like that.

There was no way out. We were caught . . . . I thought right away it was a set-up or something like that because it was so easy the first time. We all had that feeling. They took our keys and found the identification in the briefcase Eduardo had left in our room."[16]

* * *

Acting FBI Director Patrick Gray told Senator Gurney that "the replacement of the tapes on the Watergate doorlocks" made the FBI consider a double-agent theory. Gurney asked if the matter was investigated and Gray answered, "Can't tell you a thing."[17]

Minority Counsel Fred Thompson to Barker: "Was it McCord who urged you to go ahead despite the fact of discovering that obviously someone had untaped the doors?"

Barker: "Mr. McCord was of this opinion .... I was against entry at that time and, to the best of my recollection, so was Mr. Hunt, my superior. To the best of my knowledge, Mr. Martinez asked if he had taken off the tapes and Mr. McCord replied yes."[18]

Let us spell out the story of these fragments. McCord went inside the Watergate when the doors were still open and put a piece of tape across the latch on a certain door so that it would not lock. He placed the tape horizontally, so that it showed outside the door.[19] When the entry team arrived at this door hours later expecting to find it thus taped open, they found it shut. The tape had been removed; therefore it must have been discovered, which must have aroused suspicion. The Plumbers then went back across the street to their Howard Johnson's nest to discuss what to do. Everyone but McCord was of a mind to postpone the operation. McCord insisted that they go in anyway and ordered Martinez to pick the lock. Hunt and the Cubans reluctantly went to do so while McCord went someplace else for five minutes, it is not known where or for what purpose. The Cubans left tape on the door for McCord on a faith that one of the world's great intelligence specialists would have presence of mind enough, after all that had happened, to remove the tape behind him so as not to arouse still further the guard certain to return on rounds. McCord neglected to remove this tape when he followed along from his mysterious solitude five minutes later. Martinez was bright enough to ask McCord explicitly if he had remembered the tape, and McCord answered explicitly that he had. Security guard Wills came by, found the door taped open a second time, and notified the police. McCord's acquaintance, Shoffler, was standing by a minute away with his special police unit. He responded instantly.

This sequence of seeming blunders from an evidently accomplished professional that tended uniformly toward a single disastrous result is what aroused one's curiosity about McCord to begin with. The curiosity was not put to rest by the additional incongruity of such accidental details as the early role of McCord's hired man Baldwin in the exposure of the Plumbers' basic relationship to the CRP and the White House.

Nor was it weakened by the unfolding spectacle of McCord's post-Watergate role.

After the Break-in

Here is an outline of McCord's activity in the post-Watergate period: *First*, he refused to go along with, and thereby obstructed, a White House plan to make the CIA the Watergate scapegoat. *Second*, he set up intensive covert contacts with a CIA-Intelligence agent and opened a direct line to Helms, whom he apprised immediately of the White House's every Watergate move as he knew it from the lawyers. *Third*, he mounted an intense campaign of his own within the Nixon apparatus to intimidate its agents. *Fourth*, he prepared and carried out (brilliantly) the whole larger public-education phase of Watergate by means of his thunderbolt of March 19, the letter to Sirica, and his testimony before Ervin. *Fifth*, at a critical moment, he formed a key relationship with an anti-Nixon attorney.

Let us take these up one by one.

1. *McCord Alone Scotched Nixon's CIA Strategy*

Jack Caulfield met McCord at the second overlook in July 1972 and speaking for the president offered McCord a guarantee of executive clemency, no more than eleven months in prison, plus generous expense allotments, essentially the same offer Alch delivered again that October. But McCord would not consent to the plan of blaming the Watergate break-in on the CIA. Alone among the Plumbers McCord declined to go along with this deal. Only because of McCord's solitary and unanticipated resistance did Watergate escalate to become a White House crisis rather than deflate to the scale of mere CIA scandal.

Look how it might have turned out had McCord gone along with Nixon's "CIA-dunnit" theory. First, the story would have been drifted out that the CIA had found evidence of Castro money flowing to the McGovern campaign through some conduit buried in the Democratic party. It would have been let out that Castro had given the Democrats and McGovern a detailed itemization of all CIA-backed activity against the Cuban revolution. Yes, Nixon might have said, the CIA was operating outside its legal limit in searching for the threads of this suspected relationship inside domestic space, in the DNC, but it was after all in key respects a legitimately foreign intrigue (Nixon might have said), so that one could at least follow the CIA's reasoning.

Nixon could thus have denounced in fine patriotic colors the motive of the overzealous CIA wrongdoers while at the same time preserving and amplifying the anti-McGovern effects of their activity. "What? McGovern was being manipulated by Castro?" Round One for Nixon. In Round Two, leading now with his left, Nixon could explain that the CIA was nevertheless out of bounds. Helms would have to go. There would have to be a big purge. Indeed, while Nixon clung to power, Helms did go, there was a great purge of the Intelligence side of the CIA, the cooperative Schlesinger and

Colby did come to power. In this purge, of course, had it
continued, Nixon would further have rid the CIA of its anti-
Nixon people and more deeply penetrated it with his own.

There is indeed no way this scheme could *not* have
worked if McCord had played along. There was no way in
the world for the CIA to demonstrate that Hunt, McCord,
and the Cubans were *not* CIA agents. They patently *were*
CIA agents. How could an operation carried out by so many
CIA agents *not* be a CIA operation? Nixon would have
delivered a fatal blow to the McGovern campaign, knocked
out his biggest enemies in the CIA Intelligence Division and
established a monopoly on all national intelligence estimates, acquitted himself personally and politically from all
responsibility, and probably acquired as well a popular
mandate to carry the war against national insecurity to new
points of compass. Back to the Bay of Pigs! It almost tempts
one to fancy that this was the way the plot was hatched to
run, after all, that the White House set up its own Plumbers
at Watergate to look like a CIA team in order to smear
McGovern, get rid of Helms, purge the Yankees out of CIA-
Intelligence, cook up a grand Red scare and smell like a rose.
In any case, *only McCord's refusal kept the blame-the-CIA
plan from working*.

2. *Post-Watergate McCord-CIA Contact Was Intense*

On July 29, McCord wrote a letter to Helms (marked
"personal" in McCord's hand on the envelope), reading as
follows:

> A few interesting bits of information you will be
> interested in:
> 1. When Paul O'Brian was engaged by the
> Committee [to Re-Elect the President] as their lawyer in
> this case, the Committee told him that the operation

was a CIA operation. He says he did not learn otherwise until one of the defendants told him the facts, and says he blew up over it.

2.   The prosecution, under Silbert, had of course begun that line with Judge Belson from the very first hearing. Although never coming right out and saying so, it was inferred by him in every hearing that I witnessed, and learned that he did so with the other defendants in the bond hearings.

3.   Now that the CIA story has not held water, or more correctly [get this:], will not be allowed to stand by CIA, the prosecution is now planning to charge that Liddy stole the money for the operation from the Committee and in turn bribed McCord and Hunt to participate, giving McCord a $16,000 bribe on one occasion witnessed by a participant who has turned state's evidence.

Rest assured that I will not be a patsy to this latest ploy. They will have to dream up a better one than this latest story. The state's witness cannot only be impeached on the stand, but can be charged with perjury before the grand jury, and to federal officials (the FBI), if he has made such a statement to them about me. If Committee officials have alleged that Liddy stole the funds for the operation from the Committee, they also have perjured themselves and are subject to such prosecution. Liddy may sit still for this; I will *not*.

Recent leaks this week by the prosecution and/or the FBI to the New York TIMES still are trying to infer that this was a CIA operation. The frequent use of "ex-CIA agent" in other articles are further evidence. They still haven't given up on this tactic.

The letter concludes with two paragraphs on Washington juries. It is signed, "Jim."[20]

On December 22, 1972, McCord sent the following letter to CIA agent Paul Gaynor at his home in Arlington,

Virginia. Gaynor, recall, was already involved with the McCord operation at the time of the arrests. He researched and authored the suppressed report on the Pennington burnings at the McCord house the day after Watergate.

Dear Paul—

There is tremendous pressure to put the operation off on the company. Don't worry about me no matter what you hear.

The way to head this off is to flood the newspapers with leaks or anonymous letters that the plan is to place the blame on the company [i.e., CIA] for the operation. This is of *immediate* importance because the plans are in the formative stage now, and can be preempted now, if the story is leaked so that the press is alerted. It may not be headed off later when it is too late.

The fix is on one of the police officers in the MPD intelligence department, to testify that one of the defendants told him the defendants were company people and it was a company operation. He has probably been promised a promotion for changing his story to this effect. Be careful in your dealing with them. I will do all I can to keep you informed. Keep the faith.[21]

He writes Gaynor again the following day, December 23, 1972. He first gives him a list of action items around Nixon taps on the telephone. He concludes with an item 3:

"I have the evidence of the involvement of Mitchell and others, sufficient to convince a jury, the Congress and the Press.

"The maximum effect is accomplished if everything is held until the trial has just started, and then surface everything at once—showing beyond any doubt the hypocrisy of the whole group and how fixed the whole federal criminal justice system has now become."[22]

This last paragraph gives us a good glimpse into McCord's coordinating function, of McCord the tactician of

Watergate aiming for "the maximum effect," the maximum damage to Nixon. The letter to Sirica of March 19, 1973, already exists in McCord's scenario at least as early as December 23, 1972. Already Alch is going to be fired, the anti-Nixon Fensterwald is going to come on, the letter to Sirica is going to be sent, Nixon is going to fall. And to bring this result about, McCord is in immediate post-Watergate communication with the highest level of the CIA, not just as an informant, but indeed as the tactical commander of the over-all operation, the tactician of the Watergate plot.

Further indication of such a relationship between McCord and the CIA comes in his letter of December 29 to Gaynor, really a progress report.

Notes.

I am convinced that the fix is on Gerry Alch and Bernie Shankman [denied by both]. Too many things don't add up, namely:

1. Their persistence in wanting to let Gerry Alch call Helms to testify and to call Vic Marchetti "to lay the background re custom and tradition of CIA along this line."

Somehow the fix is on Marchetti or he is a party to this ploy in some other way. They are too persistent about it.

2. Their persistence in trying to find out how much I know about Mitchell's involvement, and the negative type approach, "well he didn't really talk to you about it did he."

3. Failure to really debrief me on my whole participation and knowledge. None has really occurred to date, and an absence of communications has been particularly noticeable from Nov. 7-Dec. 21st. The presence of what appears to be a desire to let time run out before the trial starts.

4. The fixed police officer's report—that of Gary Bittenbender (not Carl as previously reported). The

impact of his statement is one which can be read two ways, giving them a fall-back position. 1) That I claimed to him at the time of arraignment that this was a CIA operation, and b) that this was an operation which we—the Cubans and I—cooked up on our own. No such statements were made. They are absolutely false.

Bittenbender incidentally has a twin brother as I recall; I have never met him to my knowledge. I assume he also works in the intelligence division.

5.   The general focus and impact of everything that is happening is that:

a.   They are trying to put the blame for the operation on CIA and/or McCord, or both, shifting the focus away from the White House (Liddy and Hunt).

b.   The U.S. Attorney has blown the case against the Cubans by visiting personally their employers in Miami, affecting their ability to make a living, causing Frank Sturgis's employer to fire him.

c.   They appear willing to get McCord off but only on the condition that he place the blame for the operation on CIA—or take the blame himself. No go.

d.   The wording of questions such as "You really don't want Helms to be called because you don't want to be a stoolie against CIA do you." These leave no doubt whatever.

6.   Today I visited Bernard Shankman [Alch's local rep in the case] and gave the attached letter to him, telling him I planned to release it to the press today and get a new attorney. He asked that I hold off until Tuesday morning next to talk with Alch before doing anything. I may or may not wait past Saturday Dec. 30, 1972.[23]

The letter releasing Alch is included in the following category of McCord exploits against Nixon. We note the above documents (to which could be added other similar messages to Gaynor in January) as concrete proof that

McCord was in secret contact with a Helms-centered, anti-Nixon group in the CIA from the time of Watergate onward and that he consistently operated iñ that relationship as a tactician with an offensive purpose, the scuttling of Nixon.

3. McCord Campaigned for CREEP-Nixon Capitulation

In his letter of July 29 to his CREEP lawyer Gerald Alch, McCord first outlined his rejection of the White House plan to scapegoat the CIA. Half a year's struggle fending off bribes—and as Bernstein and Woodward report, threats against his life and family[24]—had deepened his philosophic perception of the events in train, as shown in the following two documents, his statement dismissing Alch in December 1972 and his Christmas letter to Caulfield. The rupture with Alch was momentarily repaired. Alch flew to Washington and convinced McCord not to publish the dismissal notice, not to take that course yet. Saying to himself, "What are they up to now," McCord went along for a little more of the ride. McCord's dismissal notice to Alch shows, by the way, that the White House had direct and unambiguous information on McCord's intentions before the turn of the year, some three months before the Sirica letter. Here is McCord's December statement releasing Alch:

I have released Mr. Gerald Alch as my defense attorney in the Watergate Case.

In meetings recently in which plans for our defense in the Watergate trial were discussed, he persisted in a proposal that I claim that the Watergate operation was a CIA operation. This is flatly untrue, and when I rejected it, he then went on to make a second proposal.

The second proposal then was that I claim that the 4 Cubans and I cooked up the bugging operation on our own. This also is untrue.

It was patently obvious that in my own interests of a

fair trial that I dismiss Mr. Alch and find myself another
attorney. I am actively engaged in doing just that. [True
enough. As we see below, Bernard Fensterwald was
already cruising McCord's waters in December, though
he would not surface as his new attorney until the
March publication of the Sirica letter.]

The implications inherent in these two proposals
imply the deepest corruption and perversion of the
criminal justice system in recent history. It smacks of
total political control of the federal investigative
process, the federal grand jury process, and the federal
prosecutors.

Never in our nation's history has the integrity of the
national intelligence system and especially of the FBI
been in such jeopardy.

It forebodes in the present direction of the FBI the
return to the politically corrupt system that Hoover
inherited. The fine organization is already crumbling.
[He is writing in the brief ignominious moment of Pat
Gray.]

When the hundreds of dedicated fine men and
women of CIA can no longer write intelligence
summaries and reports with integrity without fear of
political recrimination—when their fine director
[Helms] is being summarily discharged in order to make
way for a politician [Schlesinger] who will write
or *re*write intelligence reports the way the politicians
want them written, instead of the way truth and best
judgment dictates, our nation is in the deepest of trouble
and freedom itself was never so imperiled. Nazi
Germany rose and fell under exactly the same
philosophy of governmental operation.

This nation is truly in the deepest trouble it has been
in in 200 years.

I fully expect the most intense character assassination campaign and harassment to be mounted against

me. So be it. The integrity of the CIA and of the FBI and of the whole Federal Criminal Justice System is far more important than one man's future or life."[25]

More powerful yet, with its array of violent metaphors, McCord's Christmas letter to Caulfield:

> Jack—
> Sorry to have to write you this letter but felt you had to know. If Helms goes, and if the WG operation is laid at CIA's feet, where it does not belong, every tree in the forest will fall. It will be a scorched desert. This whole matter is at the precipice right now. Just pass the message that if they want it to blow, they are on exactly the right course. I'm sorry that you will get hurt in the fallout.[26]

4. McCord Sang

The impact of McCord's March 19 letter to Sirica[27] is lost on no one. That letter is what kicked Nixon over the precipice by conclusively identifying the Watergate Operation with the White House. Rather than repeat this familiar document here, let us simply survey the over-all addition of McCord's feats against the Nixon camp. He was the first to say (1) that John Mitchell was implicated; (2) that CREEP money was being used to hush up the Plumbers; (3) that the White House was trying to hide behind the CIA and at the same time put the CIA in its pocket; (4) that Nixon was the master of the White House cover-up operation.

It was the March 19 letter, incubating at least since late December, that in a single fusillade launched all these fatal blows against Nixon, just the way McCord seems to have planned it—to achieve "the maximum effect."

5. *McCord Acquired an Anti-Nixon Lawyer*

When McCord came out with the March 19 letter to Sirica he simultaneously dropped Alch and picked up a new lawyer, Bernard Fensterwald. Fensterwald is a subcanyon in the McCord sidecanyon and I do not mean to guess what one might come upon at the end of it, but it is worthy of brief reconnaissance.

The given version is that McCord got to know about Fensterwald when Fensterwald appeared as a volunteer in the bail-raising committee run by McCord's wife, Ruth. This committee was active in December when McCord was first considering making his move against Alch, and Fensterwald was working with it at that time.

Fensterwald is a serious figure in assassination-conspiracy research circles. He was the founder, main moneybags, and only executive officer of a small Washington organization set up in 1969 called the Committee to Investigate Assassinations. Fensterwald was more or less closely associated with New Orleans District Attorney Jim Garrison. Garrison was at that moment well embarked on a legal campaign against the late Clay Shaw that actually threatened to expose in open court a real corner of the Kennedy assassination cabal and its strange CIA ties. Fensterwald's committee was presumably formed as a kind of PR instrument of Garrison's operation at a moment when the chances seemed strong that Garrison would actually win a conviction—and from it, a string of convictions ultimately exposing the truth of Dallas.

But long after the Garrison campaign was crushed, Fensterwald kept the CTIA open. Out front, it existed to collect and selectively spread information on the assassinations of JFK, RFK, and King. Before it folded in 1975, the CTIA maintained relationships, generally based on information, not politics, with many of the small band of writers, investigators, and random eccentrics who got actively drawn into the puzzle of the presidential assassinations. Fensterwald is also attorney of record in James Earl Ray's suit for a new trial in the King case. He was alongside Andrew St. George when St. George appeared before an executive session of Symington's Senate Armed Forces Committee growing out of his *Harper's* piece to which we have several times referred. He was a State Department lawyer for six years (Harvard 1942, Harvard Law 1949) with a minor role in the Joe McCarthy drama. He was briefly attached to RFK's staff then and more extensively later in the RFK-vs.-Hoffa phase. He worked for Kefauver's anticrime committee in the 1950s. He reputedly has independent means through a family business in Nashville and is something of a political adventurer with a penchant for cases involving the hypothesis of conspiracy.

The scent of a prior relationship and a larger purpose shared between McCord and Fensterwald first arose when McCord's CREEP lawyer, Alch, came before Ervin on May 23, 1973, to defend himself against McCord's testimony that Alch had tried to involve McCord in a conspiracy to obstruct justice and hang the CIA for Watergate and so save Nixon.

"At no time," said Alch, "did I suggest to Mr. McCord that the so-called CIA defense be utilized for the defense.... I merely asked him whether or not there was a factual basis for this contention. Mr. McCord's allegation that I announced my ability to forge his CIA personnel records with the cooperation of then acting CIA Director Schlesinger is absurd and completely untrue."

Thus secured as to salient, Alch marched to the front attack. The hearts of conspiracy nuts everywhere beat faster as they heard at last one of their own questions about Watergate actually being popped in prime time, for Alch was asking what our friend Fensterwald was doing suddenly at the side of McCord.

"Subsequently," said Alch,

...I did receive several phone calls from Mr. Fensterwald ... and I recall that in one telephone conversation he said to me: "What do you think of all that is going on?" referring to the disclosures being made by Mr. McCord....I replied, "Whatever is right for Jim McCord is all right with me." Mr. Fensterwald replied, "We're going after the President of the United States." I replied that I was not interested in any vendettas against the President but only in the best interest of my client. To which Mr. Fensterwald replied, "Well, you'll see, that's who we're going after, the President."[28]

Not only this, Alch went on, but there was even a suggestion of a prior relationship between McCord and Fensterwald. McCord's story, as we have seen, is that Fensterwald volunteered to help raise bail, that they hadn't known each other or been connected in any way before. Fensterwald added the detail that he found his way to the bail committee through one Lou Russell, an old associate of his in the private-investigations business with a background in the House UnAmerican Activities Committee. At that time, Russell was employed by McCord's private intelligence outfit, Security International, Inc.

Alch told the senators that Fensterwald had volunteered to him the information that Fensterwald and McCord had "a past relationship" going before Watergate. Alch said Fensterwald referred to contributions, in fact, that McCord had made to the CTIA. What could be going on?

Two days after Alch told the world this story I visited the dilapidated downtown Washington office of Fensterwald's CTIA and tried to get some reaction to Alch's testimony from Fensterwald's (then) aide and office manager Bob Smith, a small, overwrought, pale, exasperated man of middle age, who was sarcastic and impatient with the idea of a prior McCord-Fensterwald relationship or that something between them might be hidden. Then what about the contributions Alch says Fensterwald says McCord made to the CTIA? Were there any such contributions? To my surprise, Smith sputtered and said that there were of course no contributions, but that there had been certain irrelevant money transactions involving McCord, Fensterwald, and the CTIA going back well before Watergate.

Oh?

Smith's story was that Fensterwald's old friend Russell materialized in McCord's ambit when he was hired by McCord's Security International to help handle convention security on contract to the Republican National Committee. When Russell found it difficult to cash his paychecks from McCord's security firm, said Smith, he got into the habit of bringing them around to Fensterwald's office at the CTIA. Russell would sign his McCord check over to the CTIA and Fensterwald would write him a personal check for the like amount, which Russell could then easily cash around the corner at Fensterwald's bank. Russell brought the first such check around, recalled Smith, in March 1972. The practice was current as of Watergate. There were, as Smith remembered, about a dozen such checks. The larger, he thought, were for about $500.

Indeed? A dozen checks in three months? Just in that particular period? Maybe $5000 or so flowing from McCord through Fensterwald's CTIA in the three months before Watergate? Within two months came news of Russell's sudden death due to natural causes. About a year later a disgruntled Fensterwald aide in the CTIA sent me this note:

> Lou Russell was in the Howard Johnson Motel at the very time of the Watergate break-in. He lied to the FBI about why he was there. Someone set him up after that in a penthouse with a car. He lived on Q St. 7 or 8 blocks from Fensterwald's office when he started exchanging checks in March 1972. He worked for General Security Services Co., which was protecting Watergate at the time of the break-in. Lou Russell was Nixon's chief investigator when Dirty Dick went after Hiss. Nixon knew Russell very well.

More subcanyons leading downward. We do not know that Fensterwald is CIA-connected just because he looks and acts the part, or that McCord and he were more confederates than lawyer and client just because Fensterwald exulted in the political effects of McCord's disclosures or because the two were tenuously connected beforehand. But this fragment of a mystery nevertheless teaches the broader lesson that there is an underworld to Watergate as real as the surface Watergate of John Dean's confessional destruction of Nixon for the paltry crime of cover-up.

Nixon moved to establish a presidential control over all sources of national intelligence estimates. He did this because, for whatever reason, Yankee loyalists in the CIA would not support his conviction that the antiwar movement was foreign-inspired and subversive. An anti-Nixon group around Helms responded by infiltrating an agent, McCord, into Nixon's inner security force, the Room 16 group, using the "retired intelligence officer" routine as cover. McCord delivered two key acts. The first was the door-taping "blunder" that brought about the arrests. The second was the Sirica letter, which transformed the scandal into the crisis, and brought down another president.[29]

The Derivation of Carter

...And led finally to the election of Jimmy Carter.

Carter's "populism is not fake," writes Lilliam Hellman (*Rolling Stone*, 18 November 1976). One inclines to defer to so acute a perception as hers. Certainly Carter's administration tilts visibly leftwards, he seems a great democrat in the way he addresses his appeal to the people, and I for my part willingly believe that he is an improvement upon Ford if only because he comes after him. But is this populism of Carter's, genuine as it may be, the only force in play in his election and his administration? Is it even the most important force?

Rather, the record appears to show already with startling clarity that Carter is much less the creation of upwelling popular forces than of our old familiar Yankee Establishment. That will strike different people different ways, but it is the fact. Note that I do not call him a Yankee *creature*; I say only that without the grooming, the introductions, the support of organized Yankee forces, Carter could never have become president in the first place; and without a massive Yankee presence in positions solidly around him, he very possibly would not be able to preside.

Consider that it was through the Trilateral Commission that Carter was first introduced to big-time politics and given a finishing course by kingmakers who would not normally have regarded a Southern Baptist governor as presidential timber.

The Trilateral Commission is a direct offshoot of the Round Table, the Bilderberg Group, and the Council on Foreign Relations. It was formed by David Rockefeller in 1973 on the advice of Zbigniew Brzezinsky to counter the wave of economic nationalism brought on by Nixon's Secretary of the Treasury John Connally and to articulate the common interests of the multinational corporations of North America, West Europe and Japan. It cultivates a One-Worldist philosophy and wants to reorganize the structures of world political relationships to suit the interests of the multinationals.

Why should the likes of the Trilateral have been interested in the likes of Jimmy Carter? The answer is available in a remark attributed to master Yankee strategist Averill Harriman. Discussing Democratic presidential possibilities early in 1972 with Michael Katz, Director of International Studies at Harvard, Harriman said, "We've got to get off our highhorses and look at some of these southern governors." (Peter Pringle, *London Sunday Times*, April 18, 1976.) Population and power shifts from East to West and North to South must have made him wonder how much longer the Democratic Party could maintain its prestige and position with its habitual strategy of pairing a big-city northeastern liberal presidential candidate with a country populist vice-presidential running mate. As soon as the Trilateral

Commission was formed, Carter and two other remote-province governors were brought aboard to be put through their paces.

But what was Carter's interest in the Trilateral? As he wrote in his campaign autobiography, *Why Not the Best?*,

> In order to insure the continuing opportunity for penetrating analyses of complicated, important and timely foreign policy questions, there is in operation an organization known as the Trilateral Commission. A group of leaders from the three democratic developed areas of the world meet every six months to discuss ideas of current interest... Membership on this commission has provided me with a splendid learning opportunity, and many of the other members have helped me in my study of foreign affairs."

Carter expressed his high regard for the Trilateral and its people much more pithily, however, by taking Trilateral member Walter Mondale as his running mate and appointing within his first months as president the following Trilateral members to the following positions in his administration: Cyrus Vance, Secretary of State; Harold Brown, Secretary of Defense; Zbigniew Brzezinsky, National Security Adviser; W. Michael Blumenthal, Secretary of the Treasury; Andrew Young, Ambassador to the United Nations; Richard Holbrooke, Assistant Secretary of State for East Asian and Pacific Affairs; Warren Christopher, Deputy Secretary of State; Richard N. Cooper, Undersecretary of State for Economic Affairs; C. Fred Bergsten, Assistant Secretary of Treasury for International Economic Affairs; Paul C. Warnke, Director of the Arms Control and Disarmament Agency; and only through a spike of Cowboy resistance in the Congress need we not add, Theodore C. Sorensen, Director of the CIA. Besides which, Carter's court of innermost advisers includes the following additional members of this Rockefeller international thinktank supreme: George Ball, Clark Clifford, Samuel P. Huntington, Marshall Shulman, Richard Gardner, Lane Kirkland, Leonard Woodcock, Henry Owen, Robert Roosa, J. Paul Austin—a grand tourney of Yankee knights.

And one should look too at the way the nation voted, the Eastern half for Carter, and the West for the more Cowboyish Ford. Granting that the numerical differences were slim, this still seems an interestingly general divergence. Surely it reflects the Yankee/Cowboy dynamic of current politics, just as the low voter turnout (especially for a Bicentennial) reflects against the "populist" theory of Carter.

Of course I am not at all trying to label Carter a Rockefeller stooge, a mere Southern boy of the Yankee bankers. The relationship must be exquisitely more subtle than that. And any president, stooge or no, will be obliged by the rude geometry of the office to call outsiders, people of opposition, into government with him, to widen the burden of conscience and judgment and accountability and to guarantee the federal writ in outlying provinces. Yankee Kennedy called Cowboy Johnson and Cowboy Nixon called Yankee Kissinger just as Yankee Ally Carter called Cowboy Ally Schlesinger. That is how the game seems to be played. Carter the populist is playing with and therefore *for* a Yankee team of Trilateralists.

Thus, the whole cycle of the Watergate coup, as I see it, runs from the ruination of Nixon to the installation of Carter. The essential steps and phases for this sequence are as follows.

First, a hypothetical Yankee action group determined sometime in 1969 or 1970 that Nixon, acting for a hypothetical Cowboy group, was in the process of creating a special political espionage force totally under the control of the White House, totally illegal, "something," as Dean would come to say of the Huston Plan, "out of the Third Reich." (*Blind Ambition*, p. 276.)

Second, the Yankees determined to get more information on this "presidential cancer" and keep it under close observation. Through their people at the CIA, such as Richard Helms and James McCord, they cultivated a scheme by means of which they could keep the Hunt-Liddy group in sight at all times and prepare an appropriate response. This scheme was to penetrate that group with a trusted agent, McCord, whose politics would be sufficiently ambiguous to the Nixon crowd as to make him seem ideologically credible as a Nixon secret agent. The CIA hastily sheep-dipped McCord and gave him a patina of plausibility in a new role as a private operator. McCord then maneuvered himself into the path of Nixonians who could get him inside. He became John Mitchell's number-one security chief. He was accepted into the highest circle of secret White House agents. He was made intimate with some of the dirtiest aspects of Nixon's administration.

Third, McCord pulled the plug at Watergate by putting the tape on the doorlatch twice so that it would show and be seen, thus calling the security guard's attention to the skullduggery underway within so that officer Shoffler and his special security squad would get their cue and arrive for the arrest.

We have new indirect support for our view that a CIA connected double agent was afoot within the inner circles of the Nixon White House and was responsible for the Plumbers' bust. First John Dean (*Blind Ambition*, p. 392) quoted a point made to him by Chuck Colson as they sat at Holabird prison looking back on Watergate. They had finally given all their testimony. The pressure was off. It was the first day they could unbutton. Dean quotes Colson thus:

"I tell you, John . . . I turned into something of a CIA freak on Watergate for a while, you know, and I still think there's something there. I haven't figured out how it all adds up, but I know one thing: the people with CIA connections sure did better than the rest of us. Paul O'Brien's an old CIA man, and he walked. David Young was Kissinger's CIA liaison, and he ran off to

England when he got immunity. Bennett worked for the CIA, and he ran back to Hughes. And Dick Helms skated through the whole thing somehow. Maybe those guys just knew how to play the game better than we did."

Colson's musings are always of interest, but some will give more credit to Ervin committee minority counsel Fred Thompson, who made the same point even more explicitly in *At That Point in Time* (Quadrangle, 1976, pp. 159-160), where he says:

> In my opinion, we (the minority staff) had already determined that the CIA was aware of the activities of the Watergate burglars prior to the break-in and that it perhaps knew more than that . . . . In my mind, the question was becoming one of whether the CIA had been a participant in or a benign observer of the break-in, or, in view of the bungling of the burglary and the mysterious circumstances surrounding it, whether CIA operatives had perhaps sabotaged the break-in to weaken the White House and strengthen the Agency in its struggle for survival.

But fourth, the Nixon-Colson side had meanwhile been active itself. While the Yankees were busy infiltrating Nixon's secret group, the Cowboys were busy engineering the nomination of the Democrats' weakest candidate, McGovern, by the method of dirty-tricking the heavier-weight candidates, like Muskie, out of the competition. The result was a momentary standoff. The McCord punch at Watergate was no doubt thrown in order to lose the presidency for Nixon, but the assumption of that strategy must have been that no one like McGovern, honest and independent, was going to be the Democrat nominee. Recall that the function we associate with the Ervin committee was at first to have been carried out in October

1972, in time to have an election impact that would have been hopelessly negative for Nixon. Had Muskie (or Kennedy) been the nominee and had Watergate been sprung before the election, Nixon might never have been returned to office and there would have been no need for the Watergate we actually experienced. But the trap could not be sprung for the election because the nomination of McGovern precluded it. McGovern was not a Yankee man. He could not be controlled or guaranteed. He was as dangerous in his own way as was Nixon to the interests of Yankee corporate internationalism. Why waste Watergate on him?

So, fifth, the Yankees abandoned their election strategy and moved to a backup strategy, impeachment, much more difficult and risky because it necessarily entailed the separate removal of Vice President Agnew and the insertion of a custodial figure, like Ford, sufficiently acceptable to Yankee and Cowboy sides alike as to minimize the possibility of more direct hostility. (Ford, long sympathetic to Cowboy militarism, was also one of the founding members of the Bilderberg Group, predecessor of the Trilateral Commission.)

Sixth, as a forward strategy, the Yankee side formed up the Trilateral Commission. Presidential aspirants from all over, especially the New South, were invited to take part in its deliberations and contests. Carter entered and won—first the support of the Trilateral people, then the Democrat nomination, then the election, throughout fighting with blows as soft as he could make them, especially when up against the transparently reluctant Ford. Carter proceeded to construct an administration, as we noted above, so much under the control of central Yankee figures as by any definition to be a Yankee administration behind a New South facade, and yet remaining open enough to Cowboy interests and powers, as in Schlesinger's appointment, to soothe any further Cowboy itch for what Colson called *political hardball*. Kennedy, Johnson and Nixon were polarizing presidents, men who governed through the heightening of conflict. Carter seems to aim at being, like Eisenhower, a unifying president governing through relaxation of tensions, forcing an uneasy truce in the Yankee-Cowboy War.

IV

Neither Yankee Nor Cowboy

"... Single acts of tyranny may be ascribed to the accidental opinion of the day.... A series of oppressions, begun at a distinguished period and pursued unalterably through a change of ministers, too plainly prove a deliberate and systematic plan of reducing us to slavery."

Thomas Jefferson[1]

"But nobody reads. Don't believe people read in this country. There will be a few professors that will read the report...."

Allen Dulles to the Warren Commission[2]

9

Who Killed JFK?

Those of us who *will* read find the record tells us to turn against Yankee and Cowboy elites equally; to turn against the domination and closing up of political life by all the clandestine forces and powers.

Many of us appear already well persuaded that democracy can no longer work and that we can only hope to make the technical oligarchy more receptive to individual merit. Or that the constitutional republic is made obsolete by the requirements of modern communications and control systems and the vicissitudes of the imperial stage. Or that independence either for the individual from the state or for government from a net of entangling alliances is an outmoded pastoral aspiration.

I sense a pervasive American feeling that beneath the kinds of pressures and temptations the contemporary setting brings to bear upon individual sensibility and collective consciousness, no one need bother dream of enduring. No one will *not* be jointly tempted and oppressed, no one will *not* stoop and be taken at the same time. This is just the way we live now. How *does* democracy govern a giganticized armed bureaucracy such as the country's public administration has become? How *does* our republican Constitution answer the needs of our imperial presidency? How *does* the heritage of independence express itself when the rulers choose to remake the world in the matrix of their computers?

The defeat and impotence of the tradition underlie the perverse sophistication that shows through every nuance of the Dallas-Watergate story. Democracy, republicanism, independence, our triangular base of native, traditional, public values: these are treated by the operators on high as the values of political imbeciles. They, the men of the world of Southern California and New York, having studied the world at UCLA and Harvard, know that in reality the only serious political question is the question of the acquisition and use of power.

There is a danger that Watergate and the subsequent CIA and FBI discoveries will have actually *deepened* these attitudes in the public. I have a friend whose uncle was a straight-arrow Nixonian until Watergate, a hardworking middle-class shopkeeper. When he saw the truth of the men and the system he had been following with his hand over his heart like a fool, he said to himself, "So be it," and became a robber. He was at first successful but then took a foolish risk and was brought down in flight by a single shot from a trooper's rifle, another victim of Watergate.

Will the new knowledge lead us only to accept the new state of total surveillance and to make new personal deals with the corruption and fascism implicit in its formations? Or will we turn the other way?

The sophisticated contemporary assault on native political values (as exemplified by the report of the Trilateral Commission[3]) flies wide of the mark. The challenge to democracy is not whether it too can govern the megastate, it is rather: Can it resume the struggle against it? Not whether the Constitution can be reconciled to a general prevalence of criminal practice within government, but rather: Can the true republicans resume the struggle against state crime? Not whether independence of person from the state and of government from entangling alliances are compatible with "today's needs," but rather: Can independents resume the struggle, precisely in view of "today's needs," against the entangling, entangled state?

The traditional values stand in no shame for seeming unfeasible to us. It is not the purpose of values to be feasible, probably, only to help chart the way, help define the situation. If one cannot make the tradition speak to the current predicament, that is one way of measuring the predicament, of getting a sense of its span and character.

But when we find our values incompatible with the lives we are leading, and can no longer deny this, our first response is often to try to change our values: we refute them, spit on them, call them obsolete, childish, premature, etc. This does not change the values, it only makes them more obscure; does not remove the need for values, only makes the values harder to find, harder to recognize and embrace.

Thus, to all the admonitions about practicality and the new age from Yankee and Cowboy power elites alike, a trio of democrat, republican, and independent will respond with a single music: We are not obliged to conquer Babylon, only to maintain an active position within it, a life, a forward practice.

The wheel spins. We do not come to politics to stop this spinning, only to play a role in it. Yes, we want to win an actual respite, to build a society of some grace and repose that might last a moment and leave something worth regarding. But that is the gamble of democracy, not the precondition. Independent, republican, and democrat may choose only to continue the ancient struggle.

I must make this incantation of mine about the values I am calling traditional at least this much more explicit:

By *democrats*, I mean those who believe that powers of decision in a healthy society repose sovereignly in the living generations. The state does not come from any power going beyond the human. The state comes from the people and is subservient to them equally and as a whole.

By *republicans*, I mean those for whom the legitimate state is carefully circumscribed within society by an organic and reasoned body of explicit legal relationships and limits; those for whom the law is a set of limits to make society more prosperous and happy; who believe it is in the concrete self-interest of each generation after the next to preserve and refine this structure of law.

By *independents*, I mean those for whom the state does not fill up the human universe and who believe that there are vast domains of human experience in which the state should not be allowed in any way to intrude; that parties tend easily to become instruments of the state they seek to possess and must therefore be resisted for what they represent in themselves, the will to power.

To those who can see themselves anywhere in those vicinities, the question will rapidly become what to do. How do we resist the power-elite tendency to resolve differences through state violence? To these, I propose that a major immediate effort should be to politicize the question, Who killed JFK?

That question sums up everything we need to fear in the Dallas-Watergate decade. To comprehend and solve that crime—and then the countercrime of Watergate, "Who cashiered Nixon?"—is to restore the precondition of any self-governing and republican people, the security of the public state. As we are a single nation, we have a single president whose destiny is participated in by all. When the president bleeds, all of us have to sleep in it. But then to wake up, to acknowledge the blood, to take rational action to find the truth of it and all the mysteries around it and flowing from it across the decade and a half: that would begin to make America a free country again.

No more than begin. Suppose the people successfully forced the issue, that would still be no guarantee of the next step. What indeed happens if implicit power rivalries are forced to become explicit? And as I have said before: Solve the crime, catch the conspiracy, still the food and fuel and economic and social crises remain, the Middle-East remains, the DOD and KGB remain... the dialectic remains. But the events of 11/22/63 form a central episode in the flowering of the clandestine state. Study of the JFK murder brings us close-up to the cancer Dean saw growing on the presidency, but at another of its radiant epicenters. It is the same cancer that a host of observers since Ross and Wise in 1964 have decried under one name or another—a cancer of the defense establishment, the security establishment, the foreign-policy establishment: a generalized state cancer whose growth we can trace back to the clandestine arrangements entered into by the U.S. government with the likes of Gehlen, Lansky, and the knights of the secret Round Table. The cancer attacks at Dallas 1963 and at Watergate a decade thereafter from the other side, leaving a trail of blood and disrupted function between and beyond. It now rules us.

But to get at Dallas '63 would be to get at this sickness by one of its major victories. It would be to get at the political bottom of the Vietnam war, of the structures of internal conflict that helped produce that entire decade, the decade of Dallas-Watergate and Vietnam. Understand Dallas: That is the start of the way out. As I write, there are new chances of congressional action such as have not heretofore existed, mainly stemming from the fact that Watergate and the CIA have definitively put right-wing subversion on the agenda.[4] The Congress is agitated with the question and seems beginning to grapple with it in the committee system.

But we have seen such flashes of congressional light before. What can keep this issue alive now and detonate it at the heart of American political consciousness? One thing only, a movement of ordinary people demanding that the pressure toward the truth be increased and refreshed daily, ordinary people informed on the basic issues and confident of the authority of their purpose.

As I conclude this book a new controversy is brewing. Once it becomes at last publicly indubitable that Kennedy was killed by a conspiracy hiding behind Oswald's and

Ruby's graves, immediately the angry question will surface: Then what *kind* of conspiracy was it? I have developed aspects of one view in this book: I say JFK was killed by a rightist conspiracy formed out of anti-Castro Cuban exiles, the Syndicate, and a Cowboy oligarchy, supported by renegade CIA and FBI agents. The Warren Commission thought always in terms of a lone assassin versus a *foreign* conspiracy and scarcely entertained the domestic-conspiracy option except in those hushed, frightened secret meetings (transcripts of which were declassified in 1974 and 1975) called by Warren in January 1964 to discuss the troubling news that Oswald had possibly been an FBI informant for the fourteen months prior to the assassination. So it is today. The voices of cover-up are even now saying: There was no conspiracy, but if there was, it was a pro-Castro conspiracy. This view of Oswald has already begun to crystalize. It is the counterattack against a critique which has generally prevailed.

But all of us theorizers and patient watchers who are faithful to the traditional resolve can say we are ready to face and try to deal with the truth of Dallas, whatever it turns out to be, certain indeed that if we cannot say who killed the president, then there is no respect in which we may still see ourselves as a self-governing people. We should then be obliged to celebrate our republic's anniversary by burying as a dead letter its one-time faith in people, law, and a sense of limits.

Appendix

THE OFFICIAL THEORY OF THE HUNT CRASH

First we examine the NTSB crash reconstruction, as much as is practical in the NTSB's own words. Then we test the validity of this reconstruction.

NTSB Crash Reconstruction

The NTSB concluded that the crew of 553 was distracted by the failure of the FDR at a moment in the landing process at which maximum attention ought to have been devoted to flying the airplane. As a result, when the checklist item "flight spoilers" (or "speed brake" or "air brake") was reached, and Second Officer Elder called out, "Speed brake?" copilot Coble took note of a green indicator light at the control console and answered, "armed," meaning that the spoilers were in the stowed position but readied for automatic deployment into the extended or "ground detent" position as soon as the airplane landed. The flight spoilers are flush with the wing upper surfaces in the stowed position and are not normally used in landing. They are more generally deployed only when the plane has already touched down. In deployment, they hinge upward from the top surface of the wing to spoil the airflow across it and decrease lift.

The flaps, which also figure in this drama, are aerodynamic control surfaces mounted in the trailing edge of the wing. At slower airspeeds, as at takeoff and landing, they are extended to give the airplane a broader wing and thus higher lift at some expense in air speed. They are retracted at higher speeds aloft.

Because *Elder* was worried about the FDR, theorizes the NTSB, *Coble* failed to realize that the green spoiler indicator comes on not only when the spoiler control lever is in the "armed" position, but also when it is in any position aft of that, including the "flight detent" position. In the "flight detent" position, the spoilers are deployed to their maximum in-flight extension. Had Coble taken the time to check the position of the control lever instead of relying on the green indicator light (reasoned the NTSB), which he misread, he would have known that the spoilers were extended, or more precisely, would have remembered that he had extended them shortly before. (Alas, if we had the CVR tape transcript healthy and whole, and the FDR data, we would know exactly when and why the spoilers were originally deployed.) As it was, the airplane was approaching a combination of flight-control settings, airspeed, engine thrust, and pitch angle that would culminate in a stall. When the stickshaker sounded its warning, and simultaneously the Midway tower ordered 553 to fly a missed approach, the pilot did not know—did not remember—that, according to some previous order of his to the copilot, the spoilers were deployed. He therefore did not order the copilot to retract them. Instead, he called for flaps to be decreased to 15 degrees (further decreasing aircraft lift, already degraded by the extension of the spoilers) preparatory to the application of "takeoff thrust" to fly the plane into a climbing left turn. Retracting the flaps had the immediate result that the airplane began to settle. Since he was running out of altitude (and his altimeter was fooling him by 150 feet on the high side, remember, with the visibility ceiling at only 500 feet), his reaction to this was to pull the nose up. This further deteriorated the airplane's lift and brought the airplane closer to the stall that finally precipitated the crash. In the NTSB's words:

"The rush of cockpit activities at this point, the first officer's routine callout that the spoilers were 'armed,' and the fact that the spoilers are seldom used during the final segment of an instrument approach, may well have caused the captain to overlook the position of the spoilers at level-off." (p. 28)

This theory is based on the results of four series of tests carried out by or for the NTSB: (1) A B-737 Performance Study, (2) a simulator study, (3) flight tests, and (4) a General Electric engine-thrust study. Following is a summary of the salient points of each as they bear on the NTSB's theory of the crash. The reader's close attention is invited. The material is technical and dense, but the technical shortcomings of the spoiler-error theory of the NTSB are precious enough not to miss.

1. The B-737 Performance Study

This study takes data from the ground radar record and the engine-spectrogram study and reconstructs from it the vertical flight path profile and the airspeed of the aircraft during the last moments of the flight.

"First," reads the NTSB report,

the aircraft's drag as a function of airspeed was computed for the different approach configurations (combinations of flap, landing gear, and spoiler positions) that could have been used. Next, the various drag values and the thrust values derived from the General Electric study were used to determine the resultant forces acting on the aircraft. These forces, in turn, were compared with the vertical velocity and longitudinal acceleration values shown in the approach profile, starting with the descent from 4,000 feet, and ending with the activation of the stickshaker.

The ARTS-III altitude trace shows that the aircraft momentarily levelled off at 2,200 feet mean sea level [Midway's m.s.l. altitude is 680 feet] for approximately 12 seconds, which would have resulted in a decay of airspeed to 126 knots indicated airspeed [from a theoretically calculated entry airspeed of 152 **KIAS**]. A rate of descent of approximately 1,550 ft/min was established as the aircraft passed the outer marker. This descent rate was maintained until the aircraft levelled off about 1,000 feet m.s.l. [i.e., about 320 feet off the ground]. The correlation of the CVR with the ARTS-III data indicates that the stall warning stickshaker commenced 6 to 7 seconds after the aircraft levelled off. [Note that we do not know if this takes into account the 3-to-6-second deviations from the ARTS-III time base found in the treated CVR tape.]

In order theoretically to produce such a condition, it is necessary to assume [Note:] that the aircraft was in a configuration which resulted in sufficient drag to prevent a high positive acceleration during this final descent. It was shown in this study that had 30° flaps been selected at 1426:00, and had the spoilers been extended to the flight detent position upon establishing the 1,550 ft/min descent, the aircraft would have started to level off at MDA approximately at 133 KIAS. Any configuration producing less drag would have resulted in the aircraft leveling off at a higher airspeed. (p. 17)

A higher airspeed, of course, would be inconsistent with the ARTS-III data and the subsequent events.

To make sure this much is well in hand: The B-737 Performance Study people looked at what the ARTS-III ground radar said about the altitude and airspeed descent profile of 553. Then they looked at a separate General Electric spectrogram study to determine from the CVR tape the engine thrust levels being developed from moment to moment along that profile. Also from the CVR, investigators determined the moment of stickshaker actuation. Thus they could reason: For the plane to be going this high and this fast with the engines winding this hard, what are the possible combinations of flaps, spoilers, landing gear, and aircraft pitch angle that could bring the plane to stall-warning threshold within that much elapsed time? The conclusion was that the spoilers must have been in the flight-detent or extended position, or else the warning device would not have come on when it did.

2. Simulator Tests.

Two series of simulator tests, the second based on the data from the General Electric study, "explored the effects of different techniques in recovering from the approach-to-stall flight regime." The study found that "to attain a 1,550 ft/min descent without allowing a significant speed buildup at a thrust level corresponding to 59 percent N_1, it was necessary to use [i.e., to assume] the following drag configuration: 30° flaps, landing gear down, and full flight spoiler extension." (p. 19)

That is, the simulator tests agreed with the performance study that the spoilers must have been in flight detent at the critical moment.

3. Flight Tests.

The [stall] entry configurations were established as: 30° flaps, landing gear down, and with the flight spoilers in the stowed, halfway extended, and flight-detent positions. Recovery techniques consisted of power application to between 1.7 and 1.8 EPR (approximately 8,500 pounds of thrust per engine, 17,000 pounds total thrust), reduction of the pitch attitude to an approximately level attitude, and repositioning of the wing flaps as a variable, i.e., either retracted to 15° or extended to 40° at the initiation of the recovery. Spoilers were left in their originally selected position. In all cases, recovery was effected with power application and a simultaneous decrease in pitch attitude. The pitch attitude at the onset of stickshaker activation was consistently near 12°, as shown on the captain's altitude indicator. The stablizer trim corresponding to this position was seven units noseup. Trim was not changed during the recovery sequence. A loss of altitude of 150 to 500 feet occurred during all recoveries. The differences in flight spoiler positions upon entry into stall buffeting appeared to have little effect on the loss of altitude consistent with the recovery technique. (pp. 20-21)

4. General Electric Engine Sound Spectrogram Study.

"The CVR tape contained a high-level background noise," reports the NTSB, "which tended to mask meaningful frequency data. Through special filtering techniques much of the noise was attenuated, and some discrete frequencies corresponding to sound generated by aircraft equipment became evident." By studying these sounds spectrographically, analysts could determine the speeds and thus the thrust levels of the two engines.

The CVR-tape study found that "the final acceleration" of the engines occurred at 1427:03.35, or about one second *before* the tower radioed its order for 553 to "execute a missed approach" and about two seconds *before* the actuation of the stickshaker. Allowing for discrepancies in the CVR time track possibly attributable to its oil bath and four-day special treatment, we may assume this to be the result of a pilot response to the developing situation. "Just before the acceleration," continues the report, "one engine was at 58.6 percent N_1 and the other at 57.2 percent N_1 ," for a combined thrust of approximately 11,580 pounds. Conclusion 9 of the General Electric study states in its entirety:

"The sounds of both engines were detected during the acceleration. One engine peaked at 72 percent N_1 at 1427:07.95. The other peaked at 79.2 percent N_1 at 1427:09.55" (p. 17).

In other words, plus or minus three to six seconds, within four seconds of the actuation of the stall-warning device, the airplane was developing a total thrust of 15,100 pounds. This peak was maintained or increased over the remaining fourteen seconds of the flight. (Ground eyewitnesses and survivors agreed that the engines were winding hard during the moments before the crash.)

Critique of the Spoiler Theory

The critique of the theory that 553 crashed because the pilot neglected the flight detent position of the spoilers comprises five points.

1. Thrust levels identified by the General Electric study were apparently adequate to have accelerated 553 out of the stall regime *even with the spoilers in the full flight-detent position*. The report states:

A thrust in excess of 12,500 pounds should have been sufficient to accelerate the aircraft out of the stickshaker regime if the flight spoilers had been stowed. With the spoilers in the flight detent position, however, a total thrust of 14,500 pounds would have been required merely to maintain unaccelerated level flight within the stickshaker regime.... The performance and simulator studies indicate that the B-737 has sufficient thrust capability to accelerate out of the approach-to-stall regime, even with the spoilers extended. If takeoff thrust is produced with 2 or 3 seconds of stickshaker activation, little or no altitude has to be sacrificed. (p. 29)

But as we have seen, the GE engine-sound study indicated a combined thrust during the last fourteen seconds of the flight of 15,100 pounds, easily greater than the 14,500-pound thrust needed to keep the airplane in straight and level flight within the stickshaker regime. This surge of power may even have *preceded* the actuation of the stickshaker.

2. The position of the spoilers is uncertain. We have cited NTSB text to the effect that spoilers are rarely used in an instrument landing such as 553 was flying. It is all the more important therefore that we are not shown the moment in the CVR transcript at which the captain calls for the spoilers to be deployed to flight detent, an unusual maneuver. The fragment of the transcript published with the final report shows only the routine checklist mention of the spoilers and only the routine response that the spoilers were armed for deployment upon landing, not already deployed.

3. The spoiler control lever was not found to be in the "flight detent" position, but rather in the "stowed" position. The text is clear on this point: "After the accident, the spoiler lever was found in the forward or stowed position" (p. 30).

4. Neither was any part of the left or right spoiler assembly found in the flight-detent position in the wreckage. Again the text is unambiguous: "After the accident . . . the spoilers were in the retracted position" (p. 30).

The NTSB's explanation for the above discrepancies is the crash itself: "However, the post-impact condition of the center control pedestal and the possibility of spoiler retraction when hydraulic pressure was lost during the impact make this evidence inconclusive" (p. 30). Fine word, "inconclusive."

5. The post-impact position of the horizontal stabilizer control surface indicates that the spoilers were *not* deployed:

"The post-impact position of the horizontal stabilizer trim was determined to have been 9½ units noseup, *which would correlate more closely with a spoiler-stowed configuration at speeds within the stickshaker regime*. Boeing data indicate that a trim setting of 6½ units would more nearly correspond with a 30° flaps, gear down, spoiler extended configuration" (p. 30). (Italics mine.)

To explain away this discrepancy, the NTSB states, "Although the position of the stabilizer trim as found cannot be reconciled with that which would be expected for the existing conditions, the Board believes that the significance of this condition is outweighed by the evidence regarding the deployment of spoilers during the final descent and level-off" (p. 30).

Put it together. The NTSB must make 553's spoilers come out, even if they were not out at the wing, not out at the controls, and not out in either the captain's or the copilot's mind, and even if the control setting of the horizontal stabilizer was flatly inconsistent with their being out. This is because the NTSB must somehow get the airplane into a "stickshaker" configuration at a time determined by the perhaps faulty CVR tape to be twenty seconds before crash time, call it T-minus 20. Given that the speed and the descent rate for that moment are known from ground-radar data and engine thrust levels from the GE study, the NTSB's argument becomes totally circular. If the spoilers were *not* deployed at the moment of stickshaker activation, the NTSB is saying, then the stickshaker could not have been activated at that moment. The plane was going too fast then to start the stall-warning mechanism *unless the spoilers were out*.

That is the sole technical basis (a) for assuming that an experienced and qualified flight crew deviated without comment from standard operating procedures; and (b) for flying in the face of "inconclusive" evidence indicating that the spoilers were indeed in their normal stowed position when the plane crashed, (c) that the controls also showed the spoilers stowed, (d) that the stabilizer's position was inconsistent with spoiler deployment, and (e) that even if the spoilers *had* been deployed, and never retracted at all, as the data of the GE study show, the pilot still increased engine power quickly enough to fly the plane away from the threatened stall with no loss in altitude, much less a stall and a crash.

If, on the other hand, we do *not* assume that the stickshaker-alarm actually sounded *in the cockpit*, and if we take the pilot's application of increased thrust at about T-minus 18 seconds as his response to the wave-off signal from the tower, not to a stickshaker warning, then there is no longer any need to force the spoilers to have been where only inferential considerations say they were, and where a good many positive facts indicate they were not. But then we would need another theory of the crash.

The spoiler-error theory is simply not solidly rooted in the concrete facts of the crash as the NTSB report discloses them to us. It is based on assumptions which the NTSB's own technical findings controvert. It is not an implausible theory. It might actually turn out to be right. At least it has not been "briefly and tersely dismissed" by its few critics. But as of this moment, it is not terribly well stuck together. It is a kind of "single-bullet" theory in that it takes a conclusion (Dallas was a *normal* assassination, 553 a *normal* crash) and works backward to fit the facts to its needs, as is so apparent, for one example, in the chain of convenient inferential assumptions the NTSB is willing to make about the spoilers. Thus, it is "proved" that there was no sabotage because it is "proved" that the spoilers did it, and it is "proved" that the spoilers did it because if they did not, then the "accident" cannot be explained. Yes, correct, if it was an accident.

In no way could I have remained insensible of the risks one's credibility runs in being lent to these kinds of claims, that sabotage and murder are everywhere, that our political landscape is a burning ratrace-maze of crime and conspiracy. But whatever way I turn the matter, it continually seems to me that the spoiler theory's shortcomings are intensified by the contextualizing events: the massive FBI presence at the crash scene, the Plumbers quickly scrambling and getting in deep around the investigation, the heavy White House pressure on the NTSB to put out a hasty report, the doubts surrounding the cyanide question, the pollution and "treatment" of the CVR tape, the exactly-at-the-right-moment malfunction of the Flight Data Recorder, the passage of these vital precision instruments through the hands of the Nixon-Gray FBI and Mayor Daley's Streets and Sanitation types on their way to the innocent NTSB technicians; the mirror-image double failure of the two independent altimeters; the strained NTSB effort to explain this double failure away when it can scarcely explain one failure by itself; the irregular, out-of-code utilization of the Midway landing capabilities; the instantly corrected malfunction of the Kedzie Outer Marker just as 553 passed over it; and the whole uncanny silence, the apparent indifference, the "languor" of the crew in the face of the stickshaker warning: these things, impacted in the Hunt blackmail drama at the moment of its crisis, cry for another theory of the crash, a better explanation.

Notes

CHAPTER 1

1. See chapter 7 of "Vietnam Crucible" in Carl Oglesby and Richard Shaull, *Containment and Change* (New York: Macmillan, 1967) for a treatment of the neo-imperial theme.

2. Speech by author to the SDS National Council meeting in Lexington, KY, March 1968, just before Johnson's abdication. The ideas were summarized in my three-part article appearing in the then-New-Left-oriented periodical, *National Guardian*, April 13, 20, and 27, 1968.

3. Carroll Quigley, *Tragedy and Hope* (New York: Macmillan, 1966), pp. 1245-46. I chose in this book to avoid historical treatment of the Yankee/Cowboy theme, but the above passage from Quigley indicates a usable perspective on the Civil War. That a power-struggle theory of some kind is in fact necessary from the beginnings, and that there has always been a split at the top, is suggested in a work published too late for me to note it here except through George M. Fredrickson's review "The Uses of Antislavery," *New York Review of Books*, October, 16, 1975. The work is David Brion Davis's *The Problem of Slavery in the Age of Revolution* (Ithaca, N.Y.: Cornell University Press, 1975), the second volume in a continuing history of the revolutionary period. In Fredrickson's summary of Davis's thesis, "... the cost of nationhood in the United States was not

merely a sectional compromise but also a compact between two distinct elites—a northern capitalist class that increasingly recognized the advantages of a free labor system and a southern planter class already implicitly committed to the preservation and extension of slavery.... Hence, the United States seemingly emerged from its revolutionary period without a national ruling class; it was in fact a federation of two regional ruling classes."

4. The defense industry's place in the Yankee/Cowboy analysis has been challenged by two West Coast sociologists, Steve Weissman and Steve Johnson, Weissman first (*Ramparts*, August 1974), then Johnson in much greater detail (*The Insurgent Sociologist*, Winter 1975-1976). They maintained that the defense industry as such must *not* be a foundation of Cowboy power, because the ownership pattern prevailing in the defense industry essentially mirrors the ownership pattern prevailing in the other basic national industrial sectors. That is, like steel, the defense industry is mainly owned by the big Eastern banks—or in my terms, the Yankees. The point about ownership is perhaps valid as far as it goes, although I find it strange that the criteria Johnson should set up for Cowboyhood *in my sense* should exclude from his Cowboy sample the case I have long argued is most archetypal and important, i.e., the empire of Howard Hughes (see chapter 6). More important, Johnson ignores the extent to which, in the words of a recent summary, "the emergence of the Sunbelt has been [dependent on] its ability to obtain defense contracts and space-exploration installations." (Jon Nordheimer, "Sunbelt Region Leads Nation in Growth of Population," *New York Times*, February 8, 1976). The Weissman-Johnson approach to the politics of the defense economy is to hang everything on the single criterion of ownership. My approach is to look *also* at the regional patterns in which the some $450 billion awarded in prime defense contracts since 1960 have been spent, because the money has in no sense been spread around equally. In his book *Power Shift* (New York: Random House, 1975), an

independent elaboration of the Yankee/Cowboy perspective, Kirkpatrick Sale cites a Brookings Institution finding that from 1952 to 1962 "the overall contribution of defense to...the Pacific Region (especially Southern California) and the Mountain Region (primarily Arizona and New Mexico)...[was] 21 and 27 percent, respectively....At the same time...such states as Michigan, Wisconsin and Indiana actually had negative growth rates"[in terms of the local economic impact of defense spending] (p. 25). By 1970, the Sunbelt's portion of the defense budget had grown to 44 percent (compared to 39 percent to the Northeast) and Texas had climbed past New York as the second state in total defense contracts behind California. The First National Bank of Boston and the Girard Trust of Philadelphia may own Lockheed, but Lockheed's plants are in California, Texas, and Georgia. Morgan Guarantee Trust and Chemical Bank of New York may own General Dynamics, but four out of five of General Dynamic's chief plants are in the Sunbelt (two in California and one each in Texas, Florida and New York). Assessment of the Yankee/Cowboy factor in connection with the defense industry is thus more complex than the Weissman-Johnson analysis assumes.

5. William Appleman Williams, *The Tragedy of American Diplomacy* (New York: Dell, Delta Books, 1959); also see Williams, "The Frontier Thesis and American Foreign Policy," *History as a Way of Learning* (New York: New Viewpoints, 1973). Turner argued that it was the pioneering of the Frontier that established American democracy. He paid no attention to genocide. Williams's version of this "success" is more modern and tragic, more attuned to the era of the Vietnam War.

CHAPTER 2

1. "The Baker Report," *The Senate Watergate Report*, Dell (1974), pp. 733ff.

2. In Steve Weissman, ed., *Big Brother and the Holding Company* (Palo Alto, CA: Ramparts Press, 1974), p. 313.

3. Quigley, *Tragedy and Hope*, pp. 950-56, from which the quotations in this section are borrowed.

4. Quoted in Jeff Gerth, "Nixon and the Miami Connection," in Weissman, *Big Brother*, pp. 251-75. This seminal essay is the chief basis of my treatment of Nixon here. As for who is Warren to throw stones, we test that question in chapter 4.

5. Ibid., p. 252.

6. Hank Messick, *Lansky*, Berkley Medallion Books, New York, 1971, p. 190.

7. Ibid., p. 190.

8. Rebozo was not accused of criminal conduct in cashing this stock in 1968. Bod Edler and John McDermott, Knight News Service, Boston *Globe*, November 1, 1973.

9. "The Story of Bebe Rebozo," *Newsday Special Report*, October 6-13, 1971, p. 6R.

10. Gerth, p. 257.

11. Ibid.

12. This section is based on E.H. Cookridge's *Gehlen, Spy of the Century* (New York: Random House, 1971).

13. R. Harris Smith, *OSS: The Secret History of America's First Central Intelligence Agency* (Berkeley: University of California Press, 1972), pp. 233-239, and 240. Gehlen was of course not the only high-ranking Nazi offering the United States deals just then. In April 1944, for example, Himmler's agents were floating "separate peace" balloons all over Europe. In one offer, Himmler would turn over to the United States the German treasury of intelligence data on Japan if the United States would stall the war in France and enable the Nazis to put more into their struggle with Russia. Smith does not use the Yankee/Cowboy framework or any counterpart, but his book offers an excellent analysis of the Yankee/Cowboy competition at full drive during the Cold War years within the heart of the

American foreign policy apparatus. Particularly the regional-ideological character of the split rending the CIA emerges. He shows us why, how and to what effect the CIA was partitioned.

14. Ibid., p. 240.

CHAPTER 3

1. Richard M. Nixon, "Cuba, Castro and John F. Kennedy," *Readers Digest*, November 1964.

2. L. Fletcher Prouty, *The Secret Team* (New York: Viking Press, 1973), p. 48.

3. Actually the Cuban jets were flown to another airfield the day before the invasion struck. So they would probably have survived the critical first moments of the invasion unattacked. Once off the ground, of course, they enjoyed all the advantages of jet-age fighters over piston-age bombers.

4. Tad Szulc, "Cuba on Our Mind," *Esquire*, February 1974. Hunt claims he advised the CIA to kill Castro (Howard Hunt, *Give Us This Day: The CIA and the Bay of Pigs* [New Rochelle, NY: Arlington House, 1973], but that nothing came of it. On the contrary, the would-be assassins were almost successful. They were caught in Havana on the day of the invasion and executed. Many additional attempts on Castro's life followed in the years after. See Peter Dale Scott, "The Longest Cover-up," in Weissman's *Big Brother*.

5. Ibid.

6. Smith, *OSS*, p. 377.

7. Consider the following, a broadside distributed in the Cuban exile community of Miami just after JFK ordered a cessation of military activity against Castro. The broadside was ornamented with drawings of cowboys and the Alamo and signed, "A Texan who resents the Oriental influence that has come to control, to degrade, to pollute and enslave his own people." It reads: "Only through one development will

you Cuban patriots ever live again in your homeland as freemen...[only] if an inspried Act of God should place in the White House within weeks a Texan known to be a friend of all Latin Americans...though he must under present conditions bow to the Zionists who since 1905 came into control of the United States, and for whom Jack Kennedy and Nelson Rockefeller and other members of the Council of [sic] Foreign Relations and allied agencies are only stooges and pawns. Though Johnson must now bow to these crafty and cunning Communist-hatching Jews, yet, did an Act of God suddenly elevate him into the top position [he] would revert to what his beloved father and grandfather were, and to their values and principles and loyalties" (William Manchester, *The Death of a President* [New York: Harper and Row, 1967], p. 53.)

8.   David Halberstam, *The Best and the Brightest* (New York: Random House, 1972), pp. 66-67.

9.   Nixon, "Cuba, Castro."

10.   Haynes Johnson, *The Bay of Pigs* (New York: W.W. Norton Co., 1964).

11.   Prouty, *Secret Team*, p. 38.

12.   Murray Zeitlin and Robert Scheer, *Cuba: Tragedy in Our Hemisphere* (New York: Grove Press, 1963).

13.   *Nation*, June 22, 1964.

14.   John F. Kennedy, *The Strategy of Peace*, ed. Allan Nevins (New York: Harper and Row, 1960), p. 132.

15.   Tad Szulc, "Cuba on Our Mind."

16.   Nixon, "Cuba, Castro."

17.   Halberstam, *The Best*, p. 67.

18.   Prouty, *Secret Team*, p. 35.

19.   See for example W.W. Rostow's "Guerrilla Warfare in Underdeveloped Areas," in M. Raskin and B. Fall, eds., *The Vietnam Reader* (New York: Praeger, 1965), p. 110-12.

20.   In the words of Kennedy's foreign-policy aide Roger Hilsman, "President Kennedy's policy...was to meet the guerrilla aggression within a counterguerrilla framework, with the implied corollary that if the Viet Cong could not be defeated within a counterguerrilla framework and the

allegiance of the people of Vietnam could not be won, then the United States would accept the resulting situation and would be free to enter negotiations without fatal consequences to our position in the rest of Asia" (Roger Hilsman, *To Move a Nation* [New York: Doubleday, 1967], p. 537).

21. Prouty, *Secret Team*, pp. 114-21.

22. James M. Gavin, "We Can Get Out of Vietnam," *Saturday Evening Post*, February 24, 1968.

23. *Santa Barbara News-Press*, February 11, 1975.

24. Kenneth O'Donnell, *Johnny We Hardly Knew Ye* (Boston: Little Brown & Co., 1972), p. 16.

25. *Boston Globe*, June 24, 1973.

26. *Boston Globe,* March 13, 1973.

27. *Rolling Stone*, December 6, 1973.

28. Prouty, *Secret Team*, p. 415.

29. *Stars and Stripes*, November 1, 1963.

30. *New York Times*, October 3, 1963.

31. "GOP Vietnam Study," *Congressional Record*, May 9, 1967 (the "Hickenlooper Study").

32. Peter Dale Scott, "The Death of Kennedy and the Vietnam War," *Government by Gunplay*, ed. Sid Blumenthal and Harvey Yazijian, (New York: New American Library, 1976) pp. 152-87. NSAM 273, says Scott, is still unpublished and known only from various passing references to it. Scott's impressive reconstruction is printed in the cited article on pp. 170 ff.

33. *New York Times*, "Vietnam Chronology," January 28, 1973.

34. Ibid.

35. Ibid.

36. Ibid.

37. Ibid.

38. James Hepburn, *Farewell America* (Canada and Belgium: Frontiers Publishing, 1968), p. 244.

39. This memo is from the files of the James Garrison investigation of the JFK assassination. A copy is on file with the Assassination Information Bureau, 63 Inman St., Cambridge, Mass. 02139.

40. William Turner, "The Garrison Commission on the Assassination of President Kennedy," *Ramparts*, January 1968, p. 52; Paris Flammonde, *The Kennedy Conspiracy* (New York: Meredith, 1969), p. 112.

41. Jeff Cohen, unpublished interview with Garrison, in Assassination Information Bureau files.

42. Halberstam, *The Best*, p. 411.

43. "Ten Years After," *Playboy*, November 1973.

44. Nikita Khrushchev, *Khrushchev Remembers: The Last Testament* (Boston: Little Brown & Co., 1971), p. 202.

45. Szulc, "Cuba on Our Mind." This hit was also recommended by Howard Hunt, whose hitman was Cuban physician Rolando Cubela Secades, who confessed after being arrested in Havana.

46. Tad Szulc, *Compulsive Spy* (New York: Viking Press, 1974).

CHAPTER 4

1. *Hearings before the President's Commission on the Assassination of President John F. Kennedy*, vol. 17. (Hereafter cited as *Hearings*.)

2. Ibid.

3. *Hearings*, vol. 4, pp. 136.

4. Cyril Wecht, "A Pathologist's View of the JFK Autopsy: An Unsolved Case," *Modern Medicine*, November 27, 1972.

5. Cyril Wecht, "JFK Assassination: A Prolonged and Willful Cover-Up," *Modern Medicine*, October 28, 1974.

6. Hepburn, *Farewell America*, p. 57. See also Sylvia Meagher, *Accessories After the Fact* (New York: Bobbs-Merrill, 1967), pp. 94-133.

7. Robert Healey, "Time to Reopen the Dallas Files," *Boston Globe*, April 25, 1975.

8. *Hearings*, vol. 7, p. 535.

9. *Report of the President's Commission on the*

Assassination of President John F. Kennedy, pp. 553-55. (Hereafter cited as *Report*.) Warren discounted the gunshop owner's testimony because the official reconstruction had already placed Oswald in Mexico at the time the contact was supposedly made.

10. Kaiser, "The JFK Assassination: Why Congress Should Reopen the Investigation," *Rolling Stone*, April 24, 1975.

11. But note that former CIA officer George O'Toole (see item following) implies that Oswald had no papers on him at all and that the Hidell-Oswald link was another of the preforged components of the cover-up. See O'Toole, *The Assassination Tapes* (New York: Penthouse Press, 1975).

12. Sylvia Meagher, *Accessories After the Fact* (New York: Random House, 1967), p. 50.

13. O'Toole, *Tapes*, p. 131.

14. Ibid., Chap. 4.

15. Among them, Dr. Gordon Barland of the University of Utah, who claims already to have repeated O'Toole's tests and duplicated his results. *Penthouse*, April 1975, published testimonials from a half-dozen academic and practical specialists. The only objection one hears to the PSE is that, like the standard "lie detector," it would not work with a psychopath unaware of any standard of falsity or truth. But no one ever claimed, much less proved, that this was the kind of problem Oswald had.

16. Scott, *Big Brother*.

17. Zodiac News Service release, April 30, 1975. We are in galleys as the final volume of the Church Committee's probe of the intelligence agencies is released. This volume bears on the role of the intelligence agencies in the JFK assassination and concludes, as we have argued above, that the FBI and the CIA obstructed the investigation. What the Church Committee totally failed to do, however, was investigate the relation of Oswald to the FBI, the CIA and military intelligence. Likewise, it ignored late-developing information that Jack Ruby was also an FBI informant. *The*

Investigation of the Assassination of President John F. Kennedy: Performance of the Intelligence Agencies, Final Report, Book V, published July 23, 1976, Senate Select Committee to Study Governmental Operations with respect to Intelligence Activities. (See note 53 below.)

18.   The following account borrows on investigative reports from New Orleans Police Detective Frank Meloche to Garrison dated March 13 and March 22, 1967. These documents are on file with the Assassination Information Bureau.

19.   *Hearings*, vol. 23, p. 166. See also Ed Reid and Ovid Demaris, *The Green Felt Jungle* (New York: Simon & Schuster, Pocket Books, 1963).

20.   *Hearings*, vol. 14, p. 444. See also Scott, "The Longest Cover-up," in Weissman, *Big Brother*.

21.   Senate Committee on Government Operations, "Organized Crime and Illicit Traffic in Narcotics," *Hearings*, 88th Congress, Second Session, p. 508, chart II.

22.   Warren *Hearings*, vol. 22, pp. 300, 360, and 478. I am indebted to Peter Dale Scott for pointing out the following passages in the Warren *Hearings*.

23.   *Report*, p. 793.

24.   *Hearings*, vol. 25, p. 244, Commission Exhibit 1268.

25.   Ibid.

26.   Ibid., vol. 22, p. 423.

27.   Ibid., vol. 23, p. 369.

28.   Ibid., vol. 23, p. 371.

29.   Ibid., vol. 23, p. 372.

30.   Ibid., vol. 23, p. 363.

31.   *Report*, p. 801. But from the much-later-released transcript of the Warren Commission's meeting of January 27, 1964 (its second emergency secret meeting within five days), we know for a fact that the commissioners were not always so confident of this interpretation. Chief Counsel Rankin said at that meeting: "He [Ruby] has apparently all kinds of connections with the underworld . . . . There isn't any question but what he planned to go down to Cuba, and

he did, and the story was that it was in regard to armaments.... My recollection is that one of the stories was that he was to try to sell guns and ammunition to Castro.... That is all denied, and that he was going down there to make money on other kinds of sales but not anything that was munitions or armaments. There is no explanation of where he was there, what he did, or who his connections were. He had all kinds of connections with the minor underworld, I think you would call it, in Dallas and Chicago...." (*New Republic*, September 27, 1975).

32.   Tad Szulc, "The Warren Commission in its Own Words," *New Republic*, September 27, 1975.

33.   Warren *Report*, p. 368.

34.   Warren *Hearings*, vol. 22, p. 426 and Vol. 23, p. 362.

35.   The following quotations from the Ruby interrogation are excerpted from *Hearings*, vol. 5, pp. 181-212.

36.   Ibid. vol. 14, pp. 504-70.

37.   Ibid., vol. 14, pp. 566-67.

38.   Ibid., p. 571.

39.   Ibid.

40.   Ibid., p. 572.

41.   Ibid., p. 563.

42.   Ibid., p. 572.

43.   Ibid., p. 575-76.

44.   Ibid., pp. 586, 588.

45.   Ibid., p. 590.

46.   Ibid., p. 591.

47.   Ibid.

48.   "Murdered—For Having Too Much On JFK's Killers," *Midnight*, January 18, 1977.

49.   "A staff memorandum tells the Commission that if certain rumors about the assassination—the possibility of a foreign conspiracy—are not quelled, they 'could conceivably lead the country into a war which could cost 40 million lives'" Tad Szulc, "The Warren Commission in its Own Words," *New Republic*, September 27, 1975.

50.   Anson, "JFK: The Truth," p. 22.

51. *Boston Globe*, April 27, 1975.

52. "Grief-stricken at the sudden calamity that cut the president down, Bobby Kennedy telephoned a ranking official of the CIA, who dumbfounded, heard him demand with commingled anger and emotion: 'Did your outfit have anything to do with this horror?'" (Seymour Freiden and George Bailey, *The Experts* [New York: Macmillan, 1968], p. 85).

53. The Church Committee's review of the intelligence community's relationship to the JFK assassination and its cover-up (Book V of the Church report, published in July 1976), might easily have begun correcting this remarkable distortion. The committee knew, for example, as the Warren Commission evidently did not, that Ruby had at some point enjoyed some form of cooperative relationship with the Dallas FBI, but this fact did not even find its way into a footnote. Yet at the same time, the committee devoted pages of repetitious detail to the story of a would-be assassin of Castro, Rolando Cubela (CIA code name, AMLASH), whose attempt on Castro it imagines *may* have motivated a Castro-Oswald attempt on JFK.

CHAPTER 5

1. Geoffrey Barraclough, "Wealth and Power: The Politics of Food and Oil," *New York Review of Books*, August 7, 1975.

2. *Toward a New International Order*, p. 402.

3. Barraclough, "Wealth and Power."

4. "And slowly Clifford found allies.... In late March, Johnson summoned his Senior Informal Advisory Group on Vietnam, a blue-chip Establishment group. These were the great names of the Cold War: McCloy, Acheson, Arthur Dean, MacBundy, Douglas Dillon, Robert Murphy. And over a period of days they quietly let him know that the

Establishment—yes, Wall Street—had turned on the war; it was hurting us more than it was helping us, it had all gotten out of hand, and it was time to bring it back to proportion" (David Halberstam, "Losing Big," *Esquire*, September 1972).

5. This account is based on Jeff Cohen's impressive summary "The Assassination of Martin Luther King" in Sid Blumenthal and Harvey Yazijian, eds., *Government by Gunplay* (New York: New American Library, 1976), pp. 38-56.

6. J. Edgar Hoover, "Disruption of the New Left," dated May 14, 1968, in Weissman, *Big Brother*.

7. Alex Cockburn and Betsy Langman, "Who Killed RFK?," *Harper's*, January 1975.

8. The pistol was actually test-fired by a panel of seven court-appointed experts in October 1975 with inconclusive results. See Assassination Information Bureau interview with Allard Lowenstein, October 16, 1975, WBUR-FM Boston. Also Lowenstein, "Who Killed Robert Kennedy?" in Blumenthal and Yazijian *Government by Gunplay*, p. 4.

9. The Los Angeles Police Department's "Special Unit: Senator" was formed and run by Evelle Younger, current attorney general of California. After it had completed its apparently successful cover-up of the RFK evidence, SUS was given permanent form as the Criminal Conspiracy Section, remaining under Younger's control. The CCS shortly had taken over the war against local Reds and organized blacks. In support of its antisubversive purposes, it got involved deeply in the behavior-modification work going on in the California prison system, notably at Vaccaville, a psychofactory turning out police zombies the likes of Donald "Cinque" Defreeze and others involved in the formation of the Symbionese Liberation Army. Defreeze was explicitly a CCS creature. The thesis has thus formed that the SLA was always a plaything of the CCS and through it of the Southern California far right, and that the kidnapping of Patty Hearst was part of a larger project,

possibly including also the Zebra killings of the same period
and the murder of Oakland School Superintendent Marcus
Foster, the purpose of which was to generate a public
demand for wider police repression. (Based on material
developed by Donald Freed and the Citizens Research and
Investigating Committee of Los Angeles. SLA leader Emily
Harris has denounced Freed as a conspiracy patsy.)

CHAPTER 6

1. John Keats, *Howard Hughes* (New York: Random
House, 1966).

2. *New York Times*, March 2, 1975.

3. Chronology and quotes following are from D.F.
Fleming, *The Cold War and Its Origins* (New York:
Doubleday, 1961), vol. 1.

4. Keats, *Hughes*, p. 257-58.

5. Ibid., p. 258.

6. Ibid., p. 261.

7. Gore Vidal, *New York Review of Books*, April 20,
1972.

8. Besides Keats, see also Nicholas North-Broome,
The Hughes-Nixon Loan (New York: APAI Books, 1972).

9. David B. Tinnin, *Just About Everybody vs Howard
Hughes* (New York: Doubleday, 1973). This is an extremely
powerful book.

10. *Boston Globe*, December 5, 1973.

11. Tinnin, *Just About Everybody*, p. 62.

12. Ibid.

13. Ibid., p. 63.

14. Neither Keats nor Tinnin takes up the Las Vegas
period. My reconstruction is based essentially on media
accounts.

15. Wallace Turner, *New York Times*, October 1, 1973.

16. Thomas O'Hanlon, "The High Rollers Shoot for
Power in Las Vegas," *Fortune*, January 1971.

17.   Jack Anderson, *Boston Globe*, October 16, 1973; Wallace Turner, *New York Times*, October 1, 1973; UPI, *Los Angeles Times*, January 10, 1974; Gore Vidal, *New York Review of Books*, April 20, 1974.

18.   Selected samples of the Maheu-Hughes documents were floated in Xerox around the press in 1972 and after. The quotations here are from a set of some 50 pages in my possession.

19.   Anthony J. Lukas, *Nightmare: A Narrative History of Watergate* (New York: Viking Press, 1976).

20.   James Hougan, "Hire a Spy," *Harper's*, December 1974.

21.   Richard Hammer, "History of Organized Crime," *Playboy*, April 1974.

22.   Ron Laytner, *Up Against Howard Hughes* (New York: Manor Books, 1972), pp. 39-40.

23.   *Fortune*, January 1971.

24.   The John Meier story is reconstructed from news accounts, notably: *Time*, December 21, 1970; Bernstein and Woodward in the *Washington Post*, September 6, 1973; James M. Naughton, *New York times*, September 7, 1973; Seth Kantor, *Madison Capital Times*, September 24, 1973; Jonathan Kwitny, *Wall Street Journal*, December 4, 1973; *Boston Globe*, December 12, 1973; Jerry Cohen, *Los Angeles Times*, December 20, 1973; UPI *Los Angeles Times*, December 21, 1973; Jeff Cohen and Bill Hazlett, *Los Angeles Times*, December 27, 1973; Robert Rawitch, *Los Angeles Times*, January 24, 1974; Carroll Kilpatrick, *Washington Post*, January 26, 1974; Hank Messick, *Lansky* (New York: Berkley Medallion, 1971), p. 246. Kwitny's is a key piece.

25.   Information obtained by author from member of Watergate Committee staff.

26.   The Thanksgiving coup is reconstructed from Laytner, *Up Against Howard Hughes*; Wallace Turner, "All the Hughes That's Fit to Print," *Esquire*, July 1971; an unpublished manuscript by Jim Hougan; Stephen Fay, et

al., *Hoax* (New York: Viking Press, 1972); *New York Times*, December 8, 1970; *Time*, December 21, 1970; *Newsweek*, December 21, 1970; *Newsweek*, December 28, 1970; *Fortune*, January 1971; Jack Anderson columns for January 9 and August 7, 1971; Clay Richards, *Los Angeles Times*, January 26, 1974; *Boston Globe*, September 22, 1973.

27.   Tinnin, *Just About Everybody*, p. 379.

28.   Laytner, *Up Against*, p. 75.

29.   Tinnin, *Just About Everybody*, p. 380.

30.   On February 27, 1976, Jack Anderson reported finding a handful of people who believed they had seen Hughes since 1970: New York stockbroker Julie Sedlmayr and Attorney I. Courtney Ivey in September 1972 and Nevada Governor Mike O'Callaghan and Gaming Board Chairman Phil Hanniflin in March 1973. Anderson points out, however, that the existence of a Hughes double has long been conjectured, and the main thrust of his story was that the IRS was on the verge of declaring Hughes legally dead. Anderson quoted from a February 18, 1972, memo of a "federal agent" who had "followed Hughes's movements": "It is my belief that Howard Hughes died in Las Vegas in 1970 and that key officials in charge of running his empire concealed this fact at the time in order to prevent a catastrophic dissolution of his holdings" (*Boston Globe*, February 27, 1976).

31.   Laytner, *Up Against*, p. 96.

32.   Turner, *New York Times*, October 1, 1973.

33.   Tinnin, *Just About Everybody*, p. 386.

34.   Hank Messick, *John Edgar Hoover* (New York: David McKay Co., 1972), p. 242.

35.   Tinnin, *Just About Everybody*, pp. 415-18.

36.   Ibid., p. 395.

37.   Laytner, *Up Against*, p. 94.

38.   Ibid.

39.   Ibid., p. 42.

40.   James Hougan, et al., article in manuscript.

41.   Messick, *Lansky*, pp. 234-35.

42. Laytner, *Up Against*, p. 236.

43. This section is based on the following: July 2, 1974 Baker report; Robert L. Jackson, *Los Angeles Times*, December 11, December 21, 1973; *National Observer*, February 2, 1974; UPI dispatch Las Vegas, appearing in *Rocky Mountain News* (Denver), June 12, 1973; Lawrence Meyer, *Washington Post*, December 11, 1972; *Los Angeles Times*, January 10, 1974; John Hanrahan, *Washington Post*, September 25, 1973.

44. James McCord, A Piece of Tape (Rockville, MD: Washington Media Services, Ltd., 1974), p. 21.

CHAPTER 7

1. McCord, *Tape*, p. 46.
2. *Harper's*, October 1974.
3. *New York Times*, January 8, 1973.
4. McCord, *Tape*, p. 141.
5. Szulc, *Compulsive Spy*, p. 161.
6. *Boston Globe*, May 30, 1973.
7. *Submission of Recorded Presidential Conversations to the Committee on the Judiciary of the House of Representatives by President Richard M. Nixon.* Tapes of March 21, 1973.
8. Skolnick tells the story that a federal narc named Ray Metcalf, an agent of Drug Abuse Law Enforcement, DALE, climbed out of the wrecked tail in an asbestos jumpsuit moments after the wreckage came to a rest. The Skolnickian jumpsuit detail is unconfirmed, but Metcalf was aboard 553, was seated in the tail section, and did walk away from the crash.
9. Per Skolnick.
10. "Part of John Dean's deal with the Watergate special prosecutor was that the Segretti-Kalmbach area, the whole Bremer connection, would not be explored" (Mae Brussell, "Assassination Report" aired on WBUR-FM,

Boston, September 24, 1974).

11. *New York Times*, August 20, 1973.

12. Per Skolnick.

13. U.S., Congress, Senate, "Activities of the National Transportation Safety Board," Hearings before the Committee on Commerce, Serial 93-38, May 21 and 23, 1973, p. 2.

14. Ibid., p. 105.

15. Ibid., p. 139.

16. Ibid., p. 140.

17. *New York Times*, September 5, 1974. Resigned September 4, 1974.

18. Phone conversation with author.

19. Single copies of this report are available free on request from the National Transportation Safety Board, Washington, D.C. 20591.

20. *New York Magazine*, May 21, 1973.

21. Ronald Dorfman, *Nation*, July 30, 1973.

22. Some investigators, notably Donald Freed of the Los Angeles-based Citizens Research and Investigating Committee, have claimed that the pilot and the copilot were actually not in their seats at the time of the crash. The NTSB report indirectly supports this in two passages suggesting unprecedented departure from basic flight routines on the part of the captain: "The 4-point seatbelt and shoulder harness release mechanism was found unlocked and operable. Shoulder harness straps were found retracted in the inertial reel" (p. 12). That is, if the pilot was in his seat, he had not fastened his seatbelt. And in Appendix I: "The injuries sustained by the captain, as well as the conditions of the captain's and first officer's shoulder harness in the wreckage, indicated that the shoulder harness had not been used."

23. Ronald Dorfman, *Nation*, September 3, 1973.

24. *Chicago Tribune*, December 9, 1972.

25. Ibid., December 14, 1972.

26. The NTSB report reads: "N931U was equipped with the Fairchild Model F-5424 Flight Data Recorder (FDR)

serial No. 5134. The altitude, indicated airspeed, magnetic heading, and vertical acceleration traces ended abruptly 82:14 minutes after takeoff (approximately 14 minutes before the accident) . . . . Examination of the flight recorder showed that a miter gear . . . had slipped on its shaft causing the recorder to stop functioning" (p. 8).

27.   As recorded in Appendix F of the NTSB transcript, the last eight minutes of 553's flight:

> CAPTAIN WHITEHOUSE: Recorder go off?
> SECOND OFFICER ELDER: Pardon me?
> WHITEHOUSE: Recorder go off?
> ELDER: Yeah.
> UNIDENTIFIED VOICE: (unintelligible).
> WHITEHOUSE: See what's wrong with it, will ya?

That started at Chicago time 2:19:30.5 P.M. There follows an exchange with O'Hare about runway assignment, then at 2:20:37.5 the cockpit discussion of the FDR failure resumed:

> ELDER: Braking action reported fair by a guppy. ["Braking action" could refer to the use of airbrakes, or spoilers, which indeed figure in the NTSB theory of the crash, but which are customarily not used in landings and would certainly not be used without an explicit command from the captain. In routine landings, the captain tells the copilot what to do while concentrating all his attention on the instruments and the outside environment. "Guppy" could refer to the Boeing 737 itself, dubbed "the Guppy" by pilots grateful for its great flyability. It could also refer to the small plane ahead of them, the private Aero-Commander, which was about to circle in front of them in a for-some-reason privileged missed approach.]
> WHITEHOUSE: Fair?
> ELDER: On one, ah, three one left. [Does Elder start to say runway number one-three, the glidesloped runway formerly assigned to 553?] The only change is the altimeter thirty oh five.
> UNIDENTIFIED VOICE: (Unintelligible).

WHITEHOUSE: Sounds to me a circuit breaker, perhaps.

ELDER: Hah?

UNIDENTIFIED VOICE: (Unintelligible).

WHITEHOUSE: Yeah, I just meant, I thought you'd better check everything, ah.

ELDER: It, ah,—indicates.

Sound of several clicks (appear between words "ah" and "indicates" above) (heard on all four tracks sounds similar to circuit breaker deactivated and activated repeatedly).

ELDER: A wire on the reel to test.

Sound of several clicks.

ELDER: It tests. I think it's okay. I think it's working.

UNIDENTIFIED VOICE: (unintelligible).

ELDER: It says off.

CHICAGO-O'HARE: (to Aero-Commander): Zero nine VS turn left to one three zero.

WHITEHOUSE: You got an "off" light.

ELDER: Yeah, but, ah, the signal, the encode light comes on.

UNIDENTIFIED VOICE: (unintelligible).

ELDER: And it shows, indicating tape.

28. In view of this and the technical nature of the argument, I will quote here the NTSB's explanation in full:

"Several sources for common errors in the two independent systems were considered. One was ice, which could have accumulated on the Pitot/static probes. However, since both probe heat switches were found in the "ON" position, and since examination of the filaments of the probe head indicating lights showed that probe heat was energized at the time of impact, it is unlikely that probe icing was the source of error in this case.

"Another source of error could have been the effect of the aircraft's extreme nose-high attitude during the final moments of flight. According to the Boeing Company Flight test data, pitch angles within the stall buffeting region can produce static system errors that result in altimeter readings 60 feet higher than the actual altitude.

"Also, if electrical power to the CADC was interrupted while the aircraft was in a nose-high attitude at impact, the Pitot/static sensing ports could have been 20 feet or more above the elevation of the crash site.

"Additional errors inherent in the reported barometric pressure correction at the time of impact could account for still another 15 to 20 feet.

"Since it is possible, as shown above, to account for a significant portion of the difference between impact elevation and the CADC altitude computations at the time of power interruption, the Safety Board concludes that the static system errors reflected in the CADC readings at impact do not have a bearing on the events that occurred at Midway." (p. 24)

Ignoring the splendid *non sequitur* of that last paragraph, let us boil this down.

The NTSB has to account for an error of 157 feet in the pilot's altimeter and 103 feet in the copilot's. The possible sources of error, says the NTSB, are: (a) probe icing; (b) an extreme nose-high attitude of the airplane in a *stall*; (c) an extreme nose-high attitude of the airplane at tail-first *impact*; and (d) "inherent" errors in barometric pressure sensing.

a. The NTSB determined that icing was not a source of error in the case of 553.

b. From the nose-high *stall* attitude of the aircraft, the report assumes the maximum possible deviation of 60 feet given by Boeing.

c. From the nose-high *impact* attitude, the report assumes another maximum error input of 20 feet. This even though the attitude-dependency of both these figures (b and c) probably means that the NTSB's 20 feet should be considered simply a component of Boeing's 60 feet, since both are derived from the fact that the tail-down geometry of the aircraft in a stall as well as tail-first impact puts the probe sensing ports higher than the tail.

d. From presumed sensing errors which it does not even

try to guess the cause of, the report gets another maximum of 15 to 20 feet.

Added all up, then, the NTSB explanation accounts for a total of 95-100 feet of error, assuming the maximum values from all possible error sources. Yet this still accounts for less than the known error at the copilot's altimeter (103 feet) and less than two-thirds of the error at the pilot's altimeter (157 feet).

29. Cockpit discussion of the landing-procedure anomaly takes place immediately following the discussion of the malfunctioning FDR quoted above:

FIRST OFFICER COBLE: Wonder why they put that in there, final approach from holding pattern at Kedzie not authorized.

CHICAGO/O'HARE (to Aero-Commander ahead of 553 on runway 31L): Zero nine VS turn left zero nine zero.

COBLE: What would be wrong if you were there in the holding pattern? You'd be back here anyway. Wonder why?

CAPTAIN WHITEHOUSE: I don't know. The holding pattern's probably higher than fifteen-hundred feet.

COBLE: That's probably true.

UNIDENTIFIED VOICE: (Unintelligible).

SECOND OFFICER ELDER: Or it's not aligned with the runway.

COBLE: Yeah.

This is followed by an exchange with O'Hare about approach speed and altitude, then a return to the problem of the vexatious FDR, as we have already seen.

30. MIDWAY: Nine VS, runway three one left cleared to land.

9VS: Okay.

MIDWAY: Nine VS, do ya have the right runway in sight by any chance?

9VS: Affirmative.

MIDWAY: 'ud you swing over to that and land? There's a jet about two m—and disregard that, ah, okay, I see ya now, you're cleared to land on thirty-one left.

31.   Per Skolnick. See Barboura Freed, "Flight 553: The Watergate Murder?," in Weissman, *Big Brother*, pp. 127-58.

32.   *Washington Post*, June 3, 1973.

33.   *National Transportation Safety Board* report, Appendix F.

34.   *Chicago Sun-Times*, May 1, 1973.

35.   Author interview with Skolnick and Bottos.

36.   In June he was finally allowed to give his evidence, which consisted essentially of several thousand pages of NTSB technical reports on the crash (as with the Warren Commission, the technical investigation undermines the final report). But by that time his arguments had long since been prejudged and, as Public Information Officer Dunbar put it, "briefly and tersely dismissed."

CHAPTER 8

---

1.   CBS-TV News, January 5, 1974.

2.   Ibid., February 24, 1974.

3.   Ibid., March 24, 1974.

4.   Neil Cullinin, *New Times*, September 8, 1974.

5.   *Boston Globe*, December 6, 1974.

6.   *Time*, August 27, 1973.

7.   *Boston Globe*, April 4, 1973.

8.   *Harper's*, October 1974.

9.   Andrew St. George, *Harper's*, October 1974.

10.   Baker report, p. 17.

11.   Ibid., p. 40.

12.   Ibid., p. 43.

13.   Ibid., p. 8.

14.   Ibid., p. 12.

15.   Paul Benzaquin, Boston Channel 5, December 18, 1974.

16.   *Harper's*, October 1974.

17.   Ervin Hearings, August 6, 1973.

18.   *Times* (London), June 3, 1973.

19.   J. Anthony Lukas, "The Hughes Connection," *New York Times Magazine*, January 4, 1976.

20.   McCord documents supplied by Ervin Committee.

21.   Ibid.

22.   Ibid.

23.   Ibid.

24.   Bernstein and Woodward, *All the President's Men* (New York: Simon & Schuster, 1974), p. 274.

25.   Ibid.

26.   For what it's worth, there are at least three different versions of this remarkable letter, a masterpiece of its kind. McCord prints two in *A Piece of Tape* (pp. 48 and 150) without mentioning their differences. The other is the typescript McCord gave the Ervin research staff, a photocopy of which is what I am using here. The variances are all trivial, but on the other hand, they are numerous, and to my mind there is some question why there should be any variances at all. By whom, how, and when would they have been introduced? Do they imply that McCord had memorized the text, but imperfectly, or that several hands worked it over so that several slightly variant copies came to exist? Why should anyone do that? Why else should there be any text but the one and single text McCord sent to Caulfield and gave a photocopy of to the Ervin Committee? Calling the Ervin Committee version number one and the versions at pages 48 and 150 of *Tape* numbers two and three, we can itemize the variances as follows:

1.   Where version one opens coldly and abruptly with "Jack," the *Tape* versions read "Dear Jack."

2.   Where number one continues with the McCordian clip, "Sorry to have to write," etc., two and three read, "I am sorry," etc.

3.   Version one softens the preemptory tone of the single-sentence opening paragraph, however, by continuing: "but felt you had to know." The *Tape* versions omit this whole striking clause altogether.

4.   Version one says, "and if the WG operation," where

versions two and three leave out the *if*.

5. Two and three spell out number one's "WG."

6. Version two styles *operation* with an initial cap. In version three it's lower case.

7. Versions one and two read, "at CIA's feet." Version three reads "at the feet of CIA."

8. Version one reads, "Just pass the message." Versions two and three omit *just*.

9. Versions one and two read, "I'm sorry." Version three drops the contraction, reading, "I am sorry. . . ." So to be pedantic, version one differs from version two in six trivial details and from version three in nine. Two and three differ from each other three times. The variances are undramatic, but on the other hand, patient papyrologists discard no variance at all until they know how it could have occurred.

27. The March 19 letter is reprinted in *Tape*, pp. 173-74.

28. *Washington Post*, May 24, 1973.

29. A final note for the late-breaking news that Haldeman himself appreciated the *political* magnitude of Watergate and as of mid-1976 was still open to the possibility that somebody in the CIA might have been after Nixon. In serialized excerpts from his forthcoming memoir (see Universal Press Syndicate release of June 20, 1976, "Inside the Nixon White House," Part I), Haldeman says outright that if it had not been for Watergate, "South Vietnam would not have fallen," "Henry Kissinger would not be secretary of state," and "the 1976 Republican presidential candidate would not have been either Jerry Ford or Ronald Reagan— but John Connally." And in Part IV of the above, dated June 23, 1976, he writes: "In retrospect, I'm ambivalent as to whether the [Central Intelligence] Agency was out to get Nixon. I don't dismiss it as an impossibility. I do believe that there are a number of unanswered questions about the break-in at the Watergate. The Agency had the capacity and perhaps, unknown to me, the motivation."

CHAPTER 9

1. Bernard Bailyn, *The Ideological Origins of the American Revolution* (Cambridge, MA: Harvard University Press, 1967), pp. 119-20.

2. Tad Szulc, "The Warren Commission in Its Own Words," *New Republic*, September 27, 1975, p. 47.

3. The Trilateral Commission met in 1975 to discuss the state of democracy in the First World countries. Its controversial final report, called *The Governability of Democracies*, argues that the troubles experienced by the advanced industrial democracies during the 1960s were caused by "an excess of democracy"—as though the "riot and rebellion" of that happy decade were not a thousand times over-provoked by the cowardice, arrogance, deceit, and stupidity of the ruling class elites re Vietnam, re social policy, re the environment. *Governability* implies furthermore that if the hazards facing the late twentieth century are to be handled "rationally" and "efficiently," then government will find it necessary to curtail democratic privileges everywhere.

4. And as of Thanksgiving 1975, of course, President Ford had acknowledged the need for a new investigation of one aspect of JFK's death, the question of Oswald's political connections and identity (see chapter 4). In a miracle, Ford or Church would have chosen to open up the question as a whole to a fully public airing in which all voices in this lengthy and trying dispute could be heard and fairly judged by an informed public. But following the example of his predecessor, Ford chose instead the path of the "limited hang-out" and stuck with the original Warren theory that Oswald, whoever he was, fired all the shots. Any study of Oswald taking his guilt as a foregone conclusion or an established fact will only repeat the performance of the Warren Commission.

Carl Oglesby is the author of two previous books, *Containment and Change* (with Richard Shaull), and *New Left Reader*, a popular mass paperback which he edited. Oglesby has taught courses in Political Criticism at M.I.T. and Dartmouth and Antioch Colleges.

An early president of Students for a Democratic Society, Oglesby is presently associated with the Assassination Information Bureau (67 Inman Street, Cambridge, Mass. 02139) a group organized in 1972 to politicize the question of John F. Kennedy's assassination. His interest in the assassination of Kennedy and others and his involvement with the theoretical foundations of the antiwar movement in the sixties led to his work on this book.

Index